Frommer's®

Portable
St. Maarten/
St. Martin, Anguilla &
St. Barts

3rd Edition

by Alexis Lipsitz Flippin

Sunset Beach Bar

WILEY
Wiley Publishing, Inc.

Published by:

WILEY PUBLISHING, INC.

111 River St.
Hoboken, NJ 07030-5774

ISBN 978-0-470-63099-0 (paper); ISBN 978-0-470-94011-2 (ebk); ISBN
978-0-470-44197-8 (ebk); ISBN 978-0-470-44190-9 (ebk)

Editor: Jennifer Reilly
Production Editor: Jana M. Stefanciosa
Cartographer: Andrew Murphy
Photo Editor: Richard Fox
Production by Wiley Indianapolis Composition Services

Front Cover Photo: Cupecoy Beach ©Mark Lewis / Getty Images

For information on our other products and services or to obtain technical
support, please contact our Customer Care Department within the U.S. at
877/762-2974, outside the U.S. at 317/572-3993 or fax 317/572-4002.

Wiley also publishes its books in a variety of electronic formats. Some con-
tent that appears in print may not be available in electronic formats.

Manufactured in the United States of America

5   4   3   2   1

CONTENTS

LIST OF MAPS

ACKNOWLEDGMENTS

I'd like to thank the following individuals for their enormous help and support: the Anguilla Tourism Board, Twyla Richardson, and Merlyn Rogers; Accelyn Connor; Bart van Deventer, Amelia Vanterpool-Kubisch, and Suzanne Snart, Malliouhana; Terri Maissen and Gary Thulander, Cap Juluca; Phillip Day and Virgil Napier, the Viceroy Anguilla; the Comité du Tourisme de Saint-Barthélemy and Inès Bouchaut-Choisy; Marc Thézé Nathalie Soubira, Sabine Masseglia, and Amelie Bruzat, Guanahani; Christian & Sandrine Langlade, Hotel Christopher; Rebecca Werner and the Hotel Le Toiny; Kristin Petrelluzzi, L'Esplanade; Erika Cannegieter-Smith, Radisson Blu; the St. Maarten Tourism Board; the Westin St. Maarten; and finally, my husband, Royce Flippin, for his love and support.

—Alexis Lipsitz Flippin

ABOUT THE AUTHOR

Alexis Lipsitz Flippin is a freelance writer and former Frommer's Senior Editor. She has written and edited for consumer magazines and websites such as *Self, American Health,* CNN.com, Weather.com, and *Rolling Stone*.

HOW TO CONTACT US

In researching this book, we discovered many wonderful places—hotels, restaurants, shops, and more. We're sure you'll find others. Please tell us about them, so we can share the information with your fellow travelers in upcoming editions. If you were disappointed with a recommendation, we'd love to know that, too. Please write to:

Frommer's Portable St. Maarten/St. Martin, Anguilla & St. Barts, 3rd Edition
Wiley Publishing, Inc. • 111 River St. • Hoboken, NJ 07030-5774
frommersfeedback@wiley.com

AN ADDITIONAL NOTE

Please be advised that travel information is subject to change at any time—and this is especially true of prices. We therefore suggest that you write or call ahead for confirmation when making your travel plans. The authors, editors, and publisher cannot be held responsible for the experiences of readers while traveling. Your safety is important to us, however, so we encourage you to stay alert and be aware of your surroundings. Keep a close eye on cameras, purses, and wallets, all favorite targets of thieves and pickpockets.

FROMMER'S STAR RATINGS, ICONS & ABBREVIATIONS

Every hotel, restaurant, and attraction listing in this guide has been ranked for quality, value, service, amenities, and special features using a **star-rating system.** In country, state, and regional guides, we also rate towns and regions to help you narrow down your choices and budget your time accordingly. Hotels and restaurants are rated on a scale of zero (recommended) to three stars (exceptional). Attractions, shopping, nightlife, towns, and regions are rated according to the following scale: zero stars (recommended), one star (highly recommended), two stars (very highly recommended), and three stars (must-see).

In addition to the star-rating system, we also use **seven feature icons** that point you to the great deals, in-the-know advice, and unique experiences that separate travelers from tourists. Throughout the book, look for:

Finds	Special finds—those places only insiders know about
Fun Facts	Fun facts—details that make travelers more informed and their trips more fun
Kids	Best bets for kids, and advice for the whole family
Moments	Special moments—those experiences that memories are made of
Overrated	Places or experiences not worth your time or money
Tips	Insider tips—great ways to save time and money
Value	Great values—where to get the best deals

The following **abbreviations** are used for credit cards:

AE	American Express	**DISC**	Discover	**V**	Visa
DC	Diners Club	**MC**	MasterCard		

TRAVEL RESOURCES AT FROMMERS.COM

Frommer's travel resources don't end with this guide. Frommer's website, **www. frommers.com**, has travel information on more than 4,000 destinations. We update features regularly, giving you access to the most current trip-planning information and the best airfare, lodging, and car-rental bargains. You can also listen to podcasts, connect with other Frommers.com members through our active-reader forums, share your travel photos, read blogs from guidebook editors and fellow travelers, and much more.

The Best of St. Maarten/St. Martin with Anguilla & St. Barts

St. Maarten/St. Martin and its neighbors Anguilla and St. Barts offer something for everyone: from pristine beaches and duty-free jewelry to amazing outdoor adventures and nocturnal life on the wild side. You can stay in charming Creole cottages or world-class resorts. And you can dine very well indeed at casual beach barbecues or grand temples of gastronomy. Whatever your tastes and budget, in this chapter I guide you to the best these beautiful islands have to offer.

1 FROMMER'S FAVORITE EXPERIENCES

- **Day-Tripping to Offshore Islands:** Take a trip to a real-life desert island paradise when you visit one of the tiny offshore gems on St. Martin and Anguilla. Here you can snorkel in gin-clear waters, sip rum punches, and eat lobster and barbecue fresh off the grill. There are few more relaxing diversions than wading in the gentle lagoon at Îlet Pinel (Pinel Island) near St. Martin's Orient Beach, or taking similar day trips off-island to Anguilla's Scilly Cay, Sandy Island, Prickly Pear, and Dog Island. See p. 89 and 150.
- **Watching Children Dip their Toes in the Calm, Clear Waters at Le Galion Beach, St. Martin:** It's not called the "children's beach" for nothing. Gentle waves lap a white-sand beach, where the shallow waters seem to go on forever. It's the perfect place for kids to learn the delights of swimming in the sea. See p. 91.
- **Becoming a High-Flying Yachtsman, St. Maarten:** If you've ever dreamed of racing in an America's Cup yachting competition, here's your chance. St. Maarten's 12-Metre Challenge lets you race real America's Cup boats in one of four regattas a day.

St. Maarten/St. Martin, Anguilla & St. Barts

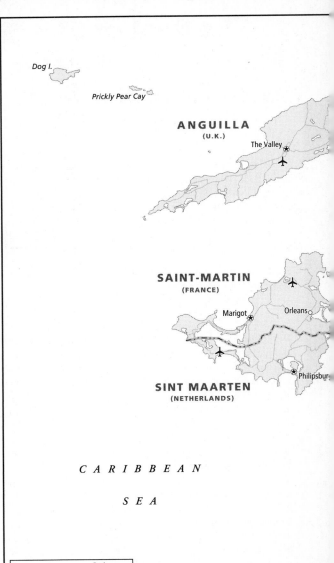

Dog I.

Prickly Pear Cay

ANGUILLA
(U.K.)

The Valley ✈

SAINT-MARTIN
(FRANCE)

✈

Marigot ⊛   Orleans○

✈

SINT MAARTEN
(NETHERLANDS)

Philipsburg ⊛

C A R I B B E A N

S E A

0   5 mi
0   5 km

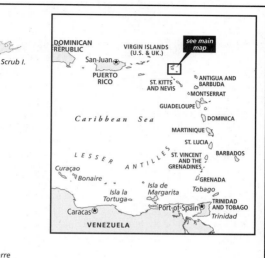

DOMINICAN
REPUBLIC
VIRGIN ISLANDS
(U.S. & UK.)

Scrub I.

San-Juan

PUERTO
RICO

ST. KITTS
AND NEVIS

see main
map

ANTIGUA AND
BARBUDA

MONTSERRAT

GUADELOUPE

C a r i b b e a n   S e a

DOMINICA

MARTINIQUE

ST. LUCIA

L E S S E R   A N T I L L E S

BARBADOS

ST. VINCENT
AND THE
GRENADINES

Curaçao

Bonaire

*Isla de
Margarita*

GRENADA

Tobago

*Isla la
Tortuga*

Caracas

Port-of-Spain

TRINIDAD
AND TOBAGO
Trinidad

VENEZUELA

I. Tintamarre

A T L A N T I C

O C E A N

I. Fourchue

I. Frégate   *I. Toc Vers*

I. Chevreau

La Tortue

SAINT BARTHÉLEMY
(FRANCE)   Gustavia

- **People-Watching at a Sidewalk Cafe:** Find yourself a prime seat on the Marigot waterfront, along the Front Street/Great Bay Boardwalk in Philipsburg (where leviathan cruise ships make the fishing dinghies look like toy boats), or in St. Barts' fairy-tale harbor town, Gustavia.

- **Dining in Grand Case, St. Martin:** This tiny fishing village has an appealing ramshackle style. But don't let its languorous style fool you: The "Gourmet Capital of the Caribbean" has an amazing concentration of top-notch eateries on one beachfront strip. See p. 76.

- **Visiting Loterie Farm, St. Martin:** Head over to this nature reserve to handle the ziplines or hike through virgin rainforest, followed by a meal at the lovely Hidden Forest Cafe. See p. 85.

- **Breakfast at La Samanna, St. Martin:** The view is extraordinary: You're high above Baie Longue, its white sands caressing the curve of the bay. The food isn't bad either: a grand buffet of breakfast favorites plus fresh island fruits and juices. See p. 56.

- **Horseback Riding, St. Maarten/St. Martin:** You actually dip into the water astride your horse during rides with **Bayside Riding Club** on the French side and **Lucky Stables** on the Dutch side (the latter also offers rugged 2-hr. jaunts down to Cay Bay). See p. 95.

- **Chilling in an Anguilla Beach Bar:** No place gets the beach-bar culture as right as Anguilla, where the vibe is laidback, the food tasty, the music toe-tapping, and the setting sublime. It'll cure whatever ails you. See p. 146.

- **Dining Out in Anguilla:** You will not have a bad meal here, I guarantee it, whether you dine in one of the island's highly touted restaurants or at a barbecue buffet at sunset. See p. 140.

- **Kitesurfing in the Grand Cul-de-Sac on St. Barts:** This stretch of water is perfect for kitesurfing. It's a thrill to do, and a thrill to watch, as the billowing kites skim the clouds and the boards skate the glassy sea. See p. 186.

- **Beach-Hopping in St. Barts:** Everyone does it, and they know *how* to do it. Grab a beach umbrella (your hotel can provide one for you)—shade is hard to find on St. Bart's beaches—towels, beach book, and delicious-smelling Ligne St. Barth coconut oil, and prepare for a day of luxuriating on some of the world's finest beaches. See p. 184.

- **Shopping in St. Barts:** When it comes to shopping, St. Barts wins the prize hands-down for the best in the Caribbean—it's Paris by the sea. And even better: It's duty and tax free. You can find stylish, high-quality clothing in even the most basic-looking shops. The pharmacies are shopping havens, where the famously exquisite French skincare lines and toiletries are a pleasure to browse. Even the grocery stores are a marvel, with imported French cheeses, pâtés, wine, and—ooh-la-la!—the French version of canned ravioli. See p. 187.

2 THE BEST BEACHES

- **Dawn Beach, St. Maarten:** The views of St. Barts, great beach bars, excellent windsurfing, and superb snorkeling enchant at any time of day. See p. 88.
- **Mullet Bay, St. Maarten:** This beautiful beach has a couple of beach shacks serving food and drinks and a sprinkling of umbrellas and chairs, but nowhere near the activity it once enjoyed as the silky strand fronting the Mullet Bay Resort, the island's first resort and now in a state of (seemingly) perpetual ruin after Hurricane Luis took it out of commission in 1995. The blue pearlescent waters are calm, and the snorkeling isn't bad along the rocks. See p. 87.
- **Simpson Bay, St. Maarten:** In spite of its proximity to the airport and the cluttered bar/casino/restaurant activity around the Simpson Bay area, this beach is quiet and peaceful, with long stretches of curving sand and sparkling turquoise seas. A good place to access the beach is at Mary's Boon Beach Resort. See p. 87.
- **Orient Bay, St. Martin:** This happening strand may be clothing optional, but it also happens to be a beautiful beach. If you're looking for watersports action and a lively beach-bar scene, this is the place to find it. See p. 90.
- **Baie Longue, St. Martin:** The longest and perhaps most private stretch of sand on St. Martin, and a fine place to spot celebrities staying at La Samanna. See p. 88.
- **Baie de l'Embouchure/Galion Beach, St. Martin:** This crescent is encircled (and protected) by a reef, making it a prime family beach. But the steady breezes lure windsurfers, too. It's a great place to glide, and learn. See p. 91.
- **Happy Bay, St. Martin:** You can only reach this pretty, remarkably deserted scimitar of sand by boat or by a short hike from Friars Bay; bring a snorkel and fins. See p. 90.
- **Pinel Island, St. Martin:** This tiny offshore cay makes for a wonderful day trip with a perfect lagoon to paddle around in. See p. 89.

- **Shoal Bay East, Anguilla:** Not to be confused with Shoal Bay West, this beach offers both rollicking beach bars and seclusion, with great snorkeling on its less-trafficked eastern flank. See p. 150.
- **Rendezvous Bay, Anguilla:** This picture-perfect beach curls and stretches its sands for nearly 3 miles—it's a great swimming beach. See p. 149.
- **Maundays Bay, Anguilla:** The prime beach for the Cap Juluca resort, Maundays Bay has calm, sparkling waters that are perfect for swimming and snorkeling. See p. 151.
- **Meads Bay, Anguilla:** Big, languorous rolls and gin-clear turquoise seas are overseen by swooping pelicans. Take your snorkeling equipment to the rocks beneath the Malliouhana resort. See p. 149.
- **Offshore Cays, Anguilla:** Head out for a castaway adventure to such delicious spits of sand as Dog Island, Prickly Pear, Sandy Island, and Scilly Cay—the latter three also have ramshackle beach bars where lobster is grilled to perfection. See p. 150.
- **St-Jean Beach, St. Barts:** This beach is split into two beaches by the Eden Rock hotel, but it's lovely nonetheless, and just steps away from great shopping and dining. See p. 184.
- **Colombier Beach, St. Barts:** This beloved beach can only be reached by two hiking trails—one a 25-minute walk along a rocky goat trail—or by boat. It's ideal for swimming and snorkeling. See p. 185.
- **Flamands Beach, St. Barts:** The island's biggest beach, Flamands has fine sand and that rarity on St. Barts beaches: shade. See p. 184.
- **Gouverneur Beach, St. Barts:** On the island's south side, this beach is just steps from the parking lot. It's a beauty, with good surf and snorkeling by the rocks. See p. 185.
- **Salines Beach, St. Barts:** From the parking lot, it's a 10- or 15-minute walk along somewhat rocky terrain to this protected cove with body-surfable waves. Like all of St. Barts' strands, it's clothing optional. Spend a morning here, then head to Grain de Sel for a spot-on Creole lunch. See p. 185.

3 THE BEST PLACES TO GET AWAY FROM IT ALL

- **Hôtel L'Esplanade,** Grand Case, St. Martin (© **590/87-06-55**), is up on a bluff overlooking Grand Case and Grand Case beach, which you can see from your private terrace. This 24-room hotel is decked out in colorful tiles and pillowed in a profusion of tropical blooms, and the rooms manage to be utterly private, beautifully outfitted, and comfortably homey all at once. You're just 5 minutes away from bustling Grand Case below, but this tranquil spot feels like a world apart. See p. 59.

- **Malliouhana,** Anguilla (© 800/835-0796). Set atop a limestone bluff overlooking Meads Bay, this venerable resort is a true getaway. The hotel sprawls over 25 acres of gently curving, beautifully landscaped property, and tiered public spaces let you move around the resort discreetly. See p. 133.
- **Palm Grove,** Anguilla (© 264/497-4224). Down a long, winding potholed road that cuts through scrub brush is this idyllic spot, the rough-hewn culinary domain of Nat Richardson and one of the sweetest snorkeling beaches on the island. Nat's place is little more than a beach shack, but his barbecued specialties (lobster, crayfish, ribs, chicken, fresh fish) are well worth the trip. The johnnycakes are first-rate, too. See p. 146.
- **Le Toiny,** St. Barts (© 800/278-6469). In your gloriously furnished villa, with its own private plunge pool, tiled terrace, and gated entrance, you don't have to see or be seen by anyone—even breakfast arrives in a hush, set out on a patio table sheathed in crisp linens and silver cutlery. From every vantage point, the sea/sky/mountain vista is soul-stirring. See p. 170.

4 THE BEST LUXURY HOTELS

- **La Samanna,** Baie Longue, St. Martin (© 800/237-1236), is rare among resorts in its class, offering posh pampering with nary a hint of pretension. The main restaurant is set high up over Baie Longue—an unbelievably beautiful setting. See p. 56.
- **Cap Juluca,** Maundays Bay, Anguilla (© 888/858-5822), is always at or near the top of everyone's "Best Of" lists—and a refashioning of the lobby and public spaces has made the place feel fresh and vigorous again. It's a favorite of celebrities and captains of industry, but regular folks get the royal treatment, too. See p. 131.
- **Malliouhana,** Mead's Bay, Anguilla (© 800/835-0796). The grande dame of Anguilla (celebrating its 25th year) may have the most beautiful *situation* in the Caribbean. Add to that thoughtful landscaping, a fine beach (with surprisingly good off-the-beach snorkeling), a world-class spa, solid new hands-on management,

and owner Leon Roydon's collecting passions on display: colorful Haitian art and arguably the Caribbean's finest wine cellar. See p. 133.

- **CuisinArt,** Anguilla (© **264/498-2000**), has a world-class beach, a lovely pool, a fabulous spa, and an amazing hydroponic farm, which supplies its on-site restaurants with fresh produce. It's a sunny, comfortable, well-managed resort, with service and amenities that just get better and better. See p. 132.

- **Viceroy,** Anguilla (© **888/622-4567**). From afar, it looks like a small city landed on the promontory between Meads Bay and Barnes Bay. Up close, this huge property's sleek white structures are smartly juxtaposed against the deep-blue sea and sky. Rooms are outfitted with every 21st-century toy and dazzling Malibu-meets-Miami interiors by Kelly Wearstler. See p. 134.

- **Eden Rock,** Baie de St-Jean, St. Barts (© **877/563-7105**). Its lodgings are staggered on either side of the titular bluff that cleaves the bay. Owners David and Jane Matthews never rest on their laurels, constantly improving one of the Caribbean's most elegant enclaves. See p. 168.

- **Hotel Christopher,** St. Barts (© **590/27-63-63**). Yes, rooms are small and the rates not even close to luxury-resort stratospheric. But this smart, sophisticated, and intimate spot is an earthy sanctuary of barefoot luxury. Every detail has been painstakingly thought out, from the impeccably (and sustainably) sourced materials and ultrafine linens to the custom-made toiletries and attentive but never obsequious service. And that view! Watch the sunset while relaxing on your terrace or lounging around the island's largest infinity pool. See p. 175.

- **Hotel Guanahani & Spa,** Grand Cul-de-Sac, St. Barts (© **590/27-66-60**), is the ultimate spot to relax and unwind and let the pros pamper you. The vibrantly colored rooms are stuffed with state-of-the-art amenities, the beach looks out on beauteous Grand Cul-de-Sac bay, and the food is terrific. The capper? All this luxury is yours without pomp or attitude. See p. 171.

- **The Villas at Le Sereno,** Grand Cul-de-Sac, St. Barts (© **590/52-83-00**), are simply spectacular, with panoramic views of Grand Cul-de-Sac. They include designer kitchens stocked with Le Creuset pots and pans and big plunge pools. See p. 170.

- **Hôtel St. Barth Isle de France,** Baie des Flamands, St. Barts (© **590/27-61-81**), is an award-winning boutique hotel (35 rooms) that is both luxurious and comfortable. It opens right onto glorious Flamands beach. See p. 169.

- **Temptation,** Cupecoy, St. Maarten (© **599/545-2254**), lives up to its admittedly silly if appropriate name with the island's most creative fare, not to mention an incredibly hip space. See p. 69.
- **Spiga,** Grand Case, St. Martin (© **590/52-47-83**), proves that Grand Case (and St. Martin) can cook Italian with equal panache. From tuna carpaccio to tiramisu, everything is perfection. See p. 78.
- **Lolos,** St. Martin/St. Maarten, is a term for basic outdoor barbecue shacks that dish out heaping helpings of Creole fare at unbelievably fair prices. The biggest concentration lies along the beach in Grand Case. See p. 77.
- **Blanchards,** Anguilla (© **264/497-6100**), ranks high on everyone's list of top beachfront eateries. Owners Bob and Melinda Blanchard have become celebrities themselves, thanks to their witty books about the joys and perils of running a Caribbean restaurant. See p. 141.
- **Da'Vida,** Anguilla (© **264/498-5433**). Anguillian Chef Guy Gumbs' restaurant is one of the island's favorite places for celebratory dinners. Da'Vida—whose motto is "Celebrate Life"—comprises a more upscale open-air restaurant and the casual **Bayside Grill.** The menu draws heavily on local seafood (crayfish, snapper, grouper) and does creative twists on traditional island cuisine. Everything is just steps from shimmering Crocus Bay. See p. 145.
- **Veya** (Anguilla; © **264/498-8392**): On an island blessed with top-caliber chefs and the Caribbean's best dining scene, this Sandy Ground "treehouse" is one of the best—and it's only been around since 2007. The Pennsylvanian chef/owners call their food the "cuisine of the sun," and it's a minxy fusion of exotic flavors from hot spots around the globe. See p. 144.
- **Le Gaïac,** Anse de Toiny, St. Barts (© **590/27-88-88**), in the Le Toiny hotel, has an ambience that is swooningly romantic at dinner and food that is sublime any time. See p. 183.
- **Dining Beachside on St. Barts:** You can do it high (**Santa Fe,** overlooking **Gouverneur Beach**) or you can do it low (**Do Brazil,** on the sands of Shell Beach) but dining on St. Barts' beaches is simply divine. Try it casual (**O'Corrail,** Grand Cul-de-Sac) or fancy (Eden Rock's **On the Rocks,** overlooking Baie St-Jean). See chapter 9.

6 THE BEST SHOPPING

- **Front Street** in Philipsburg, St. Maarten is a mind-boggling display of rampant consumerism. And it's all duty-free, from luxury watches to diamonds to Delft china. See chapter 6.
- **Marigot, French St. Martin.** Skip the icy air-conditioned and marbled West Indies Mall and explore the streets of this charming village for shops selling prêt-a-porter, atmospheric wine stores, and French pharmacies. The tiny warrens and back alleys around the marina are filled with serendipitous finds. See chapter 6.
- **Artists' ateliers** on French St. Martin are particularly notable, showcasing Gallic expats working in a variety of media and traditions. Many open their studios to visitors, offering a wonderful insight into the creative process. See chapter 6.
- **Gustavia,** the capital of St. Barts, is crammed with stores selling couture and prêt-a-porter. Many of the luxury brands are here: Bulgari, Cartier, Giorgio Armani, Louis Vuitton, and Hermès. See chapter 8.
- **St-Jean, St. Barts,** has several small shopping plazas along the main road leading toward Lorient: Les Galeries du Commerce, La Villa Creole, La Sodexa, and L'Espace Neptune, each filled with boutiques selling the stylishly casual St. Barts clothing we covet: flirty, sexy kurtas and dresses; slouchy jersey separates; gold and silver sandals or bejeweled flip-flops. See chapter 6.
- **La Ligne St. Barth,** Lorient, St. Barts (𝄞 **590/27-82-63**), produces skincare, scents, and cosmetic products made with extracts from Caribbean flowers and seeds. The company laboratory/shop on Route de Salines in Lorient often offers slightly damaged products at deep discounts. See p. 188.

7 THE BEST NIGHTLIFE

- **Bliss,** St. Maarten (𝄞 **599/545-3936**), sounds like a spa, but it's actually Bernie's equally sizzling neighbor, another multipurpose beachfront nightclub-cum-restaurant-cum-live-music-venue. See p. 110.
- **Casino Royale,** St. Maarten (𝄞 **599/545-2590**), is the island's largest and glitziest casino, but really gets the nod over its competitors for its Vegas-style showroom and upstairs high-tech disco throwback, **Tantra.** See p. 118.

- **Sunset Beach Bar,** St. Maarten (© **599/545-3998**), on the same beach as Bernie's and Bliss, is one of those places you either love or hate, but it's a "must" experience. A dive in the best or worst sense of the word, Sunset is famous for watching the planes take off and land right above your head. See p. 113.
- **Cheri's Café,** St. Maarten (© **599/545-3361**), is one of those institutions that manages to avoid becoming a cliché or a tourist trap: good relatively inexpensive food, congenial crowd, and fun entertainment. See p. 115.
- **Johnno's Beach Stop,** Sandy Ground, Anguilla (© **264/497-2728**), is another enduringly popular haunt that draws everyone from locals to the Hollywood elite for great barbecue and live music on the beach. See p. 147.
- **Dune Preserve,** Rendezvous Bay, Anguilla (© **264/497-2660**), is a multi-tiered beachfront bar that was crafted out of old boats and beach salvage. It's got lots of interesting nooks and crannies and is owned by Anguilla's best-known singer, "Bankie" Banx; the place is jammed when he performs. See p. 147.
- **Le Bête à Z'Ailes** (also known as the Baz Bar) on the harbor in Gustavia, St. Barts (© **590/92-74-09**) is a happening live music club, where an eclectic assortment of bands play soul, jazz, blues, urban folk, and indie tunes, accompanied by excellent sushi and creative cocktails. See p. 190.
- **Le Ti St. Barth,** Pointe Milou, St. Barts (© **590/27-97-71**), serves up uneven but often excellent food in a torchlit setting that lures the wealthy and beautiful for fashion shows and theme nights. See p. 190.

Planning Your Trip to St. Maarten/ St. Martin with Anguilla & St. Barts

This chapter tackles the how-tos of a trip to St. Maarten/ St. Martin and Anguilla and St. Barts, including everything from finding airfares to deciding whether to rent a car. But first, let's start with some background information about these increasingly popular destinations.

For additional help in planning your trip and for more on-the-ground resources, please see "Fast Facts," beginning on p. 191.

1 THE ISLANDS IN BRIEF

ST. MAARTEN/ST. MARTIN

For an island with a big reputation for restaurants, hotels, and energetic nightlife, St. Maarten/St. Martin is small—only 96 sq. km (37 sq. miles), about half the area of Washington, D.C. It's the smallest territory in the world shared by two sovereign states: the Netherlands and France. St. Maarten (Sint Maarten) is the Dutch half, and St. Martin is the French half.

The island was officially split in 1648, but the two nations have coexisted so peacefully since then that if you're not paying attention, you won't even know you've crossed over from one side to the next. Still, the differences are there. Returning visitors who haven't been to the island for a while are often shocked when they see today's St. Maarten. No longer a sleepy Caribbean backwater, it's now a boomtown. The Dutch capital, Philipsburg, is often bustling with cruise ship hordes: Some 1.7 million cruise-ship passengers arrive here annually. Traffic congestion, caused in large part by the 6-times-daily drawbridge openings and closings in Simpson Bay, has become a major irritant.

Despite these problems, St. Maarten continues to attract massive numbers of visitors who want a sunny Caribbean island vacation with a splash of Vegas. The old girl still has charm to spare: The landscape

St. Maarten: Cruisin'

Some 20 cruise lines and 1.7 million cruise passengers arrive in St. Maarten annually. St. Maarten has a total of six dedicated cruise berths—making it one of the Caribbean's largest cruise-ship ports—and the big ones do pull in here, including a recent visit by *Oasis of the Seas,* the 2,700-cabin behemoth that has enjoyed record-breaking passenger numbers (over 6,000). For more about the port, go to www.portofstmaarten.com.

of undulating green hills is magical, and the island's 39 sun-splashed, white-sand beaches remain unspoiled.

St. Maarten also has what many other Caribbean nations do not: a real cosmopolitanism. The island isn't known as the "crossroads of the Caribbean" for nothing. As one expat from Surinam told me: "St. Maarten is much more accepting of outsiders than on some other Caribbean islands. Here, nearly everyone is from somewhere else."

The Dutch capital, **Philipsburg,** curves like a toy village along Great Bay. The town lies on a narrow sand isthmus separating Great Bay and the Great Salt Pond. Commander John Philips, a Scot in Dutch employ, founded the capital in 1763. To protect Great Bay, Fort Amsterdam was built in 1737. Philipsburg is one of the Caribbean's busiest duty-free stopping shops (especially when the cruise ships are in port), although a handsome beachside boardwalk has made strolling the town a real pleasure.

The French side of the island has a quieter, less frenetic pace. It's sleepier than the Dutch side and much less Americanized. Most hotels tend to be smaller and more secluded than their Dutch counterparts, and you won't be overwhelmed with cruise-ship crowds. Most people come to St. Martin to relax on its lovely (clothing-optional) beaches and experience "France in the Tropics." That's because St. Martin has a distinctly French air. The towns have names like Colombier and Orléans, the streets are *rues,* and the French flag flies over the *gendarmerie* in **Marigot,** the capital. An extraordinary number of atmospheric restaurants serve authentic French cuisine with sassy Creole inflections.

About 15 minutes by car beyond Marigot is **Grand Case,** a tiny outpost of French civilization, with an inordinate number of excellent restaurants and a couple of top-notch boutique hotels. Grand Case is a French/Creole small town with dogs roaming the streets, kids doing wheelies on bikes, and bougainvillea spilling over picket fences. Top that off with a lovely beachside setting, a main street lined with seriously good restaurants, and oh, an airport where commuter-size airplanes buzz Main Street at regular intervals daily. It's like a French Mayberry, except here Aunt Bea is a 5-star chef.

In 2010, both Dutch St. Maarten and French St. Martin underwent major administrative changes. No longer governed from Guadeloupe, French St. Martin is now an overseas collectivity (COM) of France. And at press time, the deadline for the dissolution of the Netherland (or Dutch) Antilles—an autonomous territory comprised of two groups of Caribbean islands administered by the Kingdom of the Netherlands—was fast-approaching. If it comes to pass, St. Maarten will be a self-governing country within the Netherlands for the first time since 1815.

ANGUILLA

Just 20 minutes by ferry from Marigot, flat, arid, scrubby Anguilla has become one of the Caribbean's choicest destinations, despite its unprepossessing landscape and comparative lack of colonial grandeur. The reasons are obvious: The island resembles one big sugary-sand beach surrounded by luminous turquoise seas. The locals are congenial and laid-back, all beneficiaries of the excellent British education

A Little History

Excavations suggest St. Maarten was settled around 2,500 years ago by American Indian Arawaks. Christopher Columbus sighted the island during his second voyage in November 1493, naming it without setting foot on land. The Spaniards couldn't spare the expense of military maintenance after several devastating European wars, so they literally abandoned it in 1648, enabling opportunistic French and Dutch settlers from, respectively, St. Kitts and St. Eustatius, to claim the island. After initial skirmishes, mostly political, the two nations officially settled their differences later that year. Even so, St. Maarten changed hands 16 times before it became permanently Dutch, while the French side endured the usual colonial tugs-of-war through the Napoleonic era. Alas, there appears to be no truth to the colorful legend of a wine-drinking Frenchman and gin-guzzling Dutchman walking the island to determine the border.

Visitor Information

For the latest information on **Dutch St. Maarten** and **French St Martin,** go to **www.vacationstmaarten.com** and **www.st-martin.org**, respectively. You can also contact the **St. Maarten Tourist Bureau,** 675 Third Ave., Ste. 1807, New York, NY 10017 (📞 **800/786-2278** or 212/953-2084). For information on French St. Martin, contact the **St. Martin Promotional Bureau** at 825 Third Ave., New York, NY 10022 (frontdesk@saint-martin.org). In Canada, the office for information about the Dutch side of the island is located at 703 Evans Ave., Ste. 106, Toronto, ON M9C 5E9 (📞 **416/622-4300**). For information about the French side of the island, contact 1981 Ave. McGill College, Ste. 490, in Montréal (📞 **514/288-4264**).

Once on St. Maarten, go to the **Tourist Information Bureau,** Vineyard Office Park, 33 W. G. Buncamper Rd., Philipsburg, St. Maarten, N.A. (📞 **599/542-2337**), open Monday to Friday from 9am to 5pm.

The tourist board on French St. Martin, called the **Office du Tourisme,** is at Route de Sandy Ground, Marigot, 97150 St. Martin (📞 **590/87-57-21**), open Monday to Friday from 8am to 1pm and 2:30 to 5:30pm.

For details on Anguilla and St. Barts, see chapters 8 and 9.

system. You'll find almost no hawking, pushiness, or overt poverty—and correspondingly low crime rates. The leading resorts and villa complexes define luxury, and the food is among the finest in the Caribbean. And yet the vibe is pleasingly laid-back in even the toniest resorts; it's barefoot luxury at its least pretentious.

ST. BARTS

A quick flight or 45-minute ferry ride 24km (15 miles) east of St. Maarten/St. Martin, this rugged, hilly, 21-sq.-km (8-sq.-mile) island ("St. Barths," to the locals) is practically synonymous with international glamour and glorious beaches. The cost for effortless chic is high, but the jet set has never minded. Despite its forbidding prices and luxury reputation—and its sometimes ostentatious display of wealth—St. Barts has retained its French soul and sunny, easy-going West Indian heart. The 8,000 locals—many descended from the original hardy Norman and Breton settlers—remain matter-of-fact and supremely unimpressed by the jet-setting crowd. And why not? Their cultural traditions are firmly entrenched in a fairy-tale capital, **Gustavia;** the Caribbean equivalent of the Riviera, **St-Jean;** exceptionally pretty fishing villages in **Colombier** and **Corossol;** and along a gnarled coastline, some of the world's most beautiful beaches.

2 THE THREE-ISLAND ITINERARY

It's become incredibly easy to get to these islands from North America. A number of major carriers fly direct routes from North American hubs into Dutch St. Maarten's Princess Juliana International Airport, just minutes from several of the Dutch side's top beaches. If you're heading on to another island, you won't even have to bother with a taxi. You can leave straight from the airport on a 10-minute puddle-jumper to St. Barts or hop on a private shuttle boat (30 min.) to Anguilla. If your time is limited, St. Maarten/St. Martin is a great long-weekend getaway, ideal for a quick break from the winter doldrums: You can take a direct flight out of New York City, for example, and be at the St. Maarten airport in under 4 hours. The islands are also perfect for longer stays, where you really get under the skin of a place—and as close as these islands are to one another (so near that from certain vantage points the lights of another island glitter across the sea), there's a world of difference among them, both culturally and physically. I say experience them all: These are three of the Caribbean's real gems.

Seeing **all three islands in one trip** is easy to do and highly recommended, especially if you have the time to spend at least 3 nights on each. The following itinerary does just that.

Days ❶–❷: St. Maarten/St. Martin

Fly into **Princess Juliana International Airport** in Dutch St. Maarten. You can pick up a rental car at the airport, but I suggest a 2-night stay at the **Radisson Blu,** in **Anse Marcel,** French St. Martin. It's a beautiful spot and the perfect place to ease into a tropical holiday—but it also has something the other resorts don't: a **water taxi ride** straight from the airport. Talk about instant immersion! It's a lovely 30-minute trip tracing the curves of the island's northwest coast on the catamaran *ScoobiToo.* Once you're at the resort, relax by the huge infinity pool or on the half-moon beach of this picturesque cove. On Day 2, plan a day trip to nearby **Pinel Island** or head to **Orient Beach.** See p. 81.

Days ❸–❺: St. Barts

Take a taxi to tiny **L'Esperance Airport** in nearby **Grand Case** and fly a little 6-seater on **St. Barth Commuter** for a 3-night stay on St.

Barts. The flight is just under 10 minutes, but it's a scintillating one, with sweeping views of the volcanic rocks that pepper the sea and a daredevil landing on an abbreviated strip of asphalt that ends within a hair of St. Jean beach. Whew! If you're staying at a resort, most provide airport pickup, but if you're staying at a villa, you'll probably want to rent a car at the airport. *Tip:* Drive slowly and carefully on these rollercoaster roads. You can get supplies at the **Super-U supermarket** across from the airport or hit **Maya's To Go,** also across from the airport, which sells delicious takeout specialties. (And keep in mind that even though everyone accepts dollars, the **euro** is the main currency on St. Barts and French St. Martin—and at press time gives better bang for the buck.)

If you arrive early enough, this is a good day to hit a couple of St. Barts' justly famous beaches. Head to **Grand Salines Beach** and have lunch at Grain de Sel or go to **Gouverneur Beach** and follow with a cocktail at Santa Fe, high above the beach. On the second day, head to the charming little port of Gustavia for a morning of shopping (shops close at lunch); have the daily *plat du jour* at the **Wall House,** and if it's high season, stroll the **waterfront quay** for an eye-popping primer in Yachts, Mega.

You can spend your third day taking a snorkeling trip with **Marine Service** to gorgeous **Colombier Beach** (which is only reached by boat or by climbing one of two old goat paths) or windsurfing/shopping along **St. Jean beach.** See p. 184.

Day ❻: Marigot, St. Martin

Fly back into Grand Case on St. Barth Commuter and take a 15-minute taxi to the **Port de Saint-Martin** in Marigot, the waterfront ferry depot where the Anguilla public ferry arrives and departs on a regular basis. The small ferry terminal has a luggage storage area, where you can secure your bags ($5 plus tip) while you spend a few hours sightseeing and shopping in Marigot. The village of Marigot is a colorful slice of France in the tropics. It has a rich cache of duty-free shops and tony international brands (Chanel, Cartier, Hermes) as well as French and Creole restaurants clustered around the waterfront and marina. It's a charming place to poke about—and the spot to do your shopping; Anguilla has very few shops, and what's there is exorbitant. Marigot has a number of excellent wine shops, including **Le Goût du Vin,** where you can find fine French wines at decent prices. Along Marigot's harbor side, a lively **morning market** on Wednesday and Saturday hosts vendors selling clothing, spices, and handicrafts. Have a late lunch at one of the **lolos** alongside the waterfront; I like **Enoch's Place** for its delicious and reasonably priced platter of garlicky shrimp, rice and peas, and salad. See p. 77.

Days ❻–❽: Anguilla

After your exploration of Marigot, pick up your luggage at the ferry terminal and buy your ticket for a ride on the **public ferry** to Anguilla. It's a 30-minute trip to this long, sandy, relatively flat island, a radical topographical departure from the mossy volcanic hills of St. Martin and St. Barts. (The last ferry leaves around 6:15pm.) It's a departure of a cultural kind, too; you're no longer in France but on English-speaking turf, and the dollar is the currency of choice at this self-governing British overseas territory. Once you've arrived at **Blowing Point** and passed through immigration, either your resort will pick you up or you can take a taxi to your hotel or villa. (Most car-rental agencies are happy to drop off rental cars wherever you're staying.) If you arrive before the sun sets, head to **Sandy Ground** or one of the resorts or restaurants on the **West End** to drink in the sunset. You can't go wrong anywhere on **Meads Bay,** but the **Sunset Bar** terrace at **Malliouhana,** overlooking the sweep of the sea and the pelicans roosting below, is pretty spectacular.

Anguilla is all about breathtaking beaches: On your second day in Anguilla, do a little beach hopping. Head to Meads Bay or Shoal Bay East and enjoy some of the barbecue grub at beach shacks like Gwen's. Or grab your snorkeling equipment and drive the winding, bumpy road to the beautiful beach at **Junk's Hole,** where you can dine in barefoot splendor on grilled lobster, local crayfish, or ribs at Nat Richardson's **Palm Grove Bar & Grill** on the beach.

On your third day in Anguilla, plan a snorkeling trip to an idyllic **offshore island** such as **Prickly Pear** or **Sandy Island.** Here you can snorkel, look for shells, and generally putter about a spit of sand in the castaway spirit. A couple have ramshackle beach shacks where fresh lobster and fish are always on the grill and a stiff rum drink is *de rigueur*. See p. 150.

Day ❾: Grand Case, St. Martin

Head back on an afternoon ferry to Marigot. Take a taxi to the little French village of **Grand Case.** I highly recommend a stay at the **Hotel L'Esplanade,** which is nestled into a cliff overlooking Grand Case beach. Grand Case is the culinary heart of St. Martin (some say it has the best assemblage of top restaurants in the Caribbean). This sleepy little town comes alive in the evening, when folks head to the **Calmos Café** or neighbor **Zen It** to watch the sunset. It's a favored culinary destination for visitors from all over the island, who arrive in waves of shuttle vans to descend on the narrow two-lane **Boulevard de Grand Case** to pick a place to dine. The food is largely French/Creole, with most places offering local lobster and fish. The restaurants overlooking

Day ⑩: Princess Juliana International Airport, St. Maarten

Fly home out of Princess Juliana International Airport—but before you leave, have the taxi driver take you to **Hilma's Windsor Castle,** a little trailer on Airport Road in Simpson Bay that serves some of the best johnnycakes on the island. Two dollars will get you a johnnycake filled with saltfish simmered with onions, peppers, and seasonings. It's greasy; it's great.

---

3 WHEN TO GO

THE HIGH & LOW SEASONS

Hotels on all three islands charge their highest rates during the peak winter season, from mid-December to mid-April. Christmas week rates may double those tariffs. You should make reservations months in advance for Christmas and February, especially over Presidents' Day weekend. School spring breaks are also busy family times.

The off-season on all three islands runs roughly mid-April to mid-December (though exact dates vary according to the property). Even though August can be a popular month for vacationing Europeans, it's one big summer sale: Most hotels, inns, condos, and villas slash their prices 20% to 50%. The beaches are less crowded and many top lodgings and restaurants shutter for one, even 2 months as the owners take their own vacation or perform necessary renovations. Be sure to request a room away from noise if the hotel remains open during construction. I provide closing dates wherever possible, but visitors should double-check before booking.

WEATHER

High season on all three islands features a temperate climate, rarely exceeding 90°F (32°C), with lower humidity and the famed cooling trade winds blowing in from the northeast. It's ideal beach weather, with the occasional cloudy day. Usually rain showers are brief: Islanders call them "liquid sunshine."

Rainy season runs from late May to mid-November. This doesn't mean it rains for days at a time or even every day. But this also roughly corresponds to the official Atlantic hurricane season, June 1 to November 30. Fortunately, satellite surveillance provides enough advance warning to take precautions and, rarely, evacuate.

St. Maarten/St. Martin Average Daily Temperature & Rainfall

	Jan	Feb	Mar	Apr	May	June	July	Aug	Sept	Oct	Nov	Dec
Temp. (°F)	77	77	77	79	81	81	83	83	83	81	80	79
Temp. (°C)	25	25	25	26	27	27	28	28	28	28	27	26
Rainfall (in.)	2.5	1.3	1.6	2.3	2.3	3.8	3.8	3.5	3.7	4.4	3.8	3.7

ST. MAARTEN/ST. MARTIN CALENDAR OF EVENTS

For Anguilla and St. Barts, see chapters 8 and 9.

JANUARY & FEBRUARY

Carnival. Festivities on St. Martin last for nearly 2 months starting the second Sunday in January with parade rehearsals and band tryouts.

Carnival reaches its frenzied peak on the French side in February, with jump-ups, barbecues, and pageants. It all leads to J'ouvert, the weekend before Mardi Gras, and lasts until Ash Wednesday. The dancing-in-the-streets parades represent the culmination of an entire year's preparation, from creating the feathered, sequined costumes to writing unique musical themes. The streets are crowded with young and old following trucks with enormous sound systems in Marigot until everyone congregates at "Carnival Village" come nightfall for concerts and events, including the crowning of the Carnival King and Queen.

MARCH

Heineken Regatta. Now in its third decade, this annual series of major boat races debuted in 1980. More than 200 vessels, from converted family fishing dinghies to race prototypes, compete in several categories. It's a prime excuse for partying, particularly on the Dutch side. For details, go to www.heinekenregatta.com. First weekend of March.

APRIL

Carnival. The Dutch side chimes in with its own, even more extravagant version, beginning the Wednesday after Easter Sunday and continuing for 15 riotous days of beauty pageants, costume and calypso competitions, Mas bands, parades, shows, and assorted revels.

The Carnival Village features stands dishing out spicy local fare and an enormous stage where local and international musicians perform nightly. J'ouvert, the opening jump-up, showcases local and international bands and thousands of revelers line the streets and follow the bands until they arrive at Carnival Village.

More parades are held the next morning, and the grandest of all takes place on the Queen's Birthday. Crowds pack the streets of Philipsburg vying for a spot to see the musicians, the outrageous costumes, and the colorful floats. The Last Lap, the grand finale of the Carnival, includes a symbolic burning of King Momo, a straw figure who embodies the spirit of Carnival. Island legend claims that burning the King in effigy will purge the sins and consequent bad luck of the village. Check www.stmaartencarnival.com for more information.

St. Maarten Open Golf Tournament. Residents and visitors alike are invited to participate in this 3-day 54-hole event at Mullet Bay Golf Resort. For details, go to www.stmaartengolf.com. Second weekend in April.

MAY

Ecotourism Day. Nature discovery organizations, activity operators, artisans, and local entertainers take over the Bellevue Estate on the French side for this event. You can indulge in free sea kayaking, scuba diving, horseback tours, mountain bike riding, hiking, and treasure hunts. Cultural and culinary traditions are displayed: spice-growing, pottery-making, coffee-roasting. Typical island dishes and local bands are also on the menu. Go to www.st-martin.org for updates. Usually second or third weekend of May.

Fête du Nautisme. This watersports festival organized by METIMER, the St. Martin Sea Trades Association, focuses on (re)discovering the rich marine environment. Free activities include yacht and motorboat excursions and regattas, jet-skiing, kayaking, and windsurfing, with lessons available. Usually second or third weekend of May.

JUNE

Billfish Tournament. One of the Caribbean's most prestigious fishing competitions lasts nearly the entire week, attracting anglers from Europe and the Caribbean. About 30 fishing boats battle at the "Marlin Boulevard" area, rich fishing grounds about 48km (30 miles) east of St. Maarten. Go to www.billfish-tournament.com for details. First or second week of June.

The Fishing Event. Fish the famous Marlin Boulevard area, rich fishing grounds about 48km (30 miles) east of St. Maarten. Go to www.the-fishing-event.com for details. Third or fourth week of June.

JULY

Bastille Day. The French holiday is celebrated island-wide with fanfare and fireworks, races and revelry. July 14.

Schoelcher Day. Boat and bike races are held in honor of Victor Schoelcher, a Frenchman who fought against slavery. July 21.

Regina Labega: My Favorite St. Maarten

Regina Labega, St. Maarten's Director of Tourism, is passionate about her island, both the Dutch and French sides. Instead of competing with one another, as she has famously said, the two islands "complement each other." Here are her favorite island activities:

- Going on an island tour by boat—it's beautiful and relaxing.
- Visiting my favorite beach, Friar's Bay.
- Dining at Temptation restaurant (especially for the foie gras).
- Looking out over Orient Bay.
- Seeing St. Maarten by air. I also love to watch the planes land from Sunset Beach Bar.
- Watching King Beau-Beau perform. When I think of a singer on St. Maarten, I think of Beau-Beau; he is our Frank Sinatra!
- Shopping for perfume and jewelry in Philipsburg—shops here have the most exotic pieces you can find, especially white gold.
- I love to hear the ocean and gaze at the hills. It makes me feel calm.

NOVEMBER

St. Maarten's Day. Christopher Columbus named the island St. Maarten/St. Martin because he discovered it in 1493 on November 11, the feast day of St. Martin of Tours. Island residents on both sides still celebrate it as an official holiday, organizing various sporting events, parades, and jump-ups over 2 to 3 days. November 11.

4 ENTRY REQUIREMENTS

ENTRY REQUIREMENTS
Passports

U.S. and Canadian citizens must have a passport or a combination of a birth certificate and photo ID, plus a return or ongoing ticket, to enter St. Maarten/St. Martin. Citizens of the United Kingdom, Commonwealth countries of the Caribbean, the Republic of Ireland, and E.U. countries must also have a current passport. See p. 120 and p. 158 for information on Anguilla and St. Barts.

All travelers coming from the Caribbean, including Americans, are now required to have a passport to enter or re-enter the United States. Those returning to Canada are also required to show passports. Cruise ship passengers must also meet the requirement. You'll certainly need identification at some point, and a passport is the best form of ID for speeding through Customs and Immigration. Driver's licenses are not acceptable as a sole form of ID.

CUSTOMS

Generally, you're permitted to bring in items intended for your personal use, including tobacco, cameras, film, and a limited supply of liquor—usually 40 ounces.

Just before you leave home, check with the St. Maarten/St. Martin (as well as St. Barts and Anguilla) Customs or Foreign Affairs department for the latest guidelines—including information on items that are not allowed to be brought into your home country—because the rules are subject to change and often contain some surprising oddities.

Visitors to St. Maarten/St. Martin (as well as St. Barts and Anguilla) may not carry any form of firearm, spear guns, pole spears, illegal drugs, live plants or cuttings, and raw fruits and vegetables. Visitors over 18 may bring in—duty-free—items intended for personal use (generally up to 4 liters of alcohol, a carton of cigarettes or 25 cigars), as well as laptops, cellphones, and cameras.

You should collect receipts for all purchases made abroad. You must also declare on your Customs form the nature and value of all gifts received during your stay abroad.

If you use any medication that contains controlled substances or requires injection, carry an original prescription or note from your doctor.

For specifics on what **U.S.** citizens can bring back, download the invaluable free pamphlet *Know Before You Go* online at www.cbp.gov. (Click on "Travel," then go to "Travel Smart" and click on "Know Before You Go.") Or contact the **U.S. Customs and Border Protection (CBP),** 1300 Pennsylvania Ave. NW, Washington, DC 20229 (✆ **877/287-8667**), and request the pamphlet.

U.K. citizens should contact **HM Customs & Excise** at ✆ **0845/010-9000** (✆ 020/8929-0152 from outside the U.K.), or consult its website at www.hmce.gov.uk.

Recommended Books

The Caribbean has produced numerous fine authors, including Nobel Prize laureate Derek Walcott (St. Lucia), V. S. Naipaul (Trinidad), Anthony Winkler (Jamaica), Jean Rhys (Dominica), and Jamaica Kincaid (Antigua). Alas, none of the three islands in this book boast noted native writers. But there are a few literal "beach" reads worth mentioning. *The Captain's Fund* by Raina Wissing Harris, a very purple "romance suspense" novel of murder, heiresses-in-distress, and black market diamonds, is notable for its St. Maarten/St. Martin setting with such familiar landmarks as Friar's Beach Café, the Horny Toad Guesthouse, and Joe's Jewelry International. Celebrity chef/author Anthony Bourdain's comedic crime novel *Gone Bamboo* is also inspired by St. Martin.

Melinda and Bob Blanchard's *A Trip to the Beach: Living on Island Time in the Caribbean* is the true-life restaurateurs' hilarious yet sympathetic, ungarnished version of Herman Wouk's riotous fictional account of an American hotelier in the Antilles, *Don't Stop the Carnival*. The Blanchards' most recent guide is *Changing Your Course: The 5-Step Guide to Getting the Life You Want*. *Murder in St. Barts* is a passable Gendarme Trenet novel by J. R. Ripley (note that teasing last name, mystery aficionados), better known for the Tony Kozol whodunits. Jimmy Buffet's *Tales from Margaritaville* offers fictional short stories of West Indian life, many based on his years of St. Barts residency.

For a clear summary of **Canadian** rules, write for the booklet *I Declare*, issued by the **Canada Border Services Agency** (© **800/461-9999** in Canada, or 204/983-3500; www.cbsa-asfc.gc.ca).

Citizens of **Australia** should request a helpful brochure available from Australian consulates or Customs offices called *Know Before You Go*. For more information, call the **Australian Customs Service** at © **1300/363-263,** or log on to www.customs.gov.au.

For **New Zealand** Customs information, contact **New Zealand Customs** at © **04/473-6099** or 0800/428-786, or log on to www.customs.govt.nz.

GETTING TO ST. MAARTEN/ST. MARTIN

The island has two airports. Your likely arrival point will be St. Maarten's **Princess Juliana International Airport (PJIA)** (© 599/ 546-7542; www.pjiae.com), which has grown from a military airfield built by the United States in 1943 into the second-busiest airport in the eastern Caribbean, topped only by San Juan, Puerto Rico. Princess Juliana is a thoroughly modern facility, with restaurants, snack bars, ATMs, and car-rental kiosks. The much smaller **L'Espérance Airport,** in Grand Case on French St. Martin (© 590/87-10-36), caters largely to inter-island commuter airlines and small private aircraft.

American Airlines (© 800/433-7300 in the U.S. and Canada; www.aa.com) offers more options and more frequent service into St. Maarten than any other airline—currently one daily nonstop flight from New York's JFK and one from Miami. Additional nonstop daily flights into St. Maarten are offered by American and its local affiliate, **American Eagle** (same number), from San Juan.

Continental Airlines (© 800/231-0856 in the U.S. and Canada; www.continental.com) has daily nonstop flights out of its hub in Newark, New Jersey, during the winter months (flight times vary in off season). **Delta Airlines** (© 800/241-4141 in the U.S. and Canada; www.delta.com) flies in from Atlanta and New York City (through Atlanta).

United (© 800/538-2929 in the U.S. and Canada; www.united. com) also offers flights from New York.

US Airways (© 800/428-4322 in the U.S. and Canada; www. usairways.com) offers nonstop daily service from Philadelphia and Charlotte to St. Maarten.

JetBlue Airways (© 800-JETBLUE/538-2583 in the US; www. jetblue.com) has one daily nonstop flight from New York's JFK into St. Maarten.

Spirit Airlines (© 800/772-7117 in the U.S. and Canada; www. spiritair.com) has nonstop service from Fort Lauderdale to St. Maarten.

Air Caraïbes (© 590/52-05-10; www.aircaraibes.com) offers flights from Paris's Orly airport into St. Maarten.

Caribbean Airlines (© 800/920-4225 in the U.S. and Canada, or 599/54-67660 on St. Maarten; www.caribbean-airlines.com), the national airline of Trinidad and Tobago (replacing the now-defunct BWIA) has flights from New York, Miami, Toronto, and London with connections to St. Maarten.

PLANNING YOUR TRIP

GETTING THERE & AROUND

The regional airline **LIAT** (© **888/844-5428** in the U.S. and Canada; www.liatairline.com) has direct daily 40-minute flights and connecting flights into St. Maarten from its hub in Antigua. From St. Martin, LIAT offers ongoing service to a number of other islands, including Antigua, St. Croix, Puerto Rico, St. Kitts, and Dominica.

One airline specializes in flying the short routes of the northeastern Caribbean islands, from Tortola to Montserrat. **Winair** (© **888/255-6889** in the U.S. and Canada, or 599/54-54237; www.fly-winair. com) offers island trips from its main gateway at the Princess Juliana International Airport.

GETTING AROUND ST. MAARTEN/ ST. MARTIN

Taxis

Most visitors use taxis at some point to get around the island. Taxis are plentiful at Princess Juliana International Airport; taxi stands are conveniently located just outside the airport Arrivals section. Taxis are unmetered on both sides of the island (although drivers are required to carry government-issued rate sheets based on two-person occupancy), so always determine the rate before getting into a cab.

Rates are slightly different depending on which side of the island the taxi is based, though both Dutch and French cabs service the entire island. **St. Maarten taxis** have minimum fares for two passengers, and each additional passenger pays $4 extra. One piece of luggage per person is allowed free; each additional piece is $1 extra. Typical fares around the island are as follows: Princess Juliana Airport to Grand Case: $25 for up to two passengers and all their luggage; Marigot to Grand Case, $15; Princess Juliana airport to anywhere in Marigot, $15 to $20; Princess Juliana Airport to the Maho Beach Hotel, $6; and from Princess Juliana Airport to Philipsburg, about $15. *Note:* Fares are 25% higher between 10pm and midnight, and 50% higher between midnight and 6am.

St. Martin taxi fares are also for two passengers, but you should plan to add about $1 for each suitcase or valise and $2 for each additional person. These fares are in effect from 6am to 10pm; after that, they go up by 25% until midnight, rising by 50% after midnight. On the French side, the fare from Marigot to Grand Case is $15, from Princess Juliana Airport to Marigot and from Princess Juliana Airport to La Samanna, $15.

A couple of recommended taxi drivers are **Gerard Taxi Service** (© **599/553-4727** [Dutch side] or 0690/76-73-13 [French side]), and **Renaldo,** who drives **Taxi 257** (© **0690/87-09-97** or 718/355-8166 in the U.S.).

For late-night cab service on St. Maarten, call ✆ **147.** To reach the **Taxi Dispatch offices** in St. Maarten, call ✆ **599/54-67759** (airport) or ✆ **599/54-22359** (Philipsburg). On the French side of the island, **Taxi Service & Information Center** operates at the port of Marigot (✆ **590/87-56-54**).

Rental Cars

A car is the best way to experience and explore St. Maarten/St. Martin. And renting a car here couldn't be easier; car-rental agencies are a dime a dozen, with locations at the airports and throughout the island. It's also a cost-efficient way to see the island, with rates starting around $30 or 21€ a day, with unlimited mileage, and short distances between towns.

Many visitors rent cars upon arrival at Princess Juliana International Airport. If you haven't already made a car-rental reservation, you can choose from one of the many agencies that have kiosks at the airport, both international chains (like Budget, Avis, and Hertz) and local. To get around the law (strictly enforced by St. Maarten taxi drivers' union) that forbids anyone from picking up a car at the airport, every rental agency parks its cars at a location nearby. When you rent a car at one of the agency kiosks on the Arrivals floor of the Princess Juliana airport, you will be taken by company shuttle 5 to 10 minutes away to pick up your car.

Note: Always ask how far away from the airport rental cars are located; some of the smaller agencies are a couple of miles away—which can turn into a long trip when traffic is heavy around the airport.

Car-rental agencies at the airport include **Budget** (✆ **800/472-3325** in the U.S. and Canada, or 599/54-54030 on the Dutch side; www.budget.com), **Avis** (✆ **800/331-1212** in the U.S. and Canada, 599/54-22847 on the Dutch side, or 590/87-50-60 on the French side; www.avis-sxm.com), **Hertz** (✆ **800/654-3001** in the U.S. and Canada, or 590/545-4541 on the Dutch side; www.hertz.com), and **Alamo/National** (✆ **800/328-4567** in the U.S. and Canada, or 599/54-55546 on the Dutch side; www.nationalcar.com). Also at the Princess Juliana airport are **Best Deal Car Rental** (✆ **866/826-2205** or 599/54-53061; www.bestdealscarrental.com) and **Safari Car Rentals** (✆ **800/736-6917** or 599/54-53185; www.safaricarrentals.com).

Budget (✆ **599/543-0431**) also has an office at the cruise-ship terminal in Philipsburg.

All these companies charge roughly equivalent rates. The major car-rental agencies require that renters be at least 25 years old.

Many rental agencies will also deliver cars directly to your hotel, where an employee will complete the paperwork. Some hotels, like La Samanna, actually have a fleet of cars to rent on the premises—but try to reserve well in advance because supply is limited.

Driving is on the right side of the road. Seat belts and child car seats are mandatory. International road signs are observed, and there are no Customs formalities at the border between the French and Dutch sides—in fact, you might not even realize you crossed the border.

Expect traffic jams in and around Philipsburg during rush hours—particularly in the Simpson Bay area when the Simpson Bay drawbridge is raised to let boat traffic through (six times daily in high season). Tune your car radio to **Island 92** (91.9 FM) for traffic updates.

Public Bus

Traveling by public bus (more like a minivan) is a reasonable means of transport on St. Maarten/St. Martin if you don't mind a bit of inconvenience and overcrowding. Buses run daily from 5am to midnight and serve most major locations on both sides of the island. The most popular run is from Philipsburg on the Dutch side to Marigot on the French side. Privately owned and operated, minibuses tend to follow specific routes; the fare is $2 ($2.50 8pm–midnight). Buses accept both dollars and euros.

GETTING TO & AROUND ANGUILLA & ST. BARTS

For more information on getting to and around Anguilla and St. Barts, see "Getting There" in chapters 8 and 9, as well as the "Getting to St. Maarten/St. Martin" info above.

ANGUILLA Public ferries run between Marigot Bay, St. Martin, and Blowing Point, Anguilla (℡ **264/497-6070**) every 30 minutes. The trip takes 20 to 25 minutes, making day trips a snap. Usually, the first ferry leaves St. Martin at 8am and the last at 7pm; from Blowing Point, the first ferry leaves at 7:30am and the last at 6:15pm. The one-way fare is $15 ($10 children 2–18) plus a $3 departure tax. A departure tax of $20 (children $10) is charged on your return trip to St. Martin; day-trippers and visiting yachts pay a $5 departure tax. No reservations are necessary. Ferries vary in size, and none takes passenger vehicles. *Tip:* Keep in mind that if you have a late-arriving flight, you may quite literally miss the (ferry) boat. You can either spend the night in St. Maarten/St. Martin or arrange a charter plane connection (see above) into Anguilla.

A convenient option is to take one of the **privately run charter boats and ferries** that shuttle passengers between Anguilla and the airport in St. Maarten. Anguilla-based charter boats will pick you up at the Princess Juliana airport in St. Maarten and transport you and your luggage to Blowing Point or a hotel on the south side of Anguilla. These boats are more expensive than the public ferries, but let you avoid having to travel from the airport to the ferry port in Marigot by taxi

Tips on Dining

All three islands in this book are renowned for their fine dining, but dining out is definitely pricey. For St. Maarten/St. Martin specifics, see chapter 4. Consult chapters 8 and 9 for details on Anguilla and St. Barts. The restaurant listings have been separated into four categories in this book based on the average cost per person per meal, service charge included, but keep in mind that each island has slightly different relative costs—and many restaurants in St. Martin and St. Barts price their menu in euros. Roughly, the categories are **Very Expensive** ($35 and up); **Expensive** ($25–$40); **Moderate** ($15–$30); and **Inexpensive** ($15 and under).

To save money on St. Maarten/St. Martin, get take-out food for picnics and buy basics (snacks, soft drinks, milk, beer) at local grocery stores. See "Resources for Self-Catering," in chapter 4. Several restaurants take the sting from the euro's strength by offering 1€=$1 exchange rates for customers paying cash (this rarely applies to credit card users). Several restaurants, especially on the Dutch side, provide Internet coupons for free drinks or a second main course at half price. Lunch is generally less expensive, and the menu selection often simpler. Look for multicourse prix-fixe menus or midday *plats du jour*. Most restaurants include a service charge in the menu pricing (virtually all the restaurants in French St. Martin and St. Barts have *service compris*). The menu should state whether service is included, but always confirm whether gratuities are added. In many instances tips are pooled among the staff (including the back of the house), so it never hurts to add a little extra if you feel your server warrants it.

Note: Entrée is the French term for appetizer; *plat* means main course.

(a 10- to 15-min. trip)—a smart option for travelers with a lot of luggage or a lot of kids. Plus, the privately run boats are smaller and have fewer passengers and can even arrange full-boat charters for groups or families. Keep in mind that these boats do not run as frequently as the government-run ferry, but most do include ground transportation. **Good news:** In 2010, an agreement between the St. Maarten/Anguilla governments is designed to greatly facilitate the ease of private boat transfers (and passing through immigration) from the airport—which means that ideally you will be able to get off the plane and jump on a boat straight to Anguilla in under 30 minutes.

Check out the *GB Express* (© 264/235-6205 in Anguilla; 599/581-3568 on St. Maarten; www.anguillaferryandcharter; $55 one way, $90 round-trip); the **MV** *Shauna VI* (© 264/476-0975 or 264/772-2031 in Anguilla; 599/580-6275 on St. Maarten; myshauna6@hotmail.com; round-trip fare $60 adults, $40 children 2–12); or **Funtime Charters** (© 866/334-0047 or 264/497-6511; www.funtime-charters.com; $55 per person one-way; half-price for children 11 and under). Reservations are required.

Most Anguilla hotels will also arrange (for a fee) private boat char-ters between the airport in St. Maarten and the ferry dock at Blowing Point, Anguilla, with door-to-door ground transportation.

Tip: If you'd like to do some shopping and have lunch in Marigot before you take your ferry to Anguilla, simply store your bags at the ferry landing. The Port de Marigot has a small baggage storage area ($5, plus tip).

ST. BARTS   The **Voyager** vessels (© 590/87-10-68; www.voy12.com or www.voyager-st-barths.com) make frequent (usually twice daily, sometimes more) runs between St. Barts and either side of St. Maarten/St. Martin. The schedule varies according to the season (and the seas), but the **MV** *Voyager II* usually departs Marigot Harbor for St. Barts every morning and evening. **MV** *Voyager I* travels from Oyster Pond to Gustavia two to four times daily. Advance reservations are a good idea; fares run around 50€ to 58€ adults, 30€ children 2–12 one way (plus taxes). The trip can take around 45 minutes and can be rough; it's recommended that those with weak tummies take seasickness medication before the trip.

The technologically advanced, speedy, more luxurious and stable 65-foot aluminum mono-hull *Great Bay Express* (© 590/27-60-33; www.sbhferry.com) offers daily 20- to 40-minute crossings between St. Maarten's Bobby's Marina in Philipsburg and Gustavia. The boat can carry 130 passengers. Reservations are essential; the roundtrip fare is 56€ to 95€ adults, 40€ to 50€ children 2 to 11 years (plus taxes).

---

6 MONEY & COSTS

Frommer's lists exact prices in the local currency. The currency conver-sions quoted above were correct at press time. However, rates fluctuate, so before departing consult a currency exchange website such as **www.oanda.com/convert/classic** to check up-to-the-minute rates.

The Value of the U.S. Dollar vs. Other Popular Currencies

US$	Can$	UK£	Euro (€)	Aus$	NZ$
$1	C$1.05	£0.65	€0.80	A$1.18	NZ$1.45

Despite the dominance of the euro since January 2002 within the mother country, Holland, the legal tender on the Dutch side of St. Maarten is still the **Netherlands Antilles florin (NAf);** the official exchange rate is NAf 1.79 for each $1. **U.S. dollars** are really the coin of the realm here, and prices in hotels and most restaurants and shops are designated in dollars. On the French side (as well as on St. Barts), the official monetary unit is the **euro,** with most establishments widely quoting and accepting either dollars or NAf guilders as well. At press time, the U.S. dollar was trading at $1.20 to the euro. Anguilla's official currency is the **Eastern Caribbean Dollar,** though U.S. dollars are accepted everywhere; the exchange rate is set permanently at roughly 2.70EC to $1.

Prices throughout this book are given in U.S. dollars for establishments on the Dutch side and Anguilla, and in either euros or U.S. dollars for establishments on the French side and St. Barts according to whether establishments quoted their prices in euros or dollars at the time of publication.

As the dollar was still weaker than the euro at press time, some establishments on St. Barts and French St. Martin advertise a 1-to-1 exchange rate if you use cash. Always confirm before you get the bill.

ATMS The easiest and best way to get cash away from home is from an ATM. Be sure you know your daily withdrawal limit before you

What Things Cost in St. Maarten/St. Martin	$
Taxi from the airport to Marigot	20.00
Double room, moderate	200.00–250
Double room, inexpensive	100–140.00
Three-course dinner for one without wine, moderate	15.00–25.00
Bottle of Carib beer	1.00–1.50
Bottle of Coca-Cola	1.00
Cup of coffee	1.00–1.50
1 gallon of premium gas	5.00

leave home. Also keep in mind that many banks impose a fee every time a card is used at a different bank's ATM, and that fee can be higher for international transactions than for domestic ones. And if you use a debit card, the fees may be higher still—again, check with your bank before you leave home. On top of this, the bank from which you withdraw cash may charge its own fee. For international withdrawal fees, ask your bank before you leave home.

Note: Keep in mind that ATMs in St. Maarten give you a choice of dollars or euros, while ATMs on St. Martin only dispense euros.

For bank and ATM information on St. Maarten/St. Martin, St. Barts and Anguilla, see the "Fast Facts" chapter.

TRAVELER'S CHECKS   Traveler's checks are widely accepted on all three islands. You can get traveler's checks at almost any bank. They are offered in denominations of $20, $50, $100, $500, and sometimes $1,000. Generally, you'll pay a service charge ranging from 1% to 4%. The most popular traveler's checks are offered by American Express (✆ **800/807-6233** or 800/221-7282 for cardholders—this number accepts collect calls, offers service in several foreign languages, and exempts Amex gold and platinum cardholders from the 1% fee); **Visa** (✆ **800/732-1322**)—AAA members can obtain Visa checks for a $9.95 fee (for checks up to $1,500) at most AAA offices or by calling ✆ **866/339-3378;** and **MasterCard** (✆ **800/223-9920**).

If you carry traveler's checks, be sure to keep a record of their serial numbers separate from your checks in the event that they are stolen or lost. You'll get a refund faster if you know the numbers.

CREDIT CARDS   Major credit cards are widely accepted on all three islands. Keep in mind that you'll pay interest from the moment

What Things Cost in St. Barts	€
Taxi from the airport to Cul-de-Sac	20.00
Double room, moderate	200.00–300.00
Double room, inexpensive	125.00–175.00
Three-course dinner for one without wine, moderate	25.00
Bottle of Carib beer	1.50–2.00
Bottle of Coca-Cola	1.50
Cup of coffee	1.50
1 gallon of premium gas	5.00

What Things Cost in Anguilla	$
Taxi from the ferry to Malliouhana	22.00
Double room, moderate	200.00–300.00
Double room, inexpensive	100.00–150.00
Three-course dinner for one without wine, moderate	20.00–30.00
Bottle of Carib beer	1.50–2.00
Bottle of Coca-Cola	1.50
Cup of coffee	1.50–2.00
1 gallon of premium gas	5.00

of your withdrawal, even if you pay your monthly bills on time. Also note that many banks now assess a 1% to 3% "transaction fee" on all charges you incur abroad (whether you're using the local currency or your native currency).

Almost every credit card company has an emergency toll-free number that you can call if your wallet or purse is stolen. Credit card companies may be able to wire cash advances immediately, and in many places they can deliver an emergency credit card in a day or two. **Citicorp Visa**'s U.S. emergency number is (C) **800/336-8472.** **American Express** cardholders and traveler's check holders should call (C) **800/221-7282** for all money emergencies. **MasterCard** holders should call (C) **800/307-7309.**

7 STAYING HEALTHY

GENERAL AVAILABILITY OF HEALTH CARE

There are no particular health concerns on St. Maarten/St. Martin, Anguilla, or St. Barts. The best medical facilities are on St. Maarten/St. Martin, with good clinics on Anguilla and St. Barts. Emergency airlift to Puerto Rico is available from all three destinations.

It's fairly easy to obtain major over-the-counter medication, with most major North American brands available as well as brands manufactured in Europe under unfamiliar names. Some leading prescription drugs for such common ailments as allergies, asthma, and acid reflux are also available over the counter, albeit by European pharmaceutical companies.

Etiquette Tips

Despite the clothing-optional beaches on St. Martin, St. Maarten, and St. Barts, flaunting one's body (or any flagrant display) is frowned upon, especially on proper British Anguilla. Except at casual beach bars, men should wear some kind of shirt, women a wrap. Casual resort wear is recommended for most restaurants, especially at dinner. "Sunday dress" is appropriate when visiting churches, though ties aren't mandatory for men. In general, profanity is frowned upon.

COMMON AILMENTS

BUGS, BITES & OTHER WILDLIFE CONCERNS The biggest menaces on all three islands are mosquitoes (none are disease vectors) and no-see-ums, which appear mainly in the early evening. Window screens aren't always sufficient, so carry insect repellent. In St. Barts, many pharmacies sell the Belou line of essential oils, which includes **Belou's P Soothing Mosquito Repellent Oil,** a natural repellent. Many of the products in the **Ligne St. Barth** (www.lignestbarth.com) line of creams and sunscreens contain roucou, considered to be a natural insect repellent; its shop/laboratory is on the Route de Salines in Lorient.

SUN EXPOSURE The tropical sun can be brutal. Wear sunglasses and a hat, and apply sunscreen liberally. Increase your time on the beach gradually. If you do overexpose yourself, stay out of the sun until you recover. Sun and heatstroke are possibilities, especially if you engage in strenuous physical activity. See a doctor immediately if fever, chills, dizziness, nausea, or headaches follow overexposure.

WHAT TO DO IF YOU GET SICK AWAY FROM HOME

It's easy to find good English-speaking doctors on all three islands. You can find **hospitals** and **emergency numbers** in the "Fast Facts" chapter.

If you suffer from a chronic illness, consult your doctor before your departure. You may have to pay all medical costs up front and be reimbursed later. If you worry about getting sick away from home, you might want to consider buying medical travel insurance.

8 CRIME & SAFETY

Petty crime has become an issue of concern on Dutch St. Maarten, with thefts and break-ins an increasing problem. Travelers are urged to lock their cars and lodging doors and windows at all times. Visitors should exercise common sense and take basic precautions everywhere on the island, including being aware of one's surroundings, avoiding walking alone after dark or in remote areas, and locking all valuables in a rental or hotel safe.

Anguilla is one of the safest destinations in the Caribbean, but you should still take standard precautions. Although crime is rare here, secure your valuables. Crime is also extremely rare on St. Barts; it's one of the safest islands in the Caribbean. But it's always wise to protect your valuables. Don't leave them unguarded on the beach or in parked cars, even if locked in the trunk.

Hurricanes

The northeastern Caribbean has seen its share of destructive hurricanes; the latest to have an impact in this region was Hurricane Omar, which in 2008 eroded beaches and blew down beach shacks in the Maho Bay area in St. Maarten and also caused beach erosion on Anguilla's West End. Fortunately, modern technology and satellite surveillance provide plenty of advance warning for impending storms. Hurricane season officially begins in June and ends in late November, but high hurricane season in this neck of the woods is the month of September. A number of resorts use this time (early fall) to close for renovations, especially on St. Barts. If you are caught in a hurricane or tropical storm during your stay, follow the instructions of officials (especially in the event of an evacuation to higher ground). Keep in mind that low-lying areas may be prone to flooding, and the seas may have dangerous rip currents even after a hurricane has passed. For the latest satellite imagery and hurricane information, go to the National Oceanic and Atmospheric Administration's **National Hurricane Center** (www.nhc.noaa.gov).

9 SPECIALIZED TRAVEL RESOURCES

In addition to the destination-specific resources listed below, please visit Frommers.com for other specialized travel resources.

TRAVELERS WITH DISABILITIES

Be aware that most flights arriving into St. Maarten do not deplane through gates but down movable steps on the tarmac. Many of the newer hotels and resorts on the islands are equipped with handicapped-accessible bathrooms. Beaches can be difficult to access for those in wheelchairs, however. One surprising exception: The nudist resort, **Club Orient** (www.cluborient.com), on Orient Beach in French St. Martin, has not only wheelchair-accessible bathrooms but one of the island's few beach wheelchairs. The **oceanfront boardwalk** in Philipsburg is wide and flat, making it ideal for wheelchair travel.

LGBT TRAVELERS

The Caribbean in general isn't the LGBT-friendliest destination, perhaps because of regrettably rampant "on the DL" hypocrisy in local communities. St. Barts is by far the most open of the islands covered in this book. Anguilla, like many a British colony, is quite conservative in attitude, but individual deluxe resorts welcome gay and lesbian travelers. The French and Dutch are generally tolerant, but St. Maarten/St. Martin is a mixed bag.

The **International Gay and Lesbian Travel Association (IGLTA;** *©* **954/776-2626;** www.iglta.org) is the trade association for the gay and lesbian travel industry, and offers an online directory of gay- and lesbian-friendly travel businesses; go to its website and click on "Members."

SENIOR TRAVEL

Though the major U.S. airlines flying to St. Maarten no longer offer senior discounts or coupon books, some hotels extend deals, especially during slower periods. Members of **AARP,** 601 E St. NW, Washington, DC 20049 (*©* **888/687-2277;** www.aarp.org), get discounts on hotels, airfares, and car rentals. AARP offers members a wide range of benefits, including *AARP The Magazine* and a monthly newsletter. Anyone over 50 can join.

FAMILY TRAVEL

St. Maarten/St. Martin has a number of family-friendly resorts and restaurants featuring kids' menus. Anguilla is very family-friendly, particularly during spring break, the shoulder seasons, and summer;

the calm, clear waters are perfect for beginning swimmers. The Malliouhana resort, on Anguilla, has a wonderful children's playground (with a pirate ship) that's separate from the main section of the resort. Although a number of St. Barts resorts discourage children during high season, it's quite a kid-friendly place the rest of the year.

Even those hotels and resorts with specific adults-only aspects offer some sort of kid-friendly amenities and programs. Many of the beaches are particularly attractive for families with toddlers and young children, and older kids will have plenty of nonmotorized watersports activities (snorkeling, sailing, parasailing) to keep them happy.

To locate accommodations, restaurants, and attractions that are particularly kid-friendly, refer to the "Kids" icon throughout this guide.

10 RESPONSIBLE TOURISM

ST. MAARTEN/ST. MARTIN

Rampant development on the Dutch side of the island has been cause for concern from environmentalists for some time. At press time, reports of shoddily built plumbing systems pouring wastewater runoff onto the beach at Cupecoy were met with dismay by local environmental group **St. Maarten Pride Foundation,** which also claims that authorities have no controls in place to prevent developers from demolishing natural landmarks, overrunning the natural environment, and destroying delicate ecosystems. Also active in conservation awareness is the **Nature Foundation St. Maarten** (www.nature foundationsxm.org), established by the government in 1997.

ANGUILLA

Sustainability and "going green" are hot topics of discussion on Anguilla these days. With development at a virtual standstill from the global recession, the island's movers and shakers are using what is being seen as a gift of time to take the long view on developing ways to ensure that Anguilla's natural resources are protected and preserved. A **Sustainable Energy Committee** is looking at ways (windpower, solar power) to make the country more sustainable and less dependent on traditional energy sources. In other developments, a forward-thinking government agricultural initiative to **farm vegetables** on a large swath of land is putting fresh sweet potatoes, peppers, corn, squash, tomatoes, lettuces, and pigeon peas into the marketplace. Old farmers are rediscovering the pleasure of growing food, and new farmers (and future chefs) are being initiated in this agricultural renaissance. Local chefs are also getting in on the act, designing menus

General Resources for Responsible Travel

The following websites provide valuable wide-ranging information on sustainable travel.

- **Responsible Travel** (www.responsibletravel.com) is a great source of sustainable travel ideas; the site is run by a spokesperson for ethical tourism in the travel industry. **Sustainable Travel International** (www.sustainable travelinternational.org) promotes ethical tourism practices, and manages an extensive directory of sustainable properties and tour operators around the world.

- **Carbonfund** (www.carbonfund.org), **TerraPass** (www.terrapass.org), and **Cool Climate** (http://coolclimate.berkeley.edu) provide info on "carbon offsetting," or offsetting the greenhouse gas emitted during flights.

- **Greenhotels** (www.greenhotels.com) recommends green-rated member hotels around the world that fulfill the company's stringent environmental requirements. **Environmentally Friendly Hotels** (www.environmentally friendlyhotels.com) offers more green accommodation ratings.

- **Volunteer International** (www.volunteerinternational.org) has a list of questions to help you determine the intentions and the nature of a volunteer program. For general info on volunteer travel, visit **www.volunteer abroad.org** and **www.idealist.org**.

around **local seafood** instead of expensive imported fish. Ecotourism is on the rise, with increasingly popular eco-tours offered by the Anguilla National Trust. The Trust also makes monthly species counts on the local ponds and wetlands.

ST. BARTS

Perhaps the most environmentally enlightened of the three islands, St. Barts has long been doing its bit to protect the environment—even though getting food and goods onto the island is a massive daily (and carbon-footprint-heavy) enterprise. Islanders are **natural recyclers**—they've had to be; the island has little arable land and no fresh water. Many of the old-timers still collect rain water in cisterns; some even drink it! Most people bring recycled or cloth bags to grocery stores, and eco-conscious chefs are building menus around local and sustainable food sources. Trash is rarely seen on beaches; visitors are asked to take out whatever they bring in.

11 STAYING CONNECTED

TELEPHONES
Calling St. Maarten/St. Martin from Abroad

1. Dial the international access code: 011 from the U.S. and Canada; 00 from the U.K., Ireland, or New Zealand; or 0011 from Australia.
2. Dial the country code 599 for St. Maarten and 590 for St. Martin.
3. Dial the city code 590 (a second time) and then the six-digit number on St. Martin. The St. Maarten city code is 54, and then dial the five-digit number.

Calling Within St. Maarten/St. Martin

To call the French side from the Dutch side and vice versa is an expensive international "long distance" call, going through Byzantine routing to Europe and back. From the French to Dutch side, dial 00, then 599, 54 and the five-digit number. From the Dutch to the French side (and St. Barts), dial 00, then 590590 (590690 for cellphones) and the six-digit number.

International Calls from St. Maarten/St. Martin

From St. Maarten/St. Martin, first dial 00 and then the country code (U.S. or Canada 1, U.K. 44, Ireland 353, Australia 61, New Zealand 64). Next dial the area code and number. For example, if you wanted to call the British Embassy in Washington, D.C., you would dial 00-1-202-588-7800.

Both the Dutch side and the French side have public phones from which you can make overseas calls using prepaid phone cards. On the Dutch side there are phones from which you can also make overseas credit-card and collect calls. The public phones on the French side only accept prepaid phone cards. You can buy phone cards in $5, $10, and $20 increments throughout the island at gas stations, newsstands, phone stores, and post offices. At the Marigot post office, you can purchase a prepaid phone card called a *Télécartes,* giving you 40 units. A typical 5-minute call to the States takes up to 120 units. There are two public phones at the Marigot tourist office from which it's possible to make credit card calls. There are six public phones at the post office.

If you need operator assistance in making a call, dial 0 if you're trying to make an international call and a number within St. Maarten/St. Martin. For directory assistance, dial 150 if you're looking for a number inside St. Maarten/St. Martin, and dial 0 for numbers to all other countries.

ST. BARTS   St. Barts is linked to the Guadeloupe telephone system. To call St. Barts from home, dial your country's international access code, then **590** (the country code for Guadeloupe), and then the city code and number. To call home from St. Barts, first dial 00 and then the country code (U.S. or Canada 1, U.K. 44, Ireland 353, Australia 61, New Zealand 64), followed by the area code and number.

The island has a handful of public telephones for making local and international calls that use *Télécartes;* these prepaid phone cards are sold at the gas station across from the airport and at post offices in Gustavia and St. Jean. To reach an AT&T operator from anywhere on St. Barts, dial ✆ **0800-99-00-11.** To reach **MCI,** dial ✆ **0800-99-00-19,** and to reach **Sprint,** dial ✆ **0800-99-00-87.**

ANGUILLA   To call Anguilla from the U.S. and Canada, dial **1** and then **the 10-digit number;** to call the U.K. and New Zealand from Anguilla, dial **00** plus **1** and then the area code and number; to call Australia from Anguilla, dial **0011** plus **1** and then the area code and number.

To call the U.S. and Canada from Anguilla, dial **1** (the country code), the area code, and the seven-digit number. To call the U.K. from Anguilla, dial **011,** then **44,** then the telephone number. To call Australia from Anguilla, dial **011,** then **61,** then the area code and number. To call New Zealand from Anguilla, dial **011,** then **64,** then the area code and number.

Telephone, cable, and Telex services are offered by **LIME** (formerly Cable & Wireless Ltd.), Wallblake Road, the Valley (✆ **264/497-3100**), open Monday to Friday from 8am to 5pm. **Digicel** (✆ **264/498-3444**), with its main office by the Public Library in the Valley, usually has better rates for renting or buying a cellphone than LIME.

TOLL-FREE NUMBERS   There are no toll-free numbers on St. Maarten/St. Martin, Anguilla, or St. Barts, and calling a 1-800 number in the States from them is not toll free. In fact, it costs the same as an overseas call.

CELLPHONES

The three letters that define the islands' wireless capabilities are **GSM** (Global System for Mobile Communications), a big, seamless network that makes for easy cross-border cellphone use. If your cellphone is on a GSM system, and you have a world-capable multiband phone such as many Sony Ericsson, Motorola, or Samsung models, you can make and receive calls across the islands covered in this book. Just call your wireless operator and ask for "international roaming" to be activated on your account.

For many, **renting** a phone on one of the islands is a good idea. You can rent a phone from any number of island sites, including kiosks at airports and at car-rental agencies. Mobile phone rentals are available from **Friendly Island Cellphone Rentals** (© 599/553-7368), in Simpson Bay, St. Maarten; they'll even deliver the phone to your resort or villa. On Anguilla, you can arrange a phone rental through your hotel or resort or directly from **LIME** (formerly Cable & Wireless Ltd.), Wallblake Road, the Valley (© 264/497-3100), or **Digicel** (© 264/498-3444), with its main office by the Public Library in the Valley. On St. Barts, **Centre @lizés,** rue de la République, Gustavia (© 590/298-989) is a full-service Internet cafe that also offers cellphone and laptop rentals.

VOICE-OVER INTERNET PROTOCOL (VOIP)

If you have Web access while traveling, you might consider a broadband-based telephone service (in technical terms, **Voice over Internet protocol,** or **VoIP**) such as Skype (www.skype.com) or Vonage (www.vonage.com), which allows you to make free international calls if you use their services from your laptop or in a cybercafe. For all the details on restrictions and availability, check the websites above for details.

INTERNET/E-MAIL
Without Your Own Computer

To find cybercafes on the islands, check **www.cybercaptive.com** and **www.cybercafe.com**. For more information on Internet access on the islands, consult the "Fast Facts" chapter.

With Your Own Computer

More and more hotels, resorts, airports, cafes, and retailers are going **Wi-Fi** (wireless fidelity), becoming "hot spots" that offer free high-speed Wi-Fi access or charge a small fee for usage. Most laptops sold today have built-in wireless capability. To find public Wi-Fi hot spots on the islands, go to **www.jiwire.com**; its Hotspot Finder holds the world's largest directory of public wireless hotspots.

For dial-up access, most business-class hotels offer dataports for laptop modems.

12 TIPS ON ACCOMMODATIONS

The rates given in this book are only "rack rates"—that is, the officially posted rate that you'd be given if you just walked in off the street. Almost everyone ends up paying less than the rack rate through packages, discounts, and strategic planning. Think of the rates in this book as guidelines to help you comparison-shop. Check online for great deals and multi-day packages on hotel websites. Roughly, the price categories in this book are **Very Expensive** ($650 and up); **Expensive** ($375–$650); **Moderate** ($215–$375); and **Inexpensive** ($215 and under).

You can save big on your lodging bill simply by traveling in the off season. The high season on all three islands is the winter season, roughly from the middle of December through the middle of April. Hotels charge their peak rates during the winter, rates that spike stratospherically during the 2 weeks around the Christmas holidays. The off season is the rest of the year—although the so-called "shoulder seasons," roughly late spring and late fall (after hurricane season is over)—are increasingly popular. Expect rates to fall outside the traditional high season, however, often dramatically in the summer. You'll find that during the off season, many resorts offer deals on multi-night stays or sweeten the deal with meals or activities included in the rates.

Keep in mind that each island government imposes an occupancy or room tax (called a "tourism tax" on St. Barts), applicable to all hotels, inns, and guesthouses. On St. Maarten, a government tax of 5% is added to your hotel bill. Hotels on French St. Martin tack on a local room tax *(taxe de séjour)* of 4% to 5%. On Anguilla, the government collects a 10% tax on rooms. The St. Barts tourism tax is 5%. Ask whether taxes are included in the original rates you're quoted. Furthermore, many hotels routinely tack on 10% to 12% for "service." That means that with tax and service, some bills are 15% or even 25% higher than the price originally quoted to you!

But that's not all. Some hotels are particularly adept at charging for extras that add up quickly. The minibar is one money trap you won't want to fall into; look for a grocery or convenience store to stock up on sodas, snacks, water, and beer. Another big extra is phone charges. Making direct international calls from your hotel phone can be exorbitant, and many hotels also charge fees for local calls. If you have a GSM cellphone with international roaming capabilities, you're in business; otherwise, you may want to consider renting a cellphone or buying a prepaid cellphone when you're on one of the islands. See "Cellphones," earlier in this chapter.

TYPES OF ACCOMMODATIONS

Hotels & Resorts   All three islands have a broad range of accommodations, although the budget options on Anguilla and St. Barts are few and far between. But deals are out there, even at the priciest resorts. Be sure to get on a resort's e-mail list: Many offer terrific money-saving packages (*especially* during low season) advertised via e-mail or Twitter. Look into air/hotel packages offered by online travel agencies such as Orbitz, Travelocity, and Priceline for big savings.

Condos & Villas   Particularly if you're traveling with your family or a group of friends, a "housekeeping holiday" can be one of the least expensive ways to vacation in St. Maarten/St. Martin, Anguilla, and St. Barts. And if you like privacy and independence, it's a good way to go. The savings, especially for a large group or family, can range from 50% to 60% of what a hotel would cost. And having self-catering capabilities lets you prepare your own meals—a lot cheaper than taking all your meals at restaurants. St. Maarten offers a number of condominium rooms and suites—many of which are timeshare units; here, timeshares account for some 60% of the lodging rental market. Timeshare members of **RCI** (✆ 317/805-9000; www.rci.com) or **Interval International** (✆ 888/784-3447; www.interval world.com) can look into the feasibility of exchanges on St. Maarten. Villas are extremely popular on St. Barts and Anguilla and, to a lesser degree, on St. Maarten/St. Martin. **Wimco** (✆ 800/932-3222; www.wimco.com) is a reputable company handling properties on all three islands. For villas in St. Barts, **St. Barth Properties** (✆ 800-421-3396; www.stbarth.com) is affiliated with Sotheby's. (For other suggestions for Anguilla and St. Barts, see chapters 8 and 9.)

PLANNING YOUR TRIP

2

TIPS ON ACCOMMODATIONS

3

Where to Stay on St. Maarten/ St. Martin

Despite its small size, St. Maarten/St. Martin offers a range of accommodations: large high-rise resorts, small "bourgeois" hotels, locally owned guesthouses ranging from boutique-y to budget, not to mention villas and apartments. But timeshares comprise some 60% of the St. Maarten accommodations market. What this means is that you may be competing for rooms with timeshare owners, who generally get first dibs.

1 DUTCH ST. MAARTEN

The winding two-lane roads in Dutch St. Maarten are beginning to look like high-rise alleys, particularly along those densely developed sections of Maho Bay and Simpson Bay (and now Cupecoy, with its sprawling Porto Cupecoy complex). These areas are where the action is—where most of the casinos, clubs, and beach bars are located—so if you prefer a little peace and quiet, head to the Oyster Pond/Dawn Beach section of the island, which despite a handful of big resorts (the Westin, Princess Heights, Oyster Bay Beach Resort) still has a getaway feel. That getaway feel is present at little guesthouses like Horny Toad and Mary's Boon, close to the airport and the bustle of Simpson Bay, but still serene beachside havens.

Keep in mind that a government tax of 5% will be added to your hotel bill. On top of that, many hotels tack on a service charge of between 10% to 15%. Ask whether taxes are included in the original rates you're quoted.

VERY EXPENSIVE

Westin St. Maarten Dawn Beach Resort & Spa ★ (Kids)
When this sprawling resort opened in early 2007, one local said it looked like a prison had been plopped down on Dawn Beach. To be fair, the hotel's colonnaded beachfront facade is much more elegant than its character-free backside. And the huge freshwater infinity pool fronting Dawn Beach is beautiful. This is Dutch St. Maarten's top

lodging option, and the 306 mostly oceanview guest rooms (and six suites) have all the pampering and state-of-the-art trappings you'd expect from a Westin, including the trademark Heavenly Bed mattresses—and the rates cover a range of budgets. The lobby has a spiffy Frank Lloyd Wright feel, although it's joined at the hip by a garish casino that seems empty much of the time. Facilities include a full-service, European-style spa, fitness center, retail shops with duty-free shopping, two oceanfront restaurants, watersports, and meeting facilities. Kids get the royal treatment at Westin Kid's Club, Camp Scallywag. The Westin has a popular **Sunday champagne brunch** in the **Ocean** restaurant (noon–3pm; $48 per person).

144 Oyster Pond Rd., St. Maarten, N.A. © 800/WESTIN-1 (937-8461) or 599/543-6700. Fax 599/543-6004. www.starwoodhotels.com. 314 units. Winter $409–$578 double, $1,050–$3,150 suite; off season $324–$545 double, $735–$1,200 suite. AE, MC, V. **Amenities:** 2 restaurants; 2 lounges; babysitting; casino; concierge; casino; fitness center; outdoor pool; room service; spa; Wi-Fi (free, in lobby). *In room:* A/C, TV, hair dryer, minibar, Wi-Fi ($15/day; $50/week).

EXPENSIVE

Divi Little Bay Beach Resort ★ (Value)   Built on a slender peninsula about a 10-minute drive east of the airport, this timeshare resort/hotel originated as a simple guesthouse in 1955 and soon became famous as the vacation home of the Netherlands' Queen Juliana, Prince Bernhard, and Queen Beatrix. It's been beaten and battered by hurricanes over the years—its beach bar, **Gizmo's,** was wiped out in 2008 by Hurricane Omar—but it remains the stalwart flagship of the Divi chain. The rooms and public spaces have been nicely renovated and freshened up. The architecture evokes a European seaside village, with stucco walls and terra-cotta roofs, with some Dutch colonial touches. In the upper reaches of the property are the ruins of Fort Amsterdam, once Dutch St. Maarten's most prized military stronghold and today a decorative historical site. Gardens are carefully landscaped, and Divi improved the nearby beach after it suffered massive erosion. Divi also has a shopping promenade and an art gallery.

Accommodations are airy, accented with ceramic tiles and pastel colors, and each has its own private balcony or patio; suites (and studios) have fully equipped kitchens—the only units that don't have kitchens are the beachfront doubles. The luxury Casita one-bedroom suites even have iPod docking stations. The resort offers a variety of meal plans, including an all-inclusive option.

Little Bay Rd. (P.O. Box 961), Philipsburg, St. Maarten, N.A. © 800/367-3484 in the U.S., or 599/542-2333. Fax 599/542-4336. www.divilittlebay.com. 225 units. Winter $230–$288 double, $272–$328 1-bedroom suite, $475 2-bedroom suite; off season $180–$218 double, $178–$250 1-bedroom suite, $370 2-bedroom suite.

WHERE TO STAY ON ST. MAARTEN/ST. MARTIN

DUTCH ST. MAARTEN

ST. MARTIN
EXPLORING
Butterfly Farm **14**
Loterie Farm **11**

ACCOMMODATIONS
Alamanda Resort **12**
Club Orient Naturist Resort **15**
Esmeralda Resort **9**
Green Cay Villas **13**
Hotel La Plantation **10**
La Samanna **1**
Le Domaine de Lonvilliers **6**
Mercure St. Martin and Marina **2**
Radisson Blu Resort Marina
  & Spa, St. Martin **7**

DINING
C Le Restaurant **7**
La Cigale **3**
Le Santal **4**
Mario's Bistro **5**
Sol é Luna **8**

Airport ✈
Beach 🏖
Mountain 🏔

Pointe Arago

Pointe du Bluff

Pointe du Plum

Baie Rouge

Baie Nettlé

Baie de Marigot

Marigot

Baie aux Prunes

Nettlé Beach

2 **3** **4**

5 Marigot Fort

Baie Longue

Simpson Bay Lagoon

1

Border Monume

32

Cupecoy Bay Beach

Mullet Bay Beach

CARIBBEAN SEA

Princess Juliana Int'l Airport

31 ✈

Maho Bay Beach

30 Simpson
Bay Beach

29 **28**
22 **27**

26

25

Koolbaai

Kimsha Beach **24**

23

Cole Bay

ST. MAARTEN
EXPLORING
St. Maarten Zoological Park **20**

ACCOMMODATIONS
Divi Little Bay Beach Resort **21**
Horny Toad Guesthouse **29**
La Vista/La Vista Beach Resort **23**
Mary's Boon Beach Resort **30**
Oyster Bay Beach Resort **16**
Princess Heights **19**
Sonesta Maho Beach Hotel & Casino **31**
Turquoise Shell Inn **24**
Westin St. Maarten Dawn Beach
  Resort & Spa **18**

DINING
Halsey's **28**
La Gondola **32**
Mr. Busby's Beach Bar/
  Daniel's by the Sea **17**
Peg Leg Pub & Steakhouse **26**
Rare **32**
Saratoga **25**
Skipjack's Seafood Grill,
  Bar & Fish Market **27**
Temptation **32**
Topper's **22**

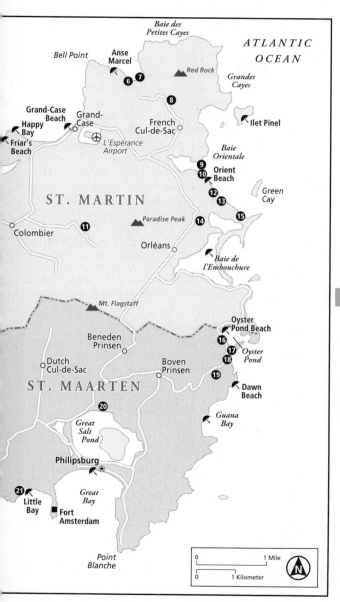

Children under 15 stay free in parent's room. AE, DC, MC, V. **Amenities:** 3 restaurants; bar; activities coordinator; gym; Internet (in Bayview Café); 3 outdoor pools; spa; 2 lit tennis courts; dive shop; watersports center and watersports equipment (extensive). *In room:* A/C, TV (DVD in some), CD player (in some), hair dryer, Jacuzzi (in suites), kitchen (in suites), MP3 docking station (in some).

Holland House Beach Hotel ★   The lobby of this polished, well-run "city" hotel runs uninterrupted from bustling Front Street to Great Bay Beach. The public areas are quite stylish, with creamy adobe walls hung with rotating local and Dutch artworks. The lively global clientele appreciates the smart little touches (free international newspapers, beach chairs, and freshwater beach shower). Most rooms have gorgeous polished hardwood floors and large, arched balconies. The one-bedroom penthouse includes a kitchenette, large-screen TV, DVD, and fax machine. The $36 surcharge is well worth it for the popular oceanview rooms, but weekly stays in any unit lasso huge savings.

The **Ocean Lounge,** a beachfront restaurant and bar (crowned by a billowing tent), is a beautiful spot to dine or sip a cocktail along the beachfront night or day. Fresh fish is the chef's specialty.

43 Front St. (P.O. Box 393), Philipsburg, St. Maarten, N.A. 🄫 **800/223-9815** in the U.S., or 599/542-2572. Fax 599/542-4673. www.hhbh.com. 54 units. Winter $229–$310 double, $425 1-bedroom suite, $650 penthouse; off season $175–$310 double, $295 1-bedroom suite, $560 penthouse. Weekly rates available. AE, MC, V. **Amenities:** Restaurant; bar; watersports equipment. *In room:* A/C and ceiling fan, TV, fridge, hair dryer, Wi-Fi (free).

Princess Heights ★   In the hills above Dawn Beach, just across the road, this boutique all-suites condo hotel has heart-stopping panoramic views. Princess Heights is reached after a 10-minute drive from Philipsburg. Opening onto St. Barts in the distance, the large suites are tastefully furnished, each containing one or two bedrooms, with separate living rooms opening onto balconies with sumptuous views. Living rooms have not only foldout sofas but foldout chairs as well. Granite-topped counters, clay-tiled terraces, marble floors throughout, and well-crafted, fully equipped kitchens make for a comfortable stay, and the hillside location spells privacy—although you either have to walk 5 minutes down a steep path or drive to get to Dawn Beach (most people have rental cars). In 2008, the hotel added 36 new ocean-view deluxe suites on the hillside slightly above the original building; ask for one—the rooms are the hotel's spiffiest.

156 Oyster Pond Rd., Oyster Pond, St. Maarten, N.A. 🄫 **599/543-6906.** Fax 599/543-6007. www.princessheights.com. 51 units. Winter $285 studio, $350–$450 suite; off season $160–$210 studio, $225–$375 suite. Children (2 maximum) under 12 stay free in parent's room. Extra person $35–$45. AE, DISC, MC, V. **Amenities:** Babysitting; fitness center; Internet; outdoor pool. *In room:* A/C, flatscreen TV, hair dryer, Jacuzzi, minibar, kitchen (in suites), kitchenette (in studios), washer/dryer (in some), Internet.

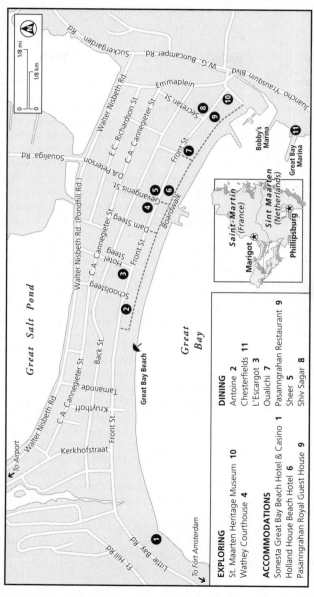

EXPLORING
St. Maarten Heritage Museum **10**
Wathey Courthouse **4**

ACCOMMODATIONS
Sonesta Great Bay Beach Hotel & Casino **1**
Holland House Beach Hotel **6**
Pasanngrahan Royal Guest House **9**

DINING
Antoine **2**
Chesterfields **11**
L'Escargot **3**
Oualichi **7**
Pasanngrahan Restaurant **9**
Sheer **5**
Shiv Sagar **8**

Sonesta Great Bay Beach Hotel & Casino ★ (Kids) Built in 1968, the second-oldest hotel in St. Maarten (after Divi) is ideally located a few minutes' walk from downtown Philipsburg. In spite of a $10-million renovation about 5 years ago, some say that it's looking a tad dowdy and due for another refreshment. No matter: The public spaces, pools, beaches, and bars are always abuzz with activity—and the setting inside a sexy curve of Great Bay beach is certainly a big draw. This resort was smartly designed around that crescent of beach. You get killer views virtually anywhere and everywhere you plop yourself, whether you're eating breakfast in the alfresco **Bay View** restaurant, sunning beside the infinity pool, or having dinner at the **Molasses** restaurant, with the lights on the harbor shimmering like diamonds before you. The rooms feature standard decorative tropical trappings, but budget travelers can save big by choosing a room with a "mountain" view (St. Maarten hills, some shrubbery, and a parking lot) over one with ocean views. The suites include kitchens and sofa beds. Friendly management, extensive facilities (including a full-service spa), and an enviable location make this a terrific choice for families.

19 Little Bay Rd. (P.O. Box 910), Philipsburg, St. Maarten, N.A. ✆ **800/223-0757** in the U.S. or 599/542-2446. Fax 599/544-3008. www.sonesta.com/greatbay. 257 units. $135–$440 double; $245–$775 suite. AE, DC, DISC, MC, V. **Amenities:** 3 restaurants; 4 bars; babysitting; casino; children's program; dive shop; fitness center; Internet cafe; 3 outdoor pools; 2 Jacuzzis; casino; spa; lit tennis court; watersports equipment (extensive). *In room:* A/C and ceiling fan, satellite TV, fridge (in some), hair dryer, kitchenette (in some), Wi-Fi ($18/day or $55/week).

Sonesta Maho Beach Hotel & Casino ★ Separated into three distinct sections, this megaresort is the island's largest hotel and practically a self-contained village. It's the closest thing on either the Dutch or French side to a Vegas-style blockbuster resort, and it's right in the thick of the Maho Bay action. It's always full of conventioneers and tour groups, but it stays slickly modern, thanks to constant renovations. Set on a 4-hectare (10-acre) tract that straddles the busy, and often congested, coastal road adjacent to the crescent-shaped Maho Beach, the hotel's scattered structures are painted a trademark cream and white. The entire Ocean Terrace building is newly renovated, and the rooms are large and comfortably furnished. Inside the main building, the premier rooms on floors 6 through 9 were refreshed in 2010 in pleasing hues of dusty lavender/rose and orange-browns. Suites have Jacuzzi tubs that open onto the bedroom and views. Each has Italian tiles, plush upholstered pieces, a walk-in closet, and good soundproofing (important, since planes taking off at the nearby Princess Juliana airport thunder overhead several times a day).

The hotel contains three separate, directly managed restaurants (the **Point** is good for steak and seafood; the open-air **Palms** is a casual beachfront cafe; the **Ocean Terrace** has all-day buffets). The glitzy **Casino Royale,** across the street from the accommodations, includes a cabaret theater for glittery shows and **Tantra** (formerly the Q Club), the island's hottest late-night dance spot. On the resort's street front, the Maho Promenade is filled with several dozen shops open late, restaurants (including Cheri's Café), a scuba-diving center, dance club, even a classy gentleman's club.

Maho Beach, 1 Rhine Rd., St. Maarten, N.A. ℂ **800/223-0757** in the U.S., or 599/545-2115. Fax 599/545-3180. www.sonesta.com/MahoBeach. 537 units. Winter $135–$470 double; $280–$620 suite. AE, DC, DISC, MC, V. **Amenities:** 3 restaurants; 1 nightclub; babysitting; casino; children's program; fitness center; 2 outdoor pools; room service; spa; 4 tennis courts. *In room:* A/C, TV, fridge (in some), hair dryer, Wi-Fi ($18/day or $55/week).

MODERATE/INEXPENSIVE

The Horny Toad Guesthouse (Value) This homey, welcoming place is run by an expatriate from Maine, Betty Vaughan. The hotel is near the airport, but the roar of jumbo jets is heard only a few times a day. Children 7 and under are not allowed, but families with older children often come here to avoid the megaresorts, and repeat visitors quickly become part of the Horned Toad family. Seven well-maintained units lie in an amply proportioned beachside house originally built in the 1950s as a private home by the island's former governor. The eighth room is in half of an octagonal "round house," with large windows and views of the sea. Guest rooms range from medium-size to spacious, and each has a fully equipped kitchen and a king-size bed. The guesthouse has no pool, no restaurant, and no organized activities of any kind, but the beach is just steps away, the island of Saba lies off in the distance, and guests have impromptu get-togethers around a pair of gas-fired barbecues.

2 Vlaun Dr., Simpson Bay, St. Maarten, N.A. ℂ **800/417-9361** in the U.S., or 599/545-4323. Fax 599/545-3316. www.thehornytoadguesthouse.com. 8 units. Winter $198 double; off season $107 double. Extra person $40 in winter, $25 off season. MC, V. No children under 7 allowed. **Amenities:** Smoke-free rooms. *In room:* A/C and ceiling fan, kitchen, Wi-Fi (free).

La Vista/La Vista Beach Resort This small timeshare resort lies at the foot of Pelican Cay. For a fee, guests can use the more elaborate facilities of the nearby Pelican Resort, with its casino, shops, and spa. The West Antillean–style resort consists of two parts—La Vista Resort, a 2-minute walk from a good sandy beach, and La Vista Beach Resort, whose units open directly onto the beach with studios and two-bedroom apartments. Rooms with a view come in seven different categories, including a junior suite, deluxe suite, and penthouse. Accommodations feature fully equipped kitchenettes or kitchens. My preference is the one-bedroom Antillean cottage with its front porch (suitable for four).

The **Hideaway Bar & Restaurant** serves well-prepared French cuisine adjacent to the pool, with live entertainment several nights a week.

53 Billy Folly Rd., Pelican Cay (P.O. Box 2086), Simpson Bay, St. Maarten, NA. ℰ **888/790-5264** or 599/544-3005. Fax 599/544-3010. www.lavistaresort.com. 50 suites. Winter $180–$210 junior and deluxe suites, $235–$330 suites for 4, $270–$300 penthouse, $210 cottage; off season $140–$160 junior and deluxe suites, $175–$225 suites for 4; $200–$215 penthouse; $160 cottage. Extra person $20. Children under 12 stay free when sharing with 2 adults. AE, DISC, MC, V. **Amenities:** Restaurant; bar; outdoor pool; Wi-Fi (free). *In room:* A/C, TV, hair dryer, kitchen or kitchenette.

Mary's Boon Beach Resort ★   Mary's Boon is one of those endearing places that draw loyal guests year after year. It's the kind of laidback spot where people not only *talk* to other people, they get downright chummy. The small, convivial bar has a fizzy happy hour, drawing local businessfolk from nearby Simpson Bay. In business for 40-plus years, Mary's Boon enjoys direct access to one of the nicest beaches on St. Maarten, uncrowded, with powdery white sand. Even better, its owner has upgraded and beautified the rooms and added spa services, and is going as green as possible on an island that doesn't recycle (yet). He has succeeded without undermining the charming, offbeat ambience.

Mary's Boon is right near the airport, so guests have to deal with the plate-rattling sounds of jets taking off at various times during the day. But it's also minutes from casinos, shops, and restaurants. Each room varies architecturally, but all have verandas or terraces; a number have big cherrywood beds and Balinese woodcarvings. Those facing the sea directly are high-ceilinged and wonderfully breezy. Renovated rooms are equipped with full fridges, granite countertops, stainless-steel appliances, and flatscreen TVs. The upstairs rooms 201 through 205 are particularly spacious, opening up to the sea on one side and the garden on the other. **Tides,** the modest beach restaurant and bar, offers satisfying, good-value food that reveals a sure hand in the kitchen—it should; the head chef, Leona, has been cooking here for almost 40 years!—and its perch over the beach, with the sea breeze wafting in, is tonic for what ails you.

117 Simpson Bay Rd., St. Maarten, N.A. (or P.O. Box 523882, Miami, FL 33152). ℰ **866/978-5899** or 599/545-7000. Fax 599/545-3403. www.marysboon.com. 37 units. Winter $135–$300 double (studios and 1-bedroom suites), $250–$425 2-bedroom suites; off season $75–$275 double, $135–$415 2-bedroom suites. Extra person $35. MC, V. Take the first right turn as you head from the airport

toward Philipsburg; then follow the signs to Mary's Boon. **Amenities:** Restaurant; bar; babysitting; outdoor pool; room service; spa; Wi-Fi (free, in lobby). *In room:* A/C, ceiling fan, TV, hair dryer, kitchen or kitchenette.

Oyster Bay Beach Resort ★   At the end of a twisting, scenic road, a 1-minute walk from Dawn Beach, this retreat was originally designed for vacationers who don't like overly commercialized megaresorts; now it's largely a timeshare. Once an intimate inn, it's been growing by leaps and bounds, having witnessed a five-fold increase in size since it was established in the 1960s. It can't be considered intimate anymore, but it's still not overwhelming. On a circular harbor on the eastern shore, near the French border, the fortresslike structure stands guard over a 14-hectare (35-acre) protected marina. There's a central courtyard and an alfresco lobby.

More than half the units have kitchens, and most have West Indian decor with lots of rattan and wicker. The bedrooms offer balconies overlooking the pond or sea; the deluxe and superior rooms are preferable to the tower suites. Rooms are airy and fairly spacious, and suites have a bathroom with a tub and a shower.

The resort restaurant, **Infinity,** serves international food for breakfast, lunch, and dinner. **Beau Beau's** (www.beaubeaus.com), facing the beach, serves seafood and Caribbean fare at lunch and dinner and offers nightly entertainment and musical cabarets from local calypso king Beau Beau. Just next door is one of the island's most popular beach bar/restaurants, **Mr. Busby's on the Beach.**

10 Emerald Merit Rd., Oyster Pond (P.O. Box 239), St. Maarten, N.A. ℂ **866/978-0212** in the U.S., or 599/543-6040. Fax 599/543-6695. www.oysterbaybeachresort. com. 178 units (of those, 153 are timeshares). Double $150–$325; suite $390–$675; deluxe loft $250–$300. Extra person $50–$60. Children under 12 stay free in parent's room. Ask about meal plans. AE, DISC, MC, V. **Amenities:** 2 restaurants; 2 bars; babysitting; fitness center; outdoor pool; spa; 4 tennis courts. *In room:* A/C, TV/DVD, Internet, kitchen or kitchenette (except for Superior rooms), hair dryer.

Pasanggrahan Royal Guest House ★ (Value   Big changes are coming to this vintage West Indian–style guesthouse, once the summer home of the Dutch Queen Wilhelmina. A new five-story addition, with underground parking and 10 new rooms, was scheduled for completion in late 2010. Pasanggrahan enjoys a prime spot on the beach in Philipsburg, sandwiched between busy, narrow Front Street and the harborside boardwalk, and set back and shaded under tall trees. One hopes that the new section isn't too jarring a contrast to this charming relic from another time. The interior has a gracious, Victorian feel, with peacock bamboo chairs, Indian spool tables, and a gilt-framed oil portrait of the queen. The small- to medium-size accommodations have queen-size, double, or king-size beds with four-poster designs; some are in the main building and others are in an adjoining annex. The finest have genuine colonial flair, with antique secretaries and four-posters swaddled in mosquito netting, madras valances, hand-stitched quilts, beamed ceilings, and still-life paintings.

Set among lush palms is the harborfront **Pasanggrahan Restaurant,** which specializes in fresh fish caught by the hotel's own deep-sea charter fishing boat and family-style dinners. Even if you aren't staying here, this is a peaceful, shady oasis for lunch or a drink after a day wrestling the cruise-ship hordes in downtown Philipsburg. The food is good and fresh, and the view of the harbor from the old wooden veranda, with Fort Amsterdam in the distance, never quits.

19 Front St. (P.O. Box 151), Philipsburg, St. Maarten, N.A. ✆ **599/542-3588. Fax** 599/542-2885. www.pasanroyalinn.com. 30 units. Winter $158–$250 double; off season $98–$250 double. Extra person winter $75, off season $55. DISC, MC, V. Closed Sept. **Amenities:** Restaurant; 2 bars; Internet (free). *In room:* A/C, ceiling fan, TV, fridge, kitchenette (in some).

Turquoise Shell Inn (Value)   The surrounding area isn't as nice and clean as this trim yellow-and-white apartment complex steps from Simpson Bay Beach, but the price and location are right. Each of the 10 one-bedroom suites has a fully equipped kitchen, though the restaurants and bars along the Simpson Bay strip are within easy walking distance (not recommended if you're alone after a night's carousing). The plumbing is noisy, the shower-only bathrooms cramped, and the decor unassuming, but the friendly, obliging management keeps everything tidy. No children under 5 are allowed.

34 Simpson Bay Rd., Simpson Bay, St. Maarten, N.A. ✆ **599/545-2875** or 545-5642. Fax 599/545-2846. www.tshellinn.com. 10 units. Winter $145 double; off season $115 double. Extra person $25–$35. Rates include tax and service charges. Ask about timeshare weeks. No children under 5. MC, V. **Amenities:** Pool. *In room:* A/C, ceiling fan, TV, Wi-Fi (free).

2 FRENCH ST. MARTIN

Unlike Dutch St. Maarten, French St. Martin has no high-rise hotels; lodgings on this side of the island are small-scale and trend toward boutique. Many, like La Samanna and the Grand Case Beach Club, are smack-dab on the beach; others, like Hotel L'Esplanade and Hotel La Plantation, are tucked into rugged green slopes above the sea. The largest French St. Martin hotel by far, the Radisson Blu, is nestled inside a protected cove, as serene and unobtrusive as Dutch St. Maarten's Sonesta Maho is in your face. *Vive le différence!*

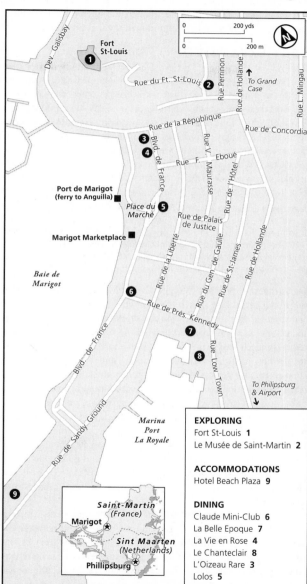

EXPLORING
Fort St-Louis **1**
Le Musée de Saint-Martin **2**

ACCOMMODATIONS
Hotel Beach Plaza **9**

DINING
Claude Mini-Club **6**
La Belle Epoque **7**
La Vie en Rose **4**
Le Chanteclair **8**
L'Oizeau Rare **3**
Lolos **5**

Hotels on French St. Martin add a 10% service charge and a *taxe de séjour*. This local room tax is 4% to 5%. Expect higher rates during Christmas week. *Note:* Rates are quoted in either euros or dollars, depending on how establishments quoted them at press time.

VERY EXPENSIVE

Green Cay Villas ★   This gated hillside community overlooking the sweep of Orient Bay features 16 fully equipped three-bedroom, 418-sq.-m (4,499-sq.-ft.) villas with private pools at—comparatively—bargain rates, especially off season. Each can be configured into individual units; even the one-bedroom contains a modern kitchen. The design emphasizes cool blue, pristine off-whites, and rich tropical accents mirroring sea, sand, and sunset. White and natural wicker and hardwood furnishings are juxtaposed with boldly hued art naïf, throw pillows, fabrics, ceramics, and whimsical touches such as painted parrots dangling from the high coffered ceilings.

Parc de la Baie Orientale (B.P. 3006), St. Martin, F.W.I. ☎ 866/592-4213 in the U.S., or 590/87-38-63. Fax 590/87-39-27. www.greencayvillas.com. 16 units. Winter $630 1-bedroom suite, $825 2-bedroom suite, $950 3-bedroom villa; off season $420 1-bedroom suite, $550 2-bedroom suite, $660 3-bedroom villa. Rates include continental breakfast. Minimum stay 4 nights. MC, V. **Amenities:** Gym; Jacuzzis; Wi-Fi (free). *In room:* A/C, TV, VCR, hair dryer, Internet, kitchen, Wi-Fi (free).

La Samanna ★★★   With low-lying Mediterranean-style villas spread out over a long stretch of one of St. Martin's finest beaches, La Samanna has earned a reputation as a world-class complex where the cognoscenti come to relax and unwind. An Orient-Express hotel, the resort is indeed lovely (the views from the hotel's signature restaurant are divine), and the colonial-style lobby and bar are handsomely atmospheric. Regardless of their size, most rooms feature private terraces. Suites and villas have spacious bedrooms with luxurious beds, fully equipped kitchens, living and dining rooms, and large patios. The bathrooms are spacious and well designed, with bidets and hand-painted Mexican tiles. Five state-of-the-art specialty suites have private terraces with sumptuous Baie Longue views. For the ultimate in luxury, eight newish villas have private wraparound infinity pools and rooftop terraces with magnificent views. The three- or four-bedroom villas come with private concierge service, private beach cabanas, and VIP airport transfers.

Despite the price tag, La Samanna isn't stuffy; everyone is treated royally here. Guests enjoy superb cuisine on a candlelit terrace spectacularly perched above Baie Longue—the ambience is pure French Riviera. (*Note:* Children under 7 are not permitted in the main restaurant for dinner.) The wine cellar, **Le Cave,** holds some 14,000 bottles.

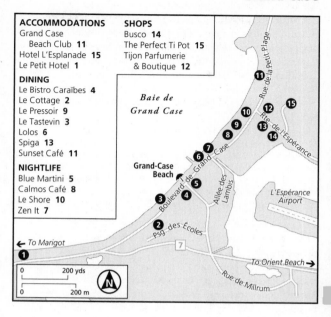

ACCOMMODATIONS
Grand Case
  Beach Club **11**
Hotel L'Esplanade **15**
Le Petit Hotel **1**

DINING
Le Bistro Caraïbes **4**
Le Cottage **2**
Le Pressoir **9**
Le Tastevin **3**
Lolos **6**
Spiga **13**
Sunset Café **11**

NIGHTLIFE
Blue Martini **5**
Calmos Café **8**
Le Shore **10**
Zen It **7**

SHOPS
Busco **14**
The Perfect Ti Pot **15**
Tijon Parfumerie
  & Boutique **12**

*Baie de
Grand Case*

Grand-Case
Beach

Rue de la Petit-Plage
Rte de l'Espérance
Rte de l'Espérance

Boulevard de Grand Case
Allée des Lambis

L'Espérance
Airport

← To Marigot

Psg. des Écoles

7

To Orient Beach →

Rue de Millrum

0 — 200 yds
0 — 200 m

The poolside grill serves lunch daily and dinner 2 nights a week. If you can't make dinner in the main restaurant, you can enjoy the same great views at the **buffet breakfasts** ★, as delicious as the setting (and included in the room rates). With the curve of Baie Longue stretched out before you, there are few better ways to start the day.

Baie Longue (B.P. 4077), 97064 St. Martin CEDEX, F.W.I. ✆ **800/237-1236** in the U.S., or 590/87-64-00. Fax 590/87-87-86. www.lasamanna.com. 81 units. Winter $995 double, $1,925–$5,275 suite; off season $450–$680 double, from $850 suite. Villas from $3,000 year-round. Extra person $75. Children 11 and under stay free in parent's room. Rates include full buffet breakfast. AE, MC, V. Closed late Aug to late Oct. **Amenities:** 2 restaurants; 2 bars; babysitting; fitness center; 2 freshwater outdoor pools; room service; spa; 3 lighted tennis courts; watersports equipment (extensive). *In room:* A/C, ceiling fan, TV/DVD, CD player (in some), hair dryer, minibar, plunge pool (in some), Wi-Fi (free).

EXPENSIVE

Alamanda Resort ★ Small and intimate, like a European beach-front inn, the Alamanda opens onto Orient Bay's beautiful beach. The resort is a cluster of Creole *cazes,* or little houses, surrounding a lushly landscaped outdoor pool quite near the beach. The Alamanda has a few drawbacks, one being that not all rooms have ocean views. Bedrooms are spacious and done up in soothing earth tones, with decorative accents in bold colors from sunflower yellow to tomato red, or pineapple patterns. The king-size beds are elegantly carved, often a four-poster. The best accommodations are the two-bedroom duplexes with a second bathroom. Our favorite place to dine here is at **Kakao Beach** beachfront restaurant, featuring both Creole and European specialties in a laid-back Caribbean atmosphere. A less expensive choice is **Cafe Alamanda,** with an inventive tropical cuisine served poolside.

Baie Orientale, St. Martin, F.W.I. ℂ **800/622-7836** in the U.S. or 590/52-87-40. Fax 590/52-87-41. www.alamanda-resort.com. 42 units. Winter $375–$490 double, $600 2-bedroom duplex, $710–$790 suite; off season $270–$340 double, $440 2-bedroom duplex, $450–$500 suite. Extra person $50. Up to two children 11 and under stay free in two parents' room. AE, MC, V. Closed Sept. **Amenities:** 2 restaurants; 2 bars; babysitting; concierge; gym; outdoor pool; room service; 2 tennis courts; watersports equipment. *In room:* A/C, ceiling fan, TV, hair dryer, kitchenette, Wi-Fi (free).

Esmeralda Resort ★   Originally conceived as a site for a single private villa, and then for a semiprivate club, this hillside housing development gives the appearance of a well-maintained compound of Creole-inspired villas on sloping terrain that's interspersed with lush gardens. It's just a 25-minute taxi ride northeast of Princess Juliana airport. Opening onto Orient Beach, the Esmeralda blossomed into a full-scale resort in the early 1990s, offering views over Orient Bay and a decidedly French focus. Each of the 18 Spanish mission–style, tile-roofed villas can be configured into four separate units by locking or unlocking the doors between rooms. Each individual unit contains a king-size or two double beds, a kitchenette, a terrace, and a private entrance. Each villa has a communal pool, which creates the feeling of a private club. The suites (one to five bedrooms) are luxuriously spacious.

The Astrolabe, with its award-winning chef, Stephane Decluseau, serves fine French-Caribbean specialties at breakfast and dinner daily. At lunch, the hotel issues an ID card that can be used for discounts at any of a half-dozen restaurants along Orient Bay.

Parc de la Baie Orientale (B.P. 5141), 97071 St. Martin, F.W.I. ℂ **590/87-36-36.** Fax 590/87-35-18. www.esmeralda-resort.com. 65 units. Winter $375–$550 double, $690–$1,020 suite; off season $270–$370 double, $440–$600 suite. Extra person 12 and over $80; children 11 and under free in parent's suite. AE, MC, V. Closed Sept. **Amenities:** 2 restaurants; bar; babysitting; horseback riding (nearby); 18 outdoor pools; room service; 2 tennis courts; watersports equipment (extensive). *In room:* A/C, ceiling fan, TV, Internet, fridge, hair dryer, kitchenette.

Grand Case Beach Club ★ (Kids)   This bundling of bougainvillea-draped buildings sits between two beaches just a short stroll from the action in "downtown" Grand Case. Of the several different room categories, including duplex units, all have well-stocked kitchens with granite counters and private balconies or patios (the best offering smashing views of Anguilla). The property is immaculately maintained, and you can't beat the views. Families will particularly appreciate the gated entrance (making the lovely Petite Plage practically private) and 24-hour security guard and video surveillance. Little extras include a sampling of island CDs and a bottle of wine at check-in. The general manager is conscientious, cordial, and helpful, qualities he inculcates in the staff.

The **Sunset Café** (see p. 78), set spectacularly on the rocks overlooking the water, serves hearty food at reasonable prices for breakfast, lunch, and dinner daily.

Grand Case 97150, St. Martin, F.W.I. ℂ **800/344-3016** in the U.S. or 590/87-51-87. Fax 590/87-59-93. www.grandcasebeachclub.com. 73 units. Winter $320–$395 studio double, $375–$530 1-bedroom suite, $530–$565 2-bedroom suite; off season $150–$220 studio double, $170–$283 1-bedroom suite, $280–$295 2-bedroom suite. Rates include continental breakfast. Children under 12 stay free in parent's room. Extra person $35. AE, MC, V. **Amenities:** Restaurant; bar; fitness center; outdoor pool; tennis court; watersports equipment (extensive). *In room:* A/C, fan, TV, CD player, hair dryer, kitchen.

Hotel Beach Plaza

This is the best hotel within a reasonable distance of Marigot's commercial heart. A three-story building that centers on a soaring atrium festooned with live banana trees and climbing vines, it's within a cluster of buildings mostly composed of condominiums. Built in 1996, and painted in shades of blue and white, it's set midway between the open sea and the lagoon, giving all rooms water views. The white interiors are accented with varnished, dark-tinted woods and a tropical motif. Each room contains a balcony, tile floors, native art, and simple hardwood furniture, including a writing desk and comfortable beds. The hotel's restaurant, **Le Corsaire,** serves French food except for the all-you-can-eat buffets 2 nights a week, which feature Creole and seafood, respectively.

Baie de Marigot, 97150 St. Martin, F.W.I. ℂ **800/221-5333** in the U.S., or 590/87-87-00. Fax 590/87-18-87. www.hotelbeachplazasxm.com. 144 units. Winter 220€–379€ double, 448€–506€ suite; off season 150€–295€ double, 342€ suite. One child 11 and under stays free in parent's room. Rates include buffet breakfast. AE, MC, V. **Amenities:** Restaurant; 2 bars; babysitting; bikes; outdoor pool; room service; watersports equipment (extensive). *In room:* A/C, TV, fridge, hair dryer, Wi-Fi (free).

Hôtel L'Esplanade ★★

This lovely, beautifully managed small hotel just gets better and better. Along with its sister hotel, Le Petit—located directly on Grand Case Beach—it's easily one of the nicest places to stay on the entire island. Everything is wonderfully maintained; you won't see a tatter here or a loose thread there. With a collection of suites set on a steeply sloping hillside above the village of Grand Case, it almost has the feel of a boutique inn in the French Alps. Flowered vines frame terraces with gorgeous views of the village and sea below. The resort is connected by a network of steps and terraced gardens; cascades of bougainvillea drape walls accented with hand-painted tiles and blue slate roofs. The lovely pool is just steps down the hill, and access to a beach is via a 6-minute walk down a winding pathway. There's no restaurant, but the village of Grand Case is famous for its many fine restaurants.

All guest rooms have private terraces that angle out toward the sea and the sun setting behind Anguilla. Each individually decorated unit contains a kitchen with up-to-date cookware, Italian porcelain tile floors, beamed ceilings, plasma-screen TVs, DVDs, mahogany and wicker furniture, and very comfortable queen- or king-size beds (many four-poster). Slate and tumbled marble bathrooms are beautifully equipped. The loft suites on the upper floors are worth the extra charge—they include a sofa bed downstairs, an upstairs master bedroom with a king-size bed, and a partial bathroom downstairs. The cordial owners, Marc and Kristin Petrelluzzi have completely redone each suite; additional, even posher villas are in the works.

Grand Case (B.P. 5007), 97150 St. Martin, F.W.I. © **866/596-8365** in the U.S., or 590/87-06-55. Fax 590/87-29-15. www.lesplanade.com. 24 units. Winter $395 studio, $445–$495 loft, $495 suite; off season $245 studio, $295–$345 loft, $345 suite. Extra person winter $70, off season $50. AE, MC, V. **Amenities:** Bar (winter); babysitting; outdoor pool. *In room:* A/C, ceiling fan, TV, CD player, hair dryer, Internet (free), kitchen, minibar.

Le Domaine de Lonvilliers ★ This attractive resort sprawls over 60 hectares (148 acres) of palm-fringed gardens and follows the lovely curve of the beach at Anse Marcel. It and the neighboring Radisson (originally one hotel) are the only inhabitants of this beguiling secluded cove. The comfortable rooms are done in cool creams and browns or bold reds set against ivory walls and white tile floors. All have spacious bathrooms and either a private balcony or terrace. The hotel has recently opened a beachside restaurant, **La Table du Marché,** the Caribbean twin to its St. Tropez sister and a thrilling new addition to the St. Martin gastronomic scene.

Anse Marcel, 97150 St. Martin, F.W.I. © **590/52-35-35.** Fax 590/29-10-81. www.hotel-le-domaine.com. 141 units. Winter 280€–500€ double, 560€–1,450€ suite; off season 235€–420 double, 470€–1,090€ suite. Extra person 60€. One child under 12 stays free in parent's room. Rates include buffet breakfast. DISC, MC, V. Closed Sept 1 to mid-Oct. **Amenities:** Restaurant; beach bar; lounge; fitness center; outdoor pool; room service; spa; 2 tennis courts; watersports equipment (extensive). *In room:* A/C, TV, kitchen (in some), Wi-Fi (free).

Le Petit Hotel ★★ (Finds) This well-managed, thoughtfully designed hotel opens directly onto the sands of Grand Case Beach. It practically defines quiet chic, starting with the hand-painted tiles throughout the public spaces and hallways. It shares the same strong management, meticulous attention to detail, and sense of stylish comfort that distinguishes its splendid sister property, L'Esplanade (see above). Furnishings and accents are sourced from around the globe, including Balinese teak and Brazilian mahogany; natural wicker beds are topped with white down duvets and pillows. Luxurious touches include Frette linens and Damana toiletries. The smallish bathrooms are mostly shower only, and the kitchenettes have a microwave, a fridge, and a two-burner stovetop, but no oven. Each has a huge, beautifully appointed terrace or balcony overlooking the sand. The overall effect is of serene sanctuary. Though there's no restaurant, the gracious staff offers advice on the town's superb dining options.

248 bd. de Grand Case, Grand Case, 97150 St. Martin, F.W.I. ℂ **590/29-09-65.** Fax 590/87-09-19. www.lepetithotel.com. 10 units. Winter $415–$455 double, $525 suite; off season $265–$305 double, $375 suite. Extra person (including children) $50–$70. Rates include continental breakfast. AE, MC, V. **Amenities:** Babysitting. *In room:* A/C, ceiling fan, TV, CD player, fridge, hair dryer, kitchenette, Wi-Fi (free).

Radisson Blu Resort Marina & Spa, St. Martin (Kids) ★★ This property is now a full-fledged Radisson Blu—which means it will go a little more upscale and have as much of a boutique feel as a 250-room hotel can have. It's the only resort on the island with direct access to a full-service marina, and the setting is a beaut, tucked inside the half-moon of the cove at Anse Marcel, with the lights of Anguilla twinkling across the sea. It's a full immersion in tropical flora and fauna: White egrets flutter in the folds of the mossy volcanic hills that rise sharply on either side of the cove, and lizards skitter along pathways. This property, which had a couple of incarnations before Radisson gave it a $60-million facelift, reopened in December 2008. Its location inside this secluded cove and the property's sheer sense of space (7 hectares/18 acres) give it a real getaway feel. The infinity, zero-entry pool is spectacular: at 93m (305 ft.) it's the largest freshwater pool on the island; one poolside area has been set up like a beach, with lounge chairs in sand alongside the water. The hotel is suite-heavy (63 suites), and most of the units face the flower-filled courtyard; if you want a full ocean view from your patio, ask for a room at the end of the East and West buildings. Every room has a patio/balcony and the trademark Radisson "Sleep Number" Bed, with remote controls to harden or soften the bed to your liking; bathrooms have been handsomely updated. **Le Spa** has five treatment rooms and two full cabanas for outside treatment; you can choose the color of your lighting and even bring your iPod.

C Le Restaurant (see chapter 4) is the resort's main restaurant; it's set alongside the Baie des Froussards, where sailboats are silhouetted against the starry sky. (The food is so good you may not want to head to Grand Case, 5 minutes away, for dinner; but you should, at least once). The full breakfast buffet in the cheerful **Le Marché** is copious (and included in the rates). Radisson will arrange watersports excursions that leave straight from the resort marina—you don't have to go through St. Maarten. You can get to the Radisson the prosaic way (by taxi) or the cool way: by **water taxi** ($45 one-way adult; $30 children 3–12) straight from the airport to the resort in the *Scoobi Too* catamaran (see chapter 5).

Anse Marcel (B.P. 581), 97056 St. Martin, F.W.I. (C) **800/333-3333** in the U.S. or Canada, or 590/87-67-00. Fax 590/87-30-38. www.radissonblu.com/resort-stmartin. 252 units. Winter 339€–419€ double, 589€–629€ suite; off season 209€–299€ double, 389€–549€ suite. Children 11 and under stay free in parent's room. Rates include full breakfast. AE, DC, DISC, MC, V. **Amenities:** 2 restaurants; 2 bars; ATM; babysitting; bocce court; children's program w/clubhouse and playground; concierge; fitness center; full-service marina; 2 pools; spa; watersports center/dive center; volleyball; watersports equipment (extensive); water taxi service. *In room:* A/C, flatscreen TV/DVD, hair dryer, minibar, MP3 docking station, Wi-Fi (free).

MODERATE

Club Orient Naturist Resort ★   Occupying an isolated spot, this is the only true nudist resort in the French West Indies, but it's definitely *not* a wild, swinging, party place. Celebrating some 32 years of business, it's clean, decent, middle class, even family friendly. Very few singles check in, in fact. Many of the guests are older and very conservative—just looking for a quiet, reclusive getaway to walk around naked. There's no pool on the premises, but the chalets are right on an excellent beach, with plentiful activities to facilitate hanging out (in every sense). Accommodations, set in red-pine chalets imported from Finland, sport a basic IKEA-meets-campground-cabin look, though the decor has been spruced up. All have outside showers and most have both front and back porches. At **Papagayo Restaurant,** you can dine alfresco; the popular 5-to-7pm happy hour allows guests to compare, er, notes. However, each unit has a kitchenette, and there's a general store, **La Boutique,** on-site if you want to cook your own meal.

1 Baie Orientale, 97150 St. Martin, F.W.I. (C) **800/690-0199** in the U.S., or 590/87-33-85. Fax 590/87-33-76. www.cluborient.com. 136 units. Winter 215€–230€ studio and suite, 330€–360€ chalet, 750€ villa; off season 135€–190€ studio and suite, 185€–280€ chalet, 450€–560€ villa. Extra person 12 and over 25€. Children

11 and under stay for free. AE, DC, DISC, MC, V. **Amenities:** 2 restaurants; 2 bars; babysitting; library; fitness center; 2 lighted tennis courts; wellness center (w/spa treatments); watersports equipment (extensive). *In room:* A/C, ceiling fan, kitchen, Wi-Fi (free).

Hotel La Plantation ★   Although it requires a few minutes' walk to reach the gorgeous white-sand beach, this is one of the most attractive and appealing hotels at Orient Bay. It's set on a steep, carefully landscaped slope. Seventeen colonial-style villas are scattered around the tropically landscaped grounds and pool; each villa contains a suite and two studios, which can be rented separately or combined. The spacious units are stylishly furnished in a colorful Creole theme, complete with hand-painted or hand-stenciled murals, and each sports its own ocean-view terrace. Studios have kitchenettes and queen-size or twin beds; the suites have separate bedrooms with king-size beds, big living rooms, full kitchens, and beautifully tiled full bathrooms. **Café Plantation** serves French and Creole dinners. At lunch, clients use an in-house "privilege card" to buy French/Creole/international meals at any of five beachfront restaurants loosely associated with the resort.

C 5 Parc de La Baie Orientale, Orient Bay, 97150 St. Martin, F.W.I. ⓒ **590/29-58-00.** Fax 590/29-58-08. www.la-plantation.com. 52 units. Winter $340–$360 studio for 2, from $510 suite; off season $200–$210 studio, from $275 suite. Children under 12 stay free in 2 parents' room. Rates include buffet breakfast. DISC, MC, V. Closed Sept 1 to mid-Oct. **Amenities:** Restaurant; beach bar and grill; babysitting; bikes; concierge; horseback riding; health club; outdoor pool; 2 tennis courts; watersports equipment; Wi-Fi (free, in public spaces). *In room:* A/C, ceiling fan, TV, CD player (in some), fridge, hair dryer, kitchen or kitchenette.

3

FRENCH ST. MARTIN

Mercure St. Martin and Marina Ⓥⓐⓛⓤⓔ   This is a good-value hotel on the French side of the island. The complex occupies a flat, sandy stretch of land between a saltwater lagoon and the beach, 8km (5 miles) west of Princess Juliana Airport. Decorated throughout in bold, Creole-inspired hues, its five three-story buildings are each evocative of a large, many-balconied Antillean house. In its center, a pool serves as the focal point for a bar built out over the lagoon, an indoor/outdoor restaurant, and a flagstone terrace that hosts steel bands and evening cocktail parties. Each unit offers, in addition to a kitchenette, a terrace with a view. The most desirable accommodations, on the third (top) floor, contain sloping ceilings sheltering sleeping lofts, and two bathrooms.

Baie Nettlé (B.P. 172), Marigot, 97052 St. Martin, F.W.I. ⓒ **800/221-4542** in the U.S., or 590/87-54-54. Fax 590/87-92-11. www.mercure.com/gb/hotel-1100-mercure-st-martin-and-marina/index.shtml. 169 units. Year-round $155–$205 double. Rates include buffet breakfast. AE, DC, MC, V. **Amenities:** Restaurant; bar; babysitting; billiards; outdoor pool; tennis court; dive center; watersports equipment (extensive). *In room:* A/C, TV, hair dryer, minibar, Wi-Fi (for a fee).

4

Where to Dine on St. Maarten/ St. Martin

Without a doubt, St. Maarten/St. Martin has some of the best food in the Caribbean. Both the French and Dutch sides offer epicurean experiences galore, with nearly 500 restaurants to choose from. St. Martin has become a competitive training ground for a number of classically trained culinary wizards and Michelin-bound chefs. Although the Dutch side is much more Americanized (you'll spot KFC and Burger King, among fast food chains), some of the island's most exciting international restaurants are here—this, after all, is the melting pot of the Caribbean.

Truth be told, the standards are so high on both sides of this tiny island that few restaurateurs can get away with mediocrity for long; even the hotel restaurants are way better than most. Speaking of which, I'd like to mention a couple that for space issues aren't reviewed below. La Samanna's **Le Réservé ★★** (www.lasamanna. com) offers a sublime fine-dining experience in a setting that's hard to beat: high above curving Baie Longue. At the other end of the dining spectrum, the **Tides** is a modest, old-fashioned dining room with a seaside setting at Mary's Boon Beach Resort (www.marysboon.com). The head chef, Leona, has been cooking here for almost 40 years, and the food is delicious—and you're so close to the sea that the spray practically perfumes your meal.

Yes, you can eat well pretty much wherever you go. You'll find great dining in **Marigot,** in restaurants lining the waterfront and at Marina Port la Royale. **Philipsburg,** for all its slightly tawdry tendencies, has a number of truly fine eateries on and around Front Street. Numerous options have sprouted in St. Maarten's **Maho district,** while its neighbor **Simpson Bay** has dozens of casual but topnotch watering holes overlooking the lagoon where fresh seafood reflects the community's longtime fishing heritage. But the island's true culinary mecca is the charming fishing village of **Grand Case,** perched near the northern tip of St. Martin: No other Caribbean town offers so many wonderful restaurants per capita, sitting cheek-by-jowl along the narrow mile-long Boulevard de Grand Case.

La Belle Créole

Befitting its turbulent colonial history, St. Maarten/St. Martin is a rich culinary melting pot. The local cuisine, symbol of the island's voyage on many levels, is primarily a savory blend of Arawak (the indigenous people), French, African, even East Indian influences. The Arawaks contributed native tubers like yuca (aka cassava) and dasheen (whose leaves, similar to spinach, are also used), as well as cilantro, lemongrass, and achiote for flavoring. The slave ships introduced plantains, sweet potato, green pigeon peas, and assorted peppers. The various European influences bore fruit in fresh garden staples like onions (and breadfruit imported from Tahiti because it proved cheaper for feeding slaves). The East Indians brought curry with them, an essential ingredient of Colombo, a meat or chicken dish of Tamil origin, as well as exotic spices.

True Creole cuisine is fast vanishing: It requires patience and work, long hours marinating and pounding. But you can still find authentic dishes whose seasonings ignite the palate. Look for specialties such as *crabe farci* (stuffed crab), *féroce* (avocado with shredded, spicy codfish called *chiquetaille*), *accras* (cod fritters), *blaff* (seafood simmered in seasoned soup), *boudin* (spicy blood sausage), *bébélé* and *matété* (tripe dishes stewed with anything from breadfruit to bananas). Conch *(lambi)* and whelks are found in fritters and stews with fiery *sauce chien*. Wash them down with local juices: mango, guava, papaya, and less familiar flavors such as the tart tangy tamarind; milky mouth-puckering soursop; pulpy passion fruit; bitter yet refreshing mauby (made from tree bark); and the milkshakelike, reputedly aphrodisiacal sea moss. And try a *ti' punch* aperitif: deceptively sweet, fruit-infused 100-proof rum.

—*Jordan Simon*

1 DUTCH ST. MAARTEN

Rates are quoted in dollars on Dutch St. Maarten. Unlike in French St. Martin, restaurants do not include a service charge, and gratuities are appreciated.

Expensive

Antoine ★ FRENCH In a lovely seaside setting, Antoine serves comforting bistro food with sophistication and style. The handsome room is decked out with jungle-themed Haitian masterworks, Delft tile, hurricane lanterns, old phonographs, and towering floral arrangements. Start with the chef's savory kettle of fish soup, escargots de Bourgogne, or the almost translucent sea scallops Nantaise. You can't go wrong with the baked red snapper filet delicately flavored with shallots and a white-wine butter sauce, shrimp scampi flambéed with Pastis, or grilled local lobster. And desserts are satisfyingly sinful. Antoine is also open for lunch, serving pastas, burgers, sandwiches, and salads, and has a basic kids' menu.

119 Front St., Philipsburg. ℂ **599/542-2964.** www.lagondola-sxm.com. Reservations recommended. Main courses $8.95–$24 lunch, $19–$40 dinner; lobster thermidor $46. AE, DISC, MC, V. Daily 11am–10pm.

L'Escargot ★★ FRENCH/CREOLE You can't miss the wildly painted shutters and tropical Toulouse-Lautrec murals of revelers on the yellow exterior of this 160-year-old Creole cottage. The high spirits continue within, thanks to the colorful, candlelit decor and mellow staff, which does double duty performing the Friday-night cabaret drag show, "La Cage aux Folles." The chef is deft with fish, particularly classic preparations as meunière, and hearty bistro classics. The *coeur de filet a la confiture d'oignons* (filet of beef served in a sweet onion dressing perfumed with grenadine) will melt in your mouth. And oh yes, snails, with at least six preparations on the menu (try the sampler plate), including *sur champignons* (in fresh mushroom caps); *en croustade au safran* (in a crust with Chardonnay and saffron sauce); and in cherry tomatoes with garlic butter. It's a temple to garlic and color and bonhomie—and a memorable evening out in Philipsburg.

96 Front St., Philipsburg. ℂ **599/542-2483.** www.lescargotrestaurant.com. Reservations recommended. Main courses $19–$31. AE, DISC, MC, V. Mon–Fri 11am–3pm and daily 6–10pm.

(Tips) Mapping It

For locations of dining establishments listed in this chapter, please refer to the St. Maarten/St. Martin, Marigot, Philipsburg, and Grand Case maps on p. 46, p. 55, p. 49, and p. 57, respectively.

Sheer ★ FRENCH/CARIBBEAN This upscale spot is one of Philipsburg's newest restaurants, introducing a coolly elegant tenor to the city's dining scene. The interior has a chic, fine-dining sheen, its series of mirrored rooms done in beige-and-cream monochromes. The owner, hotel professional Valentin Davis, has pulled out all the stops—and the place shows great promise in becoming a classic. Start with a crab salad with an avocado, apple, and red pepper coulis or the coconut shrimp cakes topped with lemongrass cream. For entrees, look for fresh fish or lobster tail or try the grilled pork tenderloin with a sweet potato pave and sautéed greens.

44 Front St., Promenade Mall, Philipsburg. ℂ **599/542-9635.** www.sheer restaurant.com. Reservations recommended. Main courses $28–$45. AE, MC, V. Daily 11am–3pm and 6:30–11pm.

Moderate

The harborfront **Pasanggrahan Restaurant** (19 Front St., Philipsburg; ℂ **599/54-23588;** www.pasanhotel.com) in the Pasanggrahan Inn, is a peaceful, shady oasis for lunch or a drink. The food is good and fresh, and the views of Great Bay are wonderful.

Chesterfields CARIBBEAN/INTERNATIONAL The "house" restaurant at the Great Bay Marina is the ideal spot for an après-snorkeling or sailing outing. Set right on the dock of the marina, with boats cruising in and salt air wafting, Chesterfields has an appealingly roughhewn, nautical feel, with wooden tables and walls tacked with mounted (fish) trophies. A friendly staff oversees the comings and goings of sunburned sailors, grizzled captains, and day-trippers revitalized after a morning of exploring offshore islets and cays. Look for standard pub fare such as burgers, steaks, salads, and sandwiches, as well as island specialties like garlic shrimp, stuffed mahimahi, and conch chowder. The food is good and hearty—testament to Chesterfields' nearly 30 years of solid customer service.

Dock Maarten, Great Bay Marina, Philipsburg. ℂ **599/542-3484.** www.chesterfields-restaurant.com. Lunch main courses $7.95–$16; dinner main courses $16–$23. DISC, MC, V. Daily 7:30am–10pm, Thurs–Sun 9am–10pm.

Mr. Busby's Beach Bar/Daniel's by the Sea ★ CARIBBEAN Little more than a few wooden palapas set in the sand on Dawn Beach, Mr. Busby's is the place to relax and let your hair down with a real cross section of St. Maarteners. Cooled by shady palms and sea breezes, this is just what it purports to be: a *beach bar*, but it's also a fine breakfast and lunch destination. It's a lively spot (but nowhere near as rowdy as the beach bars around Maho, say), and a supremely chill place to sip a Carib beer against a backdrop of low-key reggae or calypso music. But Mr. Busby's is serious about its food, and it shows.

Everything is fresh and tasty—homemade johnnycakes, eggs to order, and Bloody Marys make this one of the top breakfast spots on island. Lunch is jumping, too, with a menu that includes grilled Saba lobster, shrimp kebab over rice, conch or lobster salad, and Busby's own barbecued ribs. Be sure to sample the potato salad; it's addictive. Following the 4 to 6pm happy hour (try the guavaberry colada), the space becomes **Daniel's by the Sea,** which offers solid Italian fare. The restaurant is located next door to the Oyster Bay Beach Resort.

Dawn Beach. ℭ **599/543-6828.** Main courses $8–$20 (Mr. Busby's); $16–$32 (Daniel's). DISC, MC, V. Daily 7:30am–5pm (Mr. Busby's); 6–10pm (Daniel's).

Oualichi CARIBBEAN/INTERNATIONAL   With a prime spot on the Philipsburg waterfront, this brasserie is a local favorite. The best seating is on the patio, where you can listen to live music wafting across the boardwalk and watch cruise-ship passengers nervously roll by on Segways. Giant cruise ships docked across the waters of Great Bay compete with sailboats, catamarans, and rust buckets for your attention, but it's the sparkling waters set against mossy green cliffs that truly mesmerizes. The menu is a mix of pub food (excellent pizzas), local specialties (mahimahi and rice), and French specialties. And the food is very good, making this a solid choice for a filling lunch—you can even take a dip in the bay between courses. *Oualichi* was the island's original Arawak name, meaning "land of women" after its sinuous hills.

St. Rose Arcade, Front St., Philipsburg. ℭ **599/542-4313.** Main courses $13–$30. AE, MC, V. Mon–Wed 9am–6pm; Thurs–Sun 9am–10pm.

Shiv Sagar INDIAN   The island's first Indian eatery remains its best, emphasizing Kashmiri and Mughlai specialties. The best tables in the large second-floor split-level space overlook Front Street. Black lacquer chairs, hand-carved chess tables, and traditional Indian silkscreens depicting scenes from such great epics as the *Mahabharata* set the stage for tempting tandooris, Madras fish curry, and vegetarian dishes such as *saag panir* (spinach in garlicky curried yogurt), hearty enough to convert even the most dedicated carnivore.

20 Front St., Philipsburg. ℭ **599/542-2299.** www.shivsagarsxm.com. Main courses $11–$20. AE, DISC, MC, V. Mon–Sat noon–10pm; Sun noon–3pm.

MAHO & CUPECOY BEACH AREAS
Very Expensive

Rare ★★ STEAK   Dino Jagtiani, the whiz behind the adjacent Temptation (see below), opened this take on the classic chophouse in 2005. The futuristic-yet-retro space is wittily designed. The only steakhouse in St. Maarten to carry USDA Prime dry-aged certified Angus beef, Rare offers choices from a 12-ounce filet mignon to a

28-ounce porterhouse. Those seeking lighter fare can savor sashimi-grade tuna with wasabi mash, or Parmigiano-crusted salmon. Anyone could make a meal of the home-baked bread and dips (hummus, pesto, tapenade). Dino's creativity truly shines in its sauces (nine, including chipotle-ketchup and spicy peanut). Desserts include an inspired s'mores cobbler, with chocolate, graham crackers, marshmallow crust, caramel, and vanilla ice cream.

Atlantis Casino, Cupecoy. ✆ **599/545-5714.** www.daretoberare.com. Reservations required. Main courses $25–$45. AE, DISC, MC, V. Mon–Sat 6:30–10:30pm.

Temptation ★★★ NOUVEAU CARIBBEAN The name may sound like a strip club, but this innovative gem is one of the finest restaurants on the island. Owner/chef Dino Jagtiani, who hails from a multigenerational East Indian family, is a native and graduate of the prestigious Culinary Institute of America. His mother, Asha, graciously greets diners "as if it were our house, only for 100 guests." Dino's Asian-inspired cuisine is exciting, often utilizing unorthodox pairings. Main courses include "Quack Quack l'Orange," orange-ginger-glazed crispy duck breast with Asian veggie stir-fried rice; chicken 'n' shrimp pad Thai; and veal osso bucco braised in red wine. You'll find the perfect wine complement on one of the island's top wine lists.

Atlantis Casino, Cupecoy. ✆ **599/545-2254.** www.nouveaucaribbean.com. Main courses $34–$38. AE, MC, V. Tues–Sun 6:30–10:30pm.

Expensive

La Gondola ★★ ITALIAN In a large, warm room, guests dine on fresh pasta dishes and impeccably prepared Italian classics. The decor gives the place a swooning Mamma Mia ambience: The overriding palette is bordello red, accented by neoclassical cherubs and gilt. The food, too, hews to the tried-and-true. But the minestrone is pitch-perfect and the tomato sauce sparkles. For something richly decadent, try the lobster ravioli in a lobster sauce—it's not overkill, trust me—or the baked veal manicotti. The congenial staff makes this dining experience a real pleasure.

Atlantis Casino, 106 Rhine Rd., Cupecoy Beach. ✆ **599/545-3938.** www.sxmsaratoga.com. Reservations recommended. Main courses $18–$32. AE, MC, V. Daily 6–10pm.

Peg Leg Pub & Steakhouse ★ AMERICAN/STEAK In its location just inside the casino entrance at Princess Port de Plaisance, this tavern hopes to continue to do a brisk business in beer (more than 35 available at one of the Caribbean's longest bars). It's assumed that the decor—a marriage of clubby steakhouse with Jolly Roger kitsch (model boats, peg legs dangling from rafters)—has been transplanted to its new location. Kitsch or no, the food is delicious, offering a wide range of entrees from filet mignon to fettuccine Alfredo and a garlic shrimp platter. Even pub grub (coconut shrimp, beer-battered onion rings, fried calamari) is elevated to an art form. Lunch features salads, hearty deli sandwiches, and burgers.

Princess Port de Plaisance, Union Rd., Cupecoy. *©* **599/544-5859.** www.pegleg pub.com. Main courses $16–$30; $40 double-cut T-bone steak. AE, DISC, MC, V. Daily noon–11pm. Closed Sun lunch.

SIMPSON BAY AREA
Expensive
Saratoga ★ INTERNATIONAL/SEAFOOD   This restaurant owned and run by Culinary Institute of America grad John Jackson occupies a beautiful setting, resembling a Spanish colonial structure from the outside, and lined with rich mahogany inside. Seating is either indoors or on a marina-side veranda. The food is beautifully presented. Although the menu changes frequently, it leans toward light and healthy: The menu has some six different salads, a gazpacho with lobster, and lots of grilled local fish. Not that fat is banned: If you're looking for good and rich, opt for the linguine primavera, here prepared with both smoked ham and bacon. Yum. Jackson dips into Thai and classic Chinese preparations, including salt-and-pepper-fried whole black seabass.

Simpson Bay Yacht Club, Airport Rd. *©* **599/544-2421.** www.sxmsaratoga.com. Reservations recommended. Main courses $24–$37. AE, MC, V. Mon–Sat 6:30–10pm. Closed Aug to mid-Oct.

Moderate
Halsey's ★ INTERNATIONAL   Just south of the drawbridge on Simpson Bay, this waterfront restaurant takes an unfussy approach to fine dining (its motto is "fine food unrefined") and is adept at subtly updating classic dishes. Start with the prosciutto-wrapped sea scallops served with black truffle cream sauce, the maguro sashimi, or the smoked-salmon-wrapped asparagus. Fresh fish features largely in the main course, with your choice of blackened mahimahi, pan-seared grouper, or Asian tuna. You can also get good steaks, grilled veal chops, or rack of Colorado lamb. The flavors change nightly, but homemade ice cream is the smart finish.

86 Welfare Rd., Simpson Bay. *©* **599/544-2882.** www.halseysrestaurant.com. Main courses $19–$32. AE, MC, V. Daily 6–10pm; lounge opens earlier.

SkipJack's Seafood Grill, Bar & Fish Market ★ SEA-FOOD   Of the many shipshape seafood spots on Simpson Bay, this pleasant, breezy spot is one of the best. You can pick your fish on ice and both Maine and Caribbean lobster from a tank and pool, then enjoy the breezes on the handsome and expansive wooden deck, from which you can watch the big yachts muscle their way in and out of Simpson Bay. The entrees taste like they jumped from the sea to your plate, from blackened grouper to shrimp pot pie. The steamed shrimp, hot and piled on the plate, was some of the best I've ever had. Other excellent starters include tuna carpaccio, a hearty New England clam chowder, a lobster and crab salad, and crab cakes with caper mayo. SkipJack's does justice to its namesake, the old-time single-mast fishing boats that plied the Chesapeake.

Airport Rd., Simpson Bay. ℂ **599/544-2313.** www.skipjacks-sxm.com. Main courses $18–$25. MC, V. Daily noon–10:30pm. Closed Sun lunch.

Topper's ★ AMERICAN   Other travelers first clued me into this spot, raving about the big, delicious steaks and well-poured drinks served up by a gentleman of a certain age in what was essentially a roadside Creole shack. Topper's is indeed a hoot, but someone in the kitchen has a real touch with beef—where else on St. Maarten will you find delicious and tender brisket, served with homemade mashed potatoes and whisky carrots? Other classics include Caesar salad, shrimp cocktail, and meatloaf. The steaks are indeed big and good, and the atmosphere is fun. Best of all, the prices are reasonable for pricey St. Maarten.

113 Welfare Rd., Simpson Bay. ℂ **599/544-3500.** www.sxmtoppers.com. Reservations recommended. Main courses $13–$24. AE, MC, V. Mon–Sat 11am–10pm.

Inexpensive

Travelers in the know (and those who watch the Travel Channel's Anthony Bourdain as he chases his appetite around the globe) are already clued in to **Hilma's Windsor Castle,** located on the main road in Simpson Bay. Even by shack standards, Hilma's is rudimentary, basically a mini-trailer with an awning and four stools. Hilma's specialty? Johnnycakes filled with all sorts of delicious things, like ham, eggs, or cheese. The star is a saltfish johnnycake, spiced with peppers and onions ($2). Hilma's is open Monday through Saturday 7:30am to 3pm.

2 FRENCH ST. MARTIN

Locals and tourists alike have been raving about the food and genuine Parisian ambience at **Le Tropicana** ★ (ℂ **590/87-79-07;** on the Marina Port la Royale in Marigot; open daily lunch and dinner), a French restaurant that has blossomed under new management.

In the French Quarter in Orleans, **Chez Yvette** ★ (ℂ **590/87-32-03**) serves up Creole/West Indies cuisine in a vintage cottage trimmed in gingerbread. This is home cooking, St. Martin style, with superbly prepared mains like fish, conch, goat stew, ribs, and stewed chicken served with heaping platters of rice and peas and sides of freshly made johnnycakes. Yvette passed away several years ago, but her husband, Felix, is the master chef in charge. For those looking for an authentic island meal, this is it. A platter costs around $20.

Note: Rates are quoted in either euros or dollars, depending on how establishments quoted them at press time. Prices in St. Martin restaurants include taxes and a 15% service charge, but you may want to add an extra gratuity if the service warrants it.

MARIGOT
Expensive

La Vie en Rose ★★ FRENCH   The dining room in this balconied second-floor restaurant evokes a tropical version of Paris in the 1920s, thanks to flower boxes, gold gilt mirrors, arches, ceiling fans, candlelight, and time-honored culinary showmanship to match the show-stopping harbor views. The menu is classic French, although Caribbean overtones creep in. Lunches are relatively simple affairs, with an emphasis on fresh meal-size salads, simple grills like beefsteak with shallot sauce, brochettes of fresh fish, and pastas. Dinners are more elaborate (attracting a dressier crowd) and might begin with a lobster salad with passion-fruit dressing. Main courses include grilled filet of red snapper simmered in a champagne sauce with pumpkin risotto; breast of duck in a foie gras sauce; lobster paired with boneless rabbit in honey-vanilla sauce; and an unusual version of roasted rack of lamb in a mushroom and truffle sauce. The lobster bisque in puff pastry is a must.

Bd. de France at rue de la République, Marigot. ✆ **590/87-54-42.** Reservations recommended. Main courses 10€–18€ lunch, 19€–33€ dinner. AE, DISC, MC, V. Mon–Sat noon–3pm; daily 6:30–10pm.

Le Chanteclair ★ FRENCH   New ownership and a new chef have not diminished the appeal of this simple yet elegant eatery positioned perfectly on the marina boardwalk. Both decor (from turquoise deck to orange and yellow napery) and the cuisine are sun-drenched. Chef Stéphane Decluseau, formerly of L'Astrolabe, brings her award-winning cooking to Le Chanteclair. The "Chef's Discovery" and "Gastronomic Lobster" menus at 55€ are comparative bargains with aperitif and four courses. The foie gras is top notch, as is the duck in puff pastry with foie gras sauce. Among the many desserts, the Innommable ("No Name") stands out—pastry bursting with semi-sweet chocolate paired with vanilla ice cream in its own pastry shell swimming in vanilla sauce.

Marina Port la Royale, Marigot. ✆ **590/87-94-60.** www.lechanteclair.com. Reservations recommended. Main courses 25€–39€. MC, V. Daily 6–10:30pm.

Resources for Self-Catering

As a large provisioning hub for passing boats, St. Maarten has plenty of options for visitors with self-catering capabilities, whether a hotel kitchenette or a fully equipped kitchen. You can buy meats, fresh fruits and vegetables, snacks, drinks, and kitchen supplies at **Le Grand Marché,** a full-service grocery chain with three locations on the island, including one at Simpson Bay (✆ **599/545-3055;** www. legrandmarche.net). In Marigot, **Match supermarket,** in the Howell Center, has a good selection of French foods. The **U.S. Imports Super Marché** (✆ **590/52-87-14**), a supermarket chain on the French side, has a branch at the drawbridge in Sandy Ground that's open until 10pm (it also has baguettes, pastries, and a cheese selection). You can also find takeout foods at *traiteurs* (takeout/caterers), *pâtisseries* (pastry shops), and *boulangeries* (baked goods). For an excellent selection of wine and spirits, head to **Vinissimo,** at 1 Rue de Low Town, Marigot (✆ **590/877-078**). For fresh fish, head over to the **Simpson Bay Fish Market,** an open-air seafood market facing the lagoon, which sells Simpson Bay's fresh catches daily.

Mario's Bistro ★★ FRENCH The setting defines romantic, with tables staggered along a balcony overlooking Sandy Ground Bridge. The greeting from Martyne Tardif couldn't be warmer. And her husband, Mario, inspires passion with his architectural presentations and inventive cooking spiced with Asian, Moroccan, and Southwestern accents. Start with hoisin-braised duck roll and cacao foie gras or the sautéed lobster tails in puff pastry. For mains, try the crab-crusted baked mahimahi or bouillabaisse with green Thai curry and lemongrass. *Note:* Mario's does not have high chairs or booster seats for kids, although you're welcome to bring your own.

Sandy Ground Bridge, Marigot. ✆ 590/87-06-36. www.mariosbistro.com. Reservations recommended. Main courses 24€–35€. DISC, MC, V. Mon–Sat 6:30–10:30pm. Closed Aug–Sept.

Moderate
Claude Mini-Club ★ CREOLE/FRENCH For more than 3 decades, this has been a long-enduring favorite with locals and discerning visitors. The building was constructed to resemble a tree house around the trunks of old coconut palms and the Haitian

Tips **Grand Case: Dining in Foodie Haven**

No other town in the Caribbean features as many restaurants per capita as the small village of Grand Case, set near St. Martin's northernmost tip. Don't be put off by the town's ramshackle, feet-in-the-sand appearance: Behind the wooden Creole structures are French-, Italian-, and American-style restaurants managed by some very sophisticated cooks—and many of them have gorgeous beachside settings. Here are some tips on dining in Grand Case:

- **Don't pick the first restaurant you see.** Stroll down the Boulevard de Grand Case; menus are prominently displayed out front as are the nightly specials. Some restaurants even offer $1 = 1€ prices.

- **Drink to the sunset *sur la plage*.** Before you dine, do as the locals do and sip a drink as you watch the sunset melt into the sea on Grand Case Beach. One terrific spot is **Calmos Café** (40 bd. de Grand Case; ℗ **590/29-01-85;** www.calmoscafe.com), with chairs and candlelit tables in the sand for the nightly sunset ritual. The competition is neighbor **Zen It** (49 bd. de Grand Case; ℗ **590/29-01-85**), where you can sip a beer on the raised wooden porch overlooking the beach. A new, more upscale spot is **Le Shore** (28 bd. de Grand Case; ℗ **590/51-96-17**), which brings an element of Miami Beach and the Hamptons to little Grand Case, with a small pool and lounge chairs facing the beach.

decor—straw and shell handicrafts dangling from the beams and marvelous murals of local scenes—captures much of the vibrancy of that island. A big terrace opens onto the sea. Authentic Creole offerings include *lambi* (conch) in zesty tomato stew and *accras* (cod fritters) in shallot sauce, but you can also find entrecôte in green-peppercorn sauce, veal escalope with fresh morels, and such classic desserts as banana flambé and crème brûlée. The restaurant stages the island's best buffets, featuring such crowd pleasers as roast suckling pig, roast beef, quail, chicken, red snapper, and Caribbean lobster, accompanied by carafes of wine.

Bd. de la Mer, Marigot. ℗ **590/87-50-69.** Reservations required. Main courses 18€–30€; buffet 42€. AE, MC, V. Mon–Sat 11am–3pm and 6–10pm. Closed Sept.

- **Dress lightly.** Most restaurants are not air-conditioned.
- **New parking area pluses:** The big new parking lot near the airport and across from Calmos Café is a great addition for a town that only recently had traffic going both ways down the narrow two-lane Boulevard de Grand Case, traffic that had to dodge cars parked higgledy-piggledy on both sides of the street *and* pedestrians wending their way down the street. Now traffic is one way from the parking lot area—and cars have a place to park away from the main drag.
- **New parking area minuses:** On the other hand, the new parking lot also means more cars and vans. This is a peaceful place that can get overrun with tourist shuttles during the evening hours.
- **Prepare to shop.** Most clothing shops and art galleries along the Boulevard de Grand Case are open during the evening dinner hours to take advantage of the influx of visitors.
- **Don't miss "Grand Case Tuesdays":** It's Carnival every Tuesday evening during high season as the Boulevard de Grand Case is closed off to vehicular traffic for a street festival featuring musicians, food stands, and a crafts market.

L'Oizeau Rare ★ FRENCH   The "Rare Bird" serves up creative French cuisine in a blue-and-ivory antique house on a Marigot hillside with a view of a garden and three artfully landscaped waterfalls. The green tables are dressed in cream-colored linens. At lunch, served on the covered terrace, you can choose from a number of salads and crispy pizzas, as well as fish and meat courses (shrimp fricassee flamed with Pastis, say)—not to mention what is described as a "formidable" hamburger with homemade French fries. Dinner choices include fresh fish, such as snapper or grouper; roasted rack lamb with garlic breadcrumbs and fresh herbs; or penne with a shrimp and sea scallop fricassee. There are numerous daily specials and prix-fixe options, and the wine list features French options at moderate prices. Many guests come here at sundown to enjoy the harbor view over a Kir Royale and cigar from the extensive selection.

Bd. de France, Marigot Harbor. ✆ **590/87-56-38.** Reservations recommended. Main courses 15€–24€ lunch, 18€–25€ dinner. AE, MC, V. Mon–Sat 11:30am–3pm and 6:30–10:30pm. Closed June.

Inexpensive
La Belle Epoque FRENCH/PIZZA You won't find a better perch to watch the boats in the Marigot marina than this blue-awning boardwalk cafe. After window-shopping in Marigot, stop by for Belgian beers or a glass of proper rosé, grilled Creole specials, pastas, fish, steak, or utterly scrumptious special minipizzas (8€–19€), with a multitude of toppings. It's open for breakfast, serving omelets, pastry, and juices.

Marina Port la Royale, Marigot. ✆ **590/87-87-70.** www.belle-epoque-sxm.com. Salads, sandwiches, and main courses 14€–24€. MC, V. Daily 7:30am–11pm; from 5pm on Sun.

GRAND CASE
Expensive
Le Bistro Caraïbes ★ FRENCH/CARIBBEAN Brothers Thibault and Amaury Mezière, former chefs at Paul Bocuse's restaurant in Lyon, have been cooking at this charming spot for more than 15 years. Fresh lobster and the catch of the day are their specialties. Start with the homemade smoked salmon on toast points or the hot goat cheese in a pastry crust. You can do lobster any number of ways (in butter, simply grilled, or as thermidor) or go for the fisherman's platter in a rich bouillabaisse-style lobster sauce. A classic crème brûlée or the warm chocolate cake topped with hazelnut ice cream and coffee sauce provides an elegant finish.

81 bd. de Grand Case, Grand Case. ✆ **590/29-08-29.** www.bistrotcaraibes.com. Reservations recommended. Main courses 21€–27€. MC, V. Daily 6–10:30pm; closed Sat May–Dec.

Le Cottage ★ FRENCH/CREOLE This perennial favorite in a town loaded with worthy contenders is set in what looks like a private house on the inland side of the main road running through Grand Case. Its atmosphere is at least partly influenced by Burgundy-born sommelier Stéphane Emorine, who shows a canny ability to recommend the perfect wine to complement the French-Caribbean cuisine. Meals begin dramatically with mini tasting menus (the "taste of tuna," say, includes sashimi- and sushi-grade tuna). Mains include both rustic *cuisine du terroir* (such as roasted rack of lamb with breaded lamb sweetbreads dusted in panko) and Creole-influenced dishes, including monkfish and sautéed squid with chorizo, olives, and preserved

(Finds) Lolos: Local Barbecue Joints

Open-air barbecue stands are a St. Martin institution, dishing out big, delicious helpings of barbecued ribs, lobster, chicken or fish grilled on split metal drums, garlic shrimp, goat stew, rice and peas, cod fritters, and johnnycakes—all from $10 to $20, a real bargain on pricey St. Martin. In Grand Case, the two best, **Talk of the Town** (*C* 590/29-63-89) and **Sky's the Limit** (*C* 690/35-67-84), have covered seating, a waitstaff, and sea views. Several excellent lolo-style Creole restaurants are found in Marigot facing the marketplace and ferry port, including Le Goût and Chez Coco—but my favorite is **Enoch's Place** (*C* 590/29-29-88), which serves terrific garlic shrimp (10€), stew chicken (10€), and stew conch (8€); each platter comes with rice and peas, cooked plantains, and salad. Derrick Hodge's **Exclusive Bite** (no phone) is right by the city's scenic cemetery. The Dutch side has its own versions. For lunch, try **Mark's Place** (no phone) in Philipsburg's Food Center Plaza parking lot; after 6pm, head for **Johnny B's Under the Tree** (no phone) on Cay Hill Road in Cole Bay.

tomatoes. A four-course lobster tasting menu includes lobster mousse, lobster fritters, lobster salad, and lobster risotto.

97 bd. de Grand Case, Grand Case. *C* **590/29-03-30.** www.restaurantlecottage. com. Reservations recommended. Main courses 25€–32€; lobster tasting menu 57€. AE, DC, MC, V. Daily 6–11pm.

Le Pressoir ★★ FRENCH   This restaurant occupies a charming, 19th-century Creole house painted yellow and blue. The interior delights the eye with blue and white napery, periwinkle shutters, mango walls hung with homey island paintings (many for sale), carved hardwood chairs, and lace doilies as lampshades. The kitchen presents an artful combination of old and new French cuisine, the natural flavors of fresh ingredients enhanced by imaginative seasoning. Standout standards include lobster ravioli in a passion-fruit cream sauce, seafood tagliatelle, grilled sea scallops with foie gras and truffles, and grilled beef tenderloin in a Camembert sauce.

30 bd. de Grand Case, Grand Case. *C* **590/87-76-62.** Reservations recommended. Main courses 18€–35€. AE, MC, V. Daily 6–10:30pm (closed Sun in low season).

Le Tastevin ★ FRENCH/CARIBBEAN   With a warm, beautifully candlelit ambience, Le Tastevin is a favorite of locals and visitors alike. You dine on a garden terrace overlooking Grand Case bay. Daily specials are listed on the blackboard out front, but often include fresh fish such as mahimahi, red snapper, or grouper in a classic French or Asian-infused sauce. The two vegetarian dishes are among the best items on the menu. Try the white bean and vegetable pan with wild rice and mango, or the local squash in a curry, potato, black olive, and sun-dried-tomato napoleon. Le Tastevin is known for its extensive and detailed wine list.

86 bd. De Grand Case, Grand Case. © **590/87-49-48.** www.letastevin-restaurant. com. Reservations recommended. Main courses 17€–30€. AE, MC, V. Daily noon–2pm and 6–10pm. Closed Tues May–Nov.

Spiga ★★ ITALIAN The gracious husband-and-wife team of Ciro Russo (a native of Lecco, Italy) and Lara Bergamasco (second-generation St. Maarten restaurant royalty) have crafted the finest Italian restaurant on the island. Simple elegance reigns, starting with the charming 1914 Creole home. You can dine inside, where darkly stained wooden doors and windows frame salmon-pink walls, or on the candlelit patio. I loved the deeply flavorful tomato and basil lobster bisque and the handmade pappardelle with braised beef-and-mushroom sauce. A hearty cioppino is filled to the brim with shrimp, scallops, and fish in a tomato-crustacean broth. The roast pork tenderloin comes wrapped in smoked pancetta and stuffed with an mushroom ragout. End the evening with a vanilla-bean crème brûlée and raspberry panna-cotta, washed down with fiery grappa.

4 rte. de l'Espérance, Grand Case. © **590/52-47-83.** www.spiga-sxm.com. Reservations recommended. Main courses $17–$32. DISC, MC, V. Daily 6–10:30pm. Closed Tues May–Nov.

Moderate

Sunset Café (Value) FRENCH/INTERNATIONAL This open-air restaurant dramatically straddles the rocky peninsula dividing Grand Case Beach from Petite Plage. Tables are set along a narrow terrace that affords sweeping views of the setting sun, when the water is spotlit for extra effect. It's a nice, breezy spot to dine and watch the night waves. The chef/operator, Brittany-born Chef Alexandre Pele, has a resume that includes cooking stints at the Savoy in London and La Samanna here on French St. Martin. His emphasis is on seafood and French classics at reasonable prices. Lunch items are more basic: sandwiches, burgers, pastas, salads—and herons dive-bombing for their own meal.

Grand Case Beach Club, rue de Petit-Plage, Grand Case. © **590/87-51-87.** Reservations recommended for weekend dinners in winter. Main courses 11€–38€ lunch, 17€–26€ dinner. AE, MC, V. Daily 7am–midnight.

MONT VERNON
Moderate

Sol é Luna ★★★ (Finds) FRENCH   This lovely, family-run Creole *caze* is virtually pillowed in luxuriant greenery, with smashing Anse Marcel views. Set back from the road, it can be tricky to find, but the incomparable ambience, service, and food make "Sun and Moon" the perfect place for a romantic dinner. Asian influences and ingredients are combined with classic French preparations to create light yet intensely flavored dishes. You might start your meal with a roll of monkfish with pecans and red curry, or homemade crab cakes. Lamb braised for 7 hours melts off the bone and in your mouth, as do lobster ravioli served with saffron, basil, and spinach and drizzled with a cream sauce. Delicious desserts like banana crunchy cake with chocolate mousse are followed by a minitasting of artisan rums (plum–passion fruit, vanilla–ginger). The hideaway also offers quite handsomely appointed **studios and suites** from $726 a week (low season) or from $860 a week (high season).

61 Mont Vernon, Cul de Sac above Anse Marcel. ℂ 590/29-08-56. www.soleluna restaurant.com. Main courses 28€–35€. MC, V. Daily 6–10pm. Closed mid-June to mid-July and mid-Sept to Oct.

BAIE NETTLE & SANDY GROUND
Very Expensive

Le Santal ★ FRENCH   The approach to this dazzler is through a ramshackle, working-class Marigot suburb, a sharp contrast to the glam interior filled with mirrors, fresh flowers, ornately carved chairs, Villeroy & Boch china, and Christofle silver. Try to nab one of the coveted oceanfront tables, occupied at one time or another by the likes of Robert de Niro, Brooke Shields, Arab sheiks, and minor royalty. Sadly, you will no longer be greeted by owner Jean Dupont; he passed away in 2005, but his wife and children continue to run the restaurant. The fare focuses on the classics. The crepe stuffed with lobster meat, mushrooms, and scallions in a white-wine crawfish butter sauce is a formidable starter; the grilled whole red snapper flambéed in Pastis with fennel beurre blanc is deboned at your table. Superb chateaubriand au poivre is flambéed in aged Armagnac and coated with béarnaise. End your evening with crêpes Suzette prepared the old-fashioned way, tableside, a charming touch.

40 rue Lady Fish, Sandy Ground. ℂ **590/87-53-48.** www.restaurantlesantal.com. Reservations recommended. Main courses $38–$49. AE, MC, V. Daily 6–10:30pm (lunch by advance reservation for groups of 6 or more).

Expensive

La Cigale ★★ FRENCH   Celebrating 10 years in the business, this family-run establishment provides a winning combination of innovative French fare and tropical flair, beachfront setting, and warmth and intimacy. Tucked away behind the Laguna Beach hotel at the end of an alley, congenial Olivier Genet's bistro is worth a potential wrong turn or three to find. He recruited his parents from the Loire Valley to help him run the tiny operation: Mama is the hostess, papa the pastry chef (bravo to both for the molten chocolate cake soufflé). The setting and ambience are casual, but Chef Stéphane Istel's subtly seasoned food is anything but. Try the *crottin de Chavignol* (goat cheese) *en nougatine* (in filo pastry) with nuts and honey; seabass filet Provençal style; or rack of lamb baked in thyme, cabbage, and garlic. Olivier will ply you with several home-brewed rum *digestifs* and anecdotes of his Sancerre upbringing.

101 Laguna Beach, Baie Nettlé. ⓒ **590/87-90-23.** www.restaurant-lacigale.com. Reservations required. Main courses 26€–33€. MC, V. Mon–Sat 6–10:30pm.

ANSE MARCEL

C Le Restaurant ★ FRENCH/CARIBBEAN   Perhaps it's the close proximity to such a highly competitive restaurant scene (in Grand Case, 5 min. away); perhaps the gorgeous setting is an inspiration. For whatever reason, this Radisson restaurant is heads and shoulders above other hotel restaurants; in fact, it's a terrific destination restaurant in its own right. Executive Chef Bruno Brazier features duck, steak, and lamb on the menu but has a particularly deft touch with seafood. You might start with seafood tempura, fish soup, or even a great Caesar salad, served, whimsically, from a giant martini shaker. Look for inspired specials of the day. My favorite was *gambas* (large shrimp) stuffed with crab in a buttery curry sauce with wild rice and vegetables. The attached **Lounge at C** is open till midnight. The setting is magical; tables look out over the blue-black waters of Anse Marcel, the sea mirroring the bobbing sailboats, the encircling cliffs, and the glittering lights of Anguilla far in the distance. The only thing I would change? The unwieldy name.

Radisson Blu Resort, Marina & Spa, St. Martin, Anse Marcel. ⓒ **590/87-67-00.** www.c-le-restaurant.com. Reservations recommended. Main courses 21€–35€. AE, DC, DISC, MC, V. Daily 6:30–10:30pm.

What to See & Do on St. Maarten/ St. Martin

Though St. Maarten/St. Martin is most celebrated for beaches, shops, restaurants, and nightlife, it also packs a number of natural and man-made attractions into its compact terrain. From zoos to ziplines and working farms to forts, the array of diversions here suits history buffs, eco-geeks, and active types alike—and despite the island's reputation as an adult playground, it's a very family-friendly place.

1 ISLAND LAYOUT

St. Maarten/St. Martin is a hilly island; driving around you'll discover numerous lookouts with splendid panoramas of the coast and off-shore islets. One main road essentially circumnavigates the island; a detour from Marigot to Cole Bay on the Dutch side hugs the eastern shore of Simpson Bay lagoon and avoids traffic around the airport and bustling Maho area during rush hours.

The island is shaped—very roughly—like a boot. The toe at the western point encompasses the French **Lowlands (Terres Basses),** a tony residential area with several stunning beaches. Following the main road east takes you through **Sandy Ground,** a strip of land crammed with tour-group-style hotels, restaurants, shops, and beach bars. It's bordered on the north by Baie Nettlé and on the south by **Simpson Bay,** the Caribbean's largest enclosed body of water. **Marigot,** the French side's capital, is just over 2km (1¼ miles) to the northeast. Ferries depart its harbor for **Anguilla.** The main route ambles north, with turnoffs west on rutted roads to fine beaches, as well as east to **Pic du Paradis** (the island's highest peak at 424m/1,400 ft.) before reaching **Grand Case,** site of the tiny inter-island L'Espérance Airport, and beloved by foodies for its superlative eateries. The highway runs east, with a fork at Mont Vernon. The north turnoff accesses **French Cul-de-Sac** (embarkation point for ferries to the offshore cays) and a side road to Anse Marcel, home of a marina and the Radisson resort. The other turnoff accesses the beautiful **Orient Bay** beach, continuing south through the residential **Orléans** quarter, straddling the Dutch border at **Oyster Pond** and its marina.

Dawn Beach, site of increased development (and the Westin resort) is the first major strand on the Dutch side. The main highway turns slightly inland and passes the Great Salt Pond on its way to the Dutch capital, **Philipsburg,** which unfurls along **Great Bay.** The major cruise ships dock here; there are also several marinas offering boat rentals and excursions. **Pointe Blanche** forms the very flat heel. From Philipsburg, the highway parallels the south coast, rising and dipping over Cay and Cole Bay Hills. Traffic here in both directions is often dreadful, especially on weekends: the "Caribbean's longest parking lot," as locals joke. Party central begins at **Simpson Bay,** where the highway officially becomes Airport Road. Marinas, bars, restaurants, timeshare units, casinos, and strip malls line both sides, continuing almost unabated past Princess Juliana International Airport to **Maho Beach,** another nightlife nirvana. The road passes Mullet Bay and the lively **Cupecoy** area in the Dutch Lowlands before hitting the French border.

2 THE MAIN SIGHTS

DUTCH SIDE

Philipsburg ★, capital of the Dutch side, is named, perhaps surprisingly, for an 18th-century Scottish governor. The town has always enjoyed an uncommonly lovely setting at the headlands of Great Bay, on a spit of land separating the Caribbean from the Great Salt Pond. Its superb, deep natural harbor can accommodate such enormous cruise ships as the Queen Mary II. They disgorge passengers, who descend eagerly if not rapaciously on the casinos and duty-free stores lining the main drag, **Front Street** (see chapter 6). The hordes tend to obscure the many handsome colonial buildings, including the ornate white 1792 **Courthouse** (still in use) replete with cupola at Wathey Square, which roughly bisects Front Street. A series of hurricanes left Philipsburg somewhat dilapidated: one part lower-rent New Orleans, one part Reno.

Over the last several years, Philipsburg has undergone a beautification project. The face-lift added a delightful beachfront red brick boardwalk (Great Bay Beach Promenade), with newly planted royal palm trees, clock towers, and old-fashioned cast-iron street lamps and benches. The beach side of Front Street is now a pedestrian-friendly place to stroll, goggle at the cruise ships and mega-yachts, walk in the

> (Tips) **Mapping It**
>
> For locations of the sights listed in this chapter, please refer to the St. Maarten/St. Martin, Marigot, Grand Case, or Philipsburg maps on p. 46, p. 55, p. 57, and p. 49, respectively.

sand, or enjoy the sunset over an umbrella-shaded concoction in one of the many inviting cafes.

The continuing makeover includes a revamped tourist office, marinas, and expanded ferry and cruise dock, and the rejuvenation of Back Street, which now has improved pavement and sidewalks, the underground placement of electrical cables, newly planted trees and shrubs, and new streetlights. Eventually, the beautification will extend to the Great Salt Pond (where locals still fish for mullet), with paving and planting all the way north to the French border.

Fort Amsterdam ★ Built in 1631 on the peninsula between Great and Little bays as the Caribbean's first Dutch bastion, Fort Amsterdam was promptly captured by the Spaniards, who made it their most important garrison outside El Morro in San Juan before abandoning it in 1648. Only one small intact storage building, a few walls, and rusted cannons remain, but it's most noteworthy for its smashing views of Philipsburg. Easiest access is via the Divi Little Bay Beach Resort (guards will let you pass if you tell them you're hiking to the fort).

On the peninsula between Great and Little bays. No phone.

St. Maarten Heritage Museum ★ This deceptively modest-looking museum is packed with relics from the island's past. Documenting island history and culture, the museum starts with an impressive collection of indigenous Arawak tools, pottery shards, and *zemis* (spiritual totems) that date back over 2 millennia. The plantation and piracy era yields its own artifacts (including cargo salvaged from an 1801 wreck), period clothes (contrasted with slave beads), and weapons. The environment is represented by exhibits on typical flora, fauna, geology, and coral reefs. The final multimedia display recounts the catastrophic effects of Hurricane Luis in 1995. The museum also organizes guided hikes and sells terrific printed walking guides through historic Philipsburg.

7 Front St. (C) **599/542-4917.** Admission $5. Weekdays 10am–4pm; Sat 10am–2pm.

St. Maarten Zoological Park (Kids) Just east of Philipsburg, this is the largest park of its kind in the Caribbean. More than 500 animals comprising 80 different species from the Caribbean basin and Amazon rainforest inhabit this safari reserve. There are no cages or bars of any kind. Rather, cannily erected, environmentally conscious "naturalistic" boundaries carefully protect both animals and visitors while duplicating typical habitats. An example is Squirrel Monkey Island: The capuchins and vervets are separated by a moat (replicating the streams that draw them in the wild) stocked with water lilies, turtles, and freshwater fish. Nicely landscaped botanic gardens (with interpretive signs) alternate with various environments from a caiman marsh to a tropical forest to a boulder-strewn savannah. Walk-through aviaries hold more than 200 birds: macaws, toucans, and the Caribbean's largest display of exotic parrots. Other residents include capybaras, ocelots, peccaries, coatis, baboons, and such highly endangered species as the golden lion tamarin. The zoo even features the island's largest playground (slides and, of course, jungle gym).

Arch Rd., Madame Estate. 𝄌 **599/543-2030.** Admission $10, $5 children 3–11. Daily 9am–5pm.

FRENCH SIDE

Marigot, capital of the French side, is one of the Caribbean's more charming towns: gas lamps, sidewalk cafes, and traditional Creole gingerbread-trimmed wood houses ring the harbor, as well as a separate marina, **Port la Royale.** The marina area is filled with boutiques and shops (see chapter 6). The waterfront **Market** is a hub nearly every day for vendors and farmers. It's busiest early mornings as islanders converge to buy fresh-caught fish, fruits, vegetables, and herbs. A crafts market is there on Wednesdays and Saturdays, but vendors tend to offer many of the same goods: colorful dolls, spices, drums, trinkets, clothing.

A steep trail runs from the harbor-side Sous-Préfecture (by the splashy West Indies Mall) to Fort-Louis. Better preserved than its Dutch-side counterparts (forts Willem and Amsterdam), the bastion was erected to repel English incursions and completed in 1789. Its hilltop situation rewards hikers with sensational 180-degree vistas of Marigot, Simpson Bay lagoon, and most of the French coast, with Anguilla shimmering in the background.

Butterfly Farm ★ (Kids) Some 40 species of butterflies from around the world (including such rarities as the Central American postman, Malaysian malachite, and Brazilian blue morpho) flit and flutter through this miniature, hot and humid bamboo rainforest replica. The lengths that butterflies go to in order to preserve the species is nature at its canniest: Some lay eggs that look like bird poop; others have camouflaged wings. Most have a short but vivid life span;

the spectacularly beautiful blue morpho lives just 2 weeks. The atmosphere is hypnotically calming, between tinkling waterfalls, ponds stocked with splashing koi, passing chickens, and soft classical music. If you arrive early, you might witness butterflies emerging from their chrysalides; wear bright colors or floral scents and they might light on you. Multilingual docents conduct 25-minute hands-on tours following the typical life cycle from egg to caterpillar and on to adulthood. The ramshackle shop sells butterfly earrings, wind chimes, pewter figurines, fridge magnets, and framed mounted sets. The website tells you what to plant to attract butterflies.

Rte. Le Galion, Quartier d'Orléans. ✆ 590/87-31-21. www.thebutterflyfarm.com. Admission $14, $7 children 3–12. Daily 9am–3:30pm (last tour starts at 3pm).

Loterie Farm ★★ (Kids) Located along the turnoff to Pic du Paradis halfway between Marigot and Grand Case, this splendid sanctuary—by far the greenest spot on island—merits a stop. It was a famed sugar plantation between 1721 and 1848 (the original slave walls still surround the property). In its modern heyday a half-century ago, the Fleming family hosted Fortune 500 elite and celebrities (Benny Goodman, Jasper Johns, Harry Belafonte). But after Hurricane Luis ravaged the property in 1995, it became derelict. Californian B. J. Welch purchased the land in 2003 with the goal of establishing a nature retreat, preserving the island's last remaining virgin rainforest. Literally thousands of plant species, including towering mahogany, corossol (soursop), mango, papaw, and guavaberry trees, have reclaimed a hillside of rock formations and running streams. Iguanas, parrots, hummingbirds, monkeys, and mongoose run wild. Well-maintained trails zig and zag from the foothills to the top of Pic Paradis, the island's highest point, where a viewing platform offers sweeping 360-degree panoramas. You can trek on your own or take one of the farm's guided tours, from a mild sunset walk to a wild, strenuous eco-challenge. Along the way, enthusiastic guides discourse on local history, geology, wildlife, and bush medicine. The **Fly Zone** (35€) lets you fly over the forest canopy on ropes and cables suspended high in the air. The newest attraction, **Extreme Fly Zone** (55€), gives you even more adrenaline chills with a challenging hike uphill and a thrilling ride on a high-tech zipline down. Kids can fly on slightly lower suspended bridges and swinging rope on the park's **Ti' Tarzan** (20€) attraction. The **Hidden Forest Café** (see below) is a delightful place to dine. The **Tree Lounge** is a bar perched 7.5m (25 ft.) off the ground; it serves tapas and pizza (along with cocktails) and is open Tuesday to Sunday from noon to midnight.

Rte. Pic Paradis, Colombier. ✆ **590/87-86-16.** www.loteriefarm.net. Admission 5€. Tues–Sun 9am–4pm.

Finds **Dinner in the Treehouse**

Set on a *carbet* (covered wood patio) at Loterie Farm's entrance, the **Hidden Forest Café** (www.loteriefarm.net) serves delicious lunches and dinners; it's open from noon to 3pm and 6:30 to 9:30pm from Tuesday through Saturday and noon to 6pm on Sunday. It sports a funky-chic treehouse look, with photos of dreadlocked musicians, a blue-tile bar, oars dangling from the rafters, and hurricane lamps.

This is the domain of Canadian-born, self-taught chef Julia Purkis, who says her surroundings provide inspiration (and, of course, fresh ingredients from the organic gardens and forest). Her sophisticated culinary techniques and presentation (including often-edible floral garnishes) are all the more impressive given the cramped, basic kitchen and frequent power outages. You might start with cumin chicken rolls, mahimahi fingers with red pepper tartar sauce, shrimp spring roll, or brie in puff pastry with mango chutney. Standout main courses include grilled salmon with apple-ginger compote, rare duck breast with banana-mint-tamarind salsa, pan-seared sea scallops with vanilla rum sauce, and Julia's signature curried spinach-stuffed chicken.

Le Musée de Saint-Martin Subtitled "On the Trail of the Arawaks," this museum details island history and culture going back 2,500 years through the colonial era. It contains a treasure trove of maps, prints, daguerreotypes, and newspapers spanning the 18th to early 20th centuries. Ask the clerks about guided tours of the island focusing on its cultural heritage, including visiting archaeological digs (some closed to the general public), as well as discussing natural phenomena, such as the island's volcanic origins.

7 Fichot St. ✆ **690/56-78-92.** Admission $5. Mon–Sat 9am–1pm and 3–5pm.

3 BEACHES

Coves scissor the island, with 39 beautiful beaches of varying length and hue. All are public though access is often via a rutted dirt road and/or through a fancy resort. Beaches on the western leeward half are generally hotter and calmer; those on the eastern windward side are, predictably, breezier with rougher swells (when not reef-protected).

Warning: If it's too secluded, be careful. It's unwise to carry valuables; robberies have been reported on some remote strips. And never leave valuables in the car.

Wherever you stay, you're never far from the water. Beach samplers can sometimes use the changing facilities at bigger resorts for a small fee. Beach bars often rent chairs and umbrellas for roughly $6 and $3, respectively, but may waive the charge if you order lunch or drinks. Those who prefer topless sunbathing should head for the French side of the island, although the Dutch side is getting more liberal.

DUTCH SIDE

Popular **Cupecoy Beach** ★ is very close to the Dutch–French border at the island's southwest tip. It's a string of three sand beaches set against a backdrop of caves, rock formations, and dramatically eroded limestone cliffs. Locals come around with coolers of cold beer and soda for sale. The beach has two parking lots, one near Cupecoy and Sapphire beach clubs, the other a short distance to the west; parking costs $2. You must descend stone-carved steps to reach the sands. Cupecoy is also the island's major gay beach. Clothing is optional toward the northwest side of the beach. *Warning:* The steep drop-off and high swells make the beach hazardous for young children and weak swimmers; prevailing weather affects not only the surf, but the sand's width. Also: The Cupecoy area is seeing considerable new development, with disturbing reports of wastewater runoff onto the beaches.

The next strand down (west of the airport) is palm-shaded, white-sand **Mullet Bay Beach** ★, framed in seagrapes. Once it was the busiest beach on the island, but St. Maarten's largest resort, Mullet Bay, has been shuttered (save for a timeshare section) since Hurricane Luis in 1995, so it's never crowded, though locals flock here on weekends. Watersports equipment can be rented at a local kiosk, and two beach bars sell refreshments. The snorkeling is not bad along the rocks.

Near the airport, **Maho Beach,** at the Sonesta Maho Beach Hotel and Casino, is a classic Caribbean crescent, with vendors hawking colorful wares and locals inviting you to impromptu beach barbecues. This is one of the island's busiest beaches, buzzing with windsurfers—and buzzed by jumbo jets that nearly decapitate the palm trees. When you spot a 747 coming into view, hang on to your hats, towels, and partner.

West of Philipsburg before you reach the airport, the 2km-long (1¼-mile) white sands of crescent-shaped **Simpson Bay Beach** ring the lagoon and are set against a backdrop of brightly hued fishing boats, yachts, and townhomes. This beach is ideal for a stroll or a swim (beware the steep drop-off), with calm waters and surprisingly few crowds.

Great Bay Beach ★ is best if you're staying along Front Street in Philipsburg. This 2km-long (1¼-mile) beach is sandy and calm; despite bordering the busy capital, it's surprisingly clean and a splendid place to kick back after shopping, admiring the cruise ships from one of many strategic bars along the boardwalk. On a clear day, you'll have a view of Saba. Immediately to the west, at the foot of Fort Amsterdam, is picturesque **Little Bay Beach,** but it can be overrun with tourists disgorged by the cruise ships. You can actually climb up to the site of Fort Amsterdam itself. Built in 1631, it was the first Dutch military outpost in the Caribbean. The Spanish captured it 2 years later, making it their most important bastion east of Puerto Rico. Only a few of the fort's walls remain, but the view is panoramic.

On the east side of the island, **Dawn Beach** ★ is noted for its underwater life and incredible sunrises, with some of the island's most beautiful reefs immediately offshore. Dawn has plenty of wave action, but it's suitable for swimming and snorkeling. Dawn Beach is now the site of the **Westin Resort.** This, in addition to the expansion of **Oyster Bay Resort,** has diminished its peaceful allure, but its remarkable reef, soft pearly sand, and views of St. Barts remain unchanged.

FRENCH SIDE

Baie Longue (Long Bay) ★, on the west coast, is supremely conducive to R&R. Chic, expensive La Samanna hotel opens onto this beachfront, but it's otherwise blissfully undeveloped and uncrowded. Its reef-protected waters are ideal for snorkeling, but beware the strong undertow and steep drop-off. Baie Longue is to the north of Cupecoy Bay Beach, reached via the Lowlands Road. Don't leave valuables in your car, as break-ins have been reported along this stretch of highway.

Baie aux Prunes (Plum Bay) is a Cheshire grin of ivory sand, stretching luxuriantly around St. Martin's northwest point. This is a sublimely romantic sunset perch (bring your own champagne, as there are no facilities) that also offers good surfing and snorkeling near the rocks. Access it via the Lowlands Road past Baie Longue.

Baie Rouge (Red Beach) ★ is caught between two craggy headlands where flocks of gulls and terns descend at dusk—hence its western end is dubbed Falaise des Oiseaux (Birds' Bluff). The other side is marked by the Trou du Diable (Devil's Hole), a collapsed cave with two natural arches where the sea churns. You'll find superlative snorkeling here, but beware the powerful undertow. Beachwear becomes increasingly optional as you stroll west, though the modest will find several stands hawking sarongs, shorts, and sunbonnets. Baie Rouge is a charmer, from the serene waters to the views of Anguilla.

(Moments) A Grand Day on Pinel ★★

Imagine a secluded tropical island where bathers swim in a smooth, gin-clear lagoon fringed by palm trees and a curtain of jade mountains. Gentle surf laps a beach dotted with *palapas* and parasols. The scent of barbecued meat and coconut oil commingle with the salt air. Welcome to **Ilet Pinel,** a tiny islet a short boat ride from Orient Beach. A day trip to this uninhabited island is highly recommended. You'll find two delightful beach bistros, each with its own section of beach chairs and umbrellas (20€ for the day). Among them, **Karibuni ★** (© **690/39-67-00**) is the country's longest-running beach bar. Small ferryboats ($6 per passenger) run from the French Cul-de-Sac on St. Martin's northeast coast to Pinel daily on the hour from 9am to 4pm (to 5pm on Sun). Watch for the last return trip at 4:30pm. For more information, go to **www.visitpinel.com**. Or hop aboard a **Wind Adventures** catamaran from Orient Beach for a "One Day in Pinel" snorkeling safari (© **590/29-41-57;** www.wind-adventures.com; from 50€ per person for the day for 1–3 people).

Baie Nettlé (Nettle Bay) unfurls like a carpet between the Caribbean and Simpson Bay, just west of Marigot. Access is right off the main highway running through Sandy Ground. The area has become increasingly developed, with several hotels, apartment complexes, watersports franchises (waterskiing and kiteboarding are quite popular), and tiny beach bars alternating with fancier restaurants. The view on the Caribbean side frames Anguilla, Marigot's harbor to the north, and the ruins of La Belle Creole along the Pointe du Bluff to the south.

Isolated **Anse des Pères (Friar's Bay Beach) ★** lies at the end of a winding, bumpy country road; its clearly signposted entrance intersects with the main highway between Grand Case and Marigot. This is a pretty, less-visited beach with ample parking. Shelling, snorkeling, and sunset-watching are all favored. Two beloved beach bars organize raucous themed bashes. Stop in at **Kali's Beach Bar** (© **590/49-06-81**), a thatched bamboo hut splashed in Rasta colors, where Kali himself serves some of the island's best barbecue. Kali hosts "full-moon parties," featuring reggae bands on the beach along with a bonfire and plenty of drink. *Tip:* Have one of the staff here point you in the direction of relatively undiscovered **Anse Heureuse (Happy Bay)** ★, a 10-minute walk north through underbrush over a hill from Friar's Bay (pause to drink in the views of Anguilla). It richly deserves the name, thanks to the tranquillity, fine snorkeling, and white-sand beach.

Grand Case Beach, a long, narrow ribbon right in the middle of Grand Case, is a small, pleasant beach that can get crowded on weekends but has none of Orient Beach's carnival-like atmosphere. The waters are very calm, so swimming is good—although it's become a popular parking spot for visiting boats. A large section of the water has been roped off for kids to swim in safely. Unparalleled dining choices along the Caribbean's "Restaurant Row" run from *lolos* (essentially barbecue shacks) to gourmet bistros. For something in between, try **Calmos Café,** where you can watch the sun set over the beach with your feet in the sand and a drink in your hands.

To the east of Grand Case, follow the winding road up and over Pigeon Pea Hill. The spectacular setting of **Anse Marcel** comes into view. This lovely cove is home to two resorts, the **Radisson St. Martin** and **Domaine de Lonvilliers.** The adjacent **Marina Port de Lonvilliers** offers a handful of restaurants and shops, and the former le Méridien is now a Radisson, with additional recreational and gustatory opportunities. The beach itself is protected, with shallow waters ideal for families. You can swim here or else take a hike for 1½ hours north over a hill and down to one of the island's most pristine beaches, **Baie de Petites Cayes.** This is the most idyllic spot on St. Martin for a picnic. A ribbon of brilliant white sand beckons, and the waters ripple from sapphire to turquoise. Part of the fun is the hike itself, with panoramic views stretching all the way to Anguilla.

On the east coast, **Baie Orientale (Orient Beach)** ★ is where the action is. It's also a beauty of a beach. Eating, drinking, and people-watching qualify as sports, and many beach bistro/bars offer not only grilled crayfish Creole, but also live music, boutiques (with fashion shows), massages, parasailing, jet ski rentals, kiteboard instruction, and more. Of those beach bars marketing themselves as "The Five Stars of Orient Bay," **Waïkiki Beach** (© 590/87-43-19) is a favorite of the well-heeled barefoot St. Barts set, who down beluga caviar with Belvedere shots. **Kontiki** (© 590/87-43-27) has two sections: the main eatery and the Tiki Hut, serving a mix of dishes from jerk chicken to paninis, to quesadillas, to sushi. **Bikini Beach** (© 590/87-43-25), which also stays open for dinner, has a menu that runs from American-styled hamburgers to Spanish-influenced paella studded with lobster. Its southern end contains the naturist resort, **Club Orient.**

> ## (Fun Facts) A Trip to Tintamarre
>
> Pinel is just one of several Robinson Crusoe cays off the island's east coast. You can go even further afield to wild, 10-sq.-km (4-sq.-mile) **Tintamarre,** patois for "noisy sea" after the nesting birds (and bleating goats). The island features pristine snow-white beaches (including the aptly named Baie Blanche), striking ocher cliffs, and wrecks such as an upright tugboat encrusted in coral reef. You can clamber through the scrub and woodlands, discovering the ruins of a 19th-century stone farmhouse and an airport for regional carriers abandoned half a century ago. But nothing matches slathering yourself with mineral-rich mud from the flats, adding sea water, and baking avocado-colored in the sun: nature's exfoliant. **Wind Adventures** (✆ **590/29-41-57;** www.wind-adventures.com) has several different trips to Tintamarre from Orient Bay, including a 2-hour private snorkeling and eco-tour for one to three people (60€ per person).

Baie de l'Embouchure ★, embracing **Le Galion** and **Coconut Grove beaches,** just south of Orient, is part of the St. Martin Réserve Sous-Marine Régionale, established to protect migrant waterfowl habitats and rebuild mangrove swamps. A coral reef encloses the bay: The calm, shallow water (you can wade up to 100m/328 ft. out) makes it ideal for small children—it's the only beach on the French side where topless sunbathing is discouraged. Tiki carvings and blue umbrellas mark the appealing **Le Galion Restaurant** (also known as Chez Pat after owner Pat Turner; ✆ **590/87-37-25**). Up in the hills facing the bay is a handsome white house that was long the home of Romare Bearden, the celebrated American artist and collagist.

4 SPORTS & OTHER ACTIVITIES

If it's aquatic, St. Maarten/St. Martin offers it: from sailing to scuba diving, big game fishing to boogie boarding. It almost seems the island has more marinas per square mile than anywhere else on earth (one even changed its name to Dock Maarten, neatly combining two local economic mainstays—boating and shopping). Land-based excursions are less popular, though hiking and mountain biking can be rewarding.

ORGANIZED TOURS

Every seasoned sea salt seemingly ends up on St. Maarten at some point, if only to compete in the many renowned regattas. Needless to say, the island offers everything from booze cruises to eco-kayaking on all manner of pleasure craft from banana boats to catamarans to dinghies.

Longtime resident Stéphane Mazurier commandeers the sleek 23m (75-ft.) catamaran *ScoobiToo* (© **590/52-02-53;** www.scoobidoo. com), which sails from the Anse Marcel marina and Grand Case to Tintamarre, Anguilla, Prickly Pear, and St. Barts and on sunset cruises, dinner cruises, or some combination of the above; inquire about private charters and mini cruises. *Scoobifree* is an 18m (60-ft.) catamaran that specializes in luxury charters and mini cruises. *Scoobi-Cat,* launched in late 2008, is a 12m (36-ft.) catamaran that can zip passengers (18 max) to neighboring islands and coves for snorkeling trips or on shopping expeditions to Marigot or even Gustavia, St. Barts. Most outings ($55–$145) include snorkeling equipment, lunch, and an open bar. The crew spins arguably the best mix of the charter boats.

Eagle Tours at Bobby's Marina in Philipsburg (© **599/543-0068** or 599/542-3323; www.sailingsxm.com) offers lagoon sightseeing tours aboard the flatboat *Explorer,* stopping in Marigot for shopping before heading home; mimosas and rum punches flow copiously. But their pride and joy is the 23m (76-ft.), custom-designed *Golden Eagle* catamaran. Originally built for the prestigious Whitbread Around the World Race, it features a 24m-tall (80-ft.) main mast and a 7.2m (24-ft.) sail that took two men 3 weeks to paint by hand. It cruises to various deserted strands and cays for snorkeling and soaking up both tropical ambience and drinks (the pampering service includes a floating bar). The Friday jaunt ($99 per person) sails to Tintamarre and Creole Rock, puts in at Grand Case for lunch, then stops by Baie Longue for a final cooling dip. Transportation to and from your hotel is included.

Aqua Mania Adventures offers active trips out of Pelican Marina, Simpson Bay (© **599/544-2640;** www.stmaarten-activities.com). In addition to a parasail outfit, a PADI dive shop, high-speed-ferry service to Saba and St. Barts, and a boutique abounding in beach toys and resort wear, its three party-hearty boats patrol the waters several times daily. Two catamarans, *Lambada* and *Tango,* cruise to Anguilla and Prickly Pear for snorkeling and beach barbecues ($85 adults, $40 children 4–12). Or simply opt for sunset sails ($25 including open bar). *Sand Dollar* clings closer to St. Martin with a half-day snorkeling excursion to Creole Rock ($45 adults, $25 children 4–12). Kids can take turns piloting the *Calypso* in Simpson Bay's serene lagoon waters ($20), then bombard a small wreck with water balloons. Prizes and bobbing blow-up animals keep things happy. Or the family can frolic just offshore on *Playstation* ($20 per child; 9:30am–4:30pm), a converted colorful "swing, slide, and splash" catamaran that resembles an avant-garde art installation. The platform includes Tarzan swings, slides, and plenty of room to clamber. Dinner cruises (some aboard, others stopping at restaurants in Marigot's Marina Royale) are generally genial affairs; the return voyage toward St. Maarten's blazing skyline is memorable indeed.

The 12m (40-ft.) catamaran **Celine** departs Skipjack's dock at Simpson Bay (© **599/545-3961;** www.sailstmaarten.com) for a mellow sunset cruise ($25; with dinner $65). But South African skipper Neil Roebert, who built *Celine* by hand, is most (in)famous for leading a Lagoon Pub Crawl around Simpson Bay, with sons Graham and Johann as occasional accomplices. Neil calls himself the "ultimate designated driver," steering guests toward some of the better local bars. In addition to an open bar aboard, the first drink is free at each stop, along with a signature bite (from filet mignon cubes to mahimahi kabobs). Departures are at 7pm Wednesdays and Thursdays, with Mondays added in high season. The 3-hour bender costs a mere $75. Neil also charters *Celine* for full-day trips to Pinel, Tintamarre, Baie Longue, Friar's Bay, and more; the cost is $1,150 (up to 10 people; $115 each additional person).

(Moments) Come Sail Away

Ever dreamed of racing a state-of-the-art yacht? You can—and no previous sailing experience is necessary—when you sign on to crew aboard one of five famed America's Cup yachts in the **St. Maarten 12-Metre Challenge ★★** in Philipsburg at Bobby's Marina (© **599/542-0045;** www.12metre.com). Among the prestigious yachts are Dennis Conner's champion *Stars & Stripes, True North,* and *Canada II.* Each boat takes 9 to 18 sailors (12 and up) for a 3-hour race ($80–$100 per person). It's great fun and thrilling sailing: The captains and mates brief their swabs-for-a-day on the basics, from grinding a winch to tacking. Celebrate your win (or just finishing) with a complimentary rum punch.

BOATING   Day rentals are available from **Lagoon Sailboat Rental** in Simpson Bay Lagoon (② **599/557-0714;** www.lagoonsailboat rental.com). You can explore the lagoon—the largest in the Caribbean—and surrounding waters in state-of-the-art 6m (20-ft.) Sunfasts for $150 for a full day ($110 for a half-day). The congenial Cary and company also give a thorough 10-hour course for $200 (for 2–3 people) that can be broken up however you like.

DEEP-SEA FISHING   The island hosts several highly regarded competitions, including March's Marlin Cup and June's Billfish Tournament, that lure an impressive international roster of entrants. The waters teem with tuna, wahoo, snapper, grouper, jack, pompano, yellowtail, marlin, and other big game fish. The crew from **Lee's Roadside Grill** on Welfare Road 84, Simpson Bay (② **599/544-4233;** www.leesfish.com) knows where to catch the big boys, since they supply their own wildly popular seafood haunt. Charter one of its 9.3m (31-ft.) Bertrams for a half-, ¾-, or full-day excursion with a minimum of four people (maximum six). Drinks are included in the half-day trip ($150 per person) and lunch and drinks are included in the ¾- and full-day excursions ($200 and $250 per person respectively). And yes, they'll cook your trophy up at the restaurant for no extra cost.

Pelican Watersports, on the Dutch side, at the Pelican Resort Club, Simpson Bay (② **599/54-42640**), has boats available for deep-sea-fishing expeditions priced at $150 per person for a half-day (7:30–11:30am) or $300 per person for a full-day (7:30am–3pm) excursion. In high season, reservations must be made 1 week in advance.

GOLF   The **Mullet Bay Golf Course** (② **599/545-2850**) is the island's only golf course. It's a battered 18-hole Joseph Lee–designed course whose fate has hung in the balance, based on ongoing court battles, for years. The ruins of the Mullet Bay resort surround the course. The island's flagship resort was severely damaged by Hurricane Luis in 1995, and no one has ever gotten around to cleaning up the mess (more to the point: no one will take financial responsibility for the cleanup, not even its zillionaire developers). But golfers find their way here anyway and putter along on the lumpy, poorly kempt course. Greens fees are $50 for 9 holes or $80 for 18 holes; rental carts are $50.

HIKING & MOUNTAIN BIKING   Despite its small size, the island offers terrain ranging from limestone plateaus to a central volcanic ridge topped by 445m (1,482-ft.) Pic du Paradis, and ecosystems from semi-desert to tropical rainforest. Birders will sight coots, black-necked stilts, and ospreys nesting amid the swamps and cliffs.

Adrenaline junkies and eco-buffs will feel at home at **TriSport** headquarters on 14B Airport Rd. in Simpson Bay (© **599/545-4384;** www.trisportsxm.com). Bikers can rent Trek mountain bikes and hybrids ($17 half-day, $24 full day, $110 per week)—TriSport will deliver the bikes to your hotel for a $20 fee. TriSports also ventures into the open water with snorkeling/kayaking tours around Anse Guichard's hulking Henry Moore–ish boulders and Caye Verte. The 2½-hour **Simpson Bay Lagoon tour** ($49) includes instruction and a stop at deserted Grand Îlet, whose mangrove system houses unusual critters from sea cucumbers to upside-down jellies. You can rent kayaks for $15 per hour; a double kayak costs $19/hr.

HORSEBACK RIDING   In Seaside Nature Park, **Lucky Stables** (© 599/544-5255; http://luckystables.shoreadventures.net) offers a daily romantic Sunset Champagne ride ($72 per person) including a marshmallow roast or a beach and trail jaunt (from $48) into secluded, stony, unspoiled Cay Bay (aka Cape Bay) as Saba, Statia, St. Kitts, and Nevis drift on the horizon. Guides explain local folklore, fauna, and flora along the picturesque route through the closest thing to wilderness on the Dutch side. Horseback-riding lessons for adults and children are also offered in Seaside Park's Olympic-size riding ring ($20/lesson; $120 12-lesson card) Barring heavy traffic, the stables are 10 minutes from the airport and 15 minutes from Philipsburg. Its counterpart on the French side is the **Bayside Riding Club,** Rue de Le Galion, Coconut Grove, St. Martin (© **590/87-36-64;** www.baysideridingclub.com). Beach rides are a highlight ($95 1-hr. private ride, $70 1-hr. group ride).

SCUBA DIVING   Although the nearby island of **Saba** is considered to be the area's top dive sight, the scuba diving is quite good around **St. Martin,** with reef, wreck, night, cave, and drift diving; the depth of dives is 6 to 21m (20–69 ft.). Off the northeastern coast on the French side, dive sites include Ilet Pinel, for shallow diving; Green Key, a barrier reef; and Tintamarre, for sheltered coves and geologic faults. To the north, Anse Marcel and neighboring Anguilla are good choices. The waters around **St. Maarten** offer good dive wrecks, including the 1770 British man-of-war, **HMS *Proselyte,*** which came to a watery grave on a reef 2km (1¼ miles) off Philipsburg in 1801. Most of the big resorts have facilities for scuba diving and can provide information about underwater tours, photography, and night diving.

LeRoy French, the larger-than-life owner of the island's oldest dive shop, **Ocean Explorers,** at Kim Sha Beach (© **599/544-5252;** www.stmaartendiving.com), is still diving more than a half-century after he caught the bug (using some of Cousteau's first Aqua Lungs). Starry students in his 40-plus-year career have included Jackson Browne, Matthew McConaughey, and Sandra Bullock. He's been profiled by *Sports Illustrated,* and even the Cousteau team might envy his vivid videos. The personalized touch—he takes a maximum of six divers—costs a bit more ($53–$59 single-tank dive, $98–$104 double-tank) and means reservations are essential. Ocean Explorers also offers day trips ($90–$115) to the island of **Saba,** considered to be the area's premier dive site.

One of the island's premier dive operations is **Scuba Fun,** whose dive center is at the Great Bay Marina, Dock Maarten, Philipsburg (© 599/54-23966; www.scubafun.com). It offers morning and afternoon dives in deep and shallow water, wreck dives, and reef dives. A resort course for first-time divers with reasonable swimming skills costs 75€ and includes instruction in shallow water and a one-tank dive above a coral reef. A morning two-tank dive (certified divers only) costs 85€.

Another recommended dive operation is **Octopus Diving** (© 590/29-11-27; www.octopusdiving.com), in Grand Case. Its multinational staff provides PADI courses, night dives, and underwater photography to some 30 dive sites around the island. One-site dives go for $99, and two-site dives for $85 to $99, all equipment included. Dive Safaris, at Simpson Bay (© 599/545-2401; www.divestmaarten.com)—offers competitive rates and a full range of PADI certification courses, including specialty instruction in marine habitats, photography, and wreck diving. Those wanting to get up close and personal with sharks can don chain-mail-like armor to feed the sharks in their "Shark Awareness Dives" ($80 per person). Rates are $50 to $55 for single-tank dives; $95 to $100 for double-tank dives; and $75 for night dives.

SNORKELING ★★ The calm waters ringing the island's shallow reefs and tiny coves make it a snorkeler's heaven. The waters off the northeastern shores of French St. Martin have been classified as a regional underwater nature reserve, **Réserve Sous-Marine Régionale,** which protects the area around Flat Island (also known as Tintamarre), Ilet Pinel, Green Key, Proselyte, and Petite Clef. Equipment can be rented at almost any hotel, and most beaches have watersports kiosks.

Eagle Tours at Bobby's Marina in Philipsburg (© 599/543-0068 or 599/542-3323; www.sailingsxm.com) offers snorkeling, kayaking, lagoon sailing, and sightseeing tours aboard its fleet of seaworthy vessels. The 23m (76-ft.), custom-designed *Golden Eagle* catamaran (originally built for the prestigious Whitbread Around the World Race) cruises to various deserted strands and cays for snorkeling and soaking up both tropical ambience and drinks (the pampering service includes a floating bar—you *will* be dancing or leading a conga line by the end of the trip). The flatboat *Explorer* stops in Marigot for shopping before heading home; mimosas and rum punches flow copiously. The Friday jaunt ($99 per person) sails to Tintamarre and Creole Rock, puts in at Grand Case for lunch, then stops by Baie Longue for a final cooling dip. Transportation to and from your hotel is included.

Both **Scuba Fun** and **Octopus Diving** (see "Scuba Diving," above) provide guided snorkeling trips to the island's teeming offshore reefs. Snorkeling trips with Scuba Fun cost 30€ for a half-day, plus 7.50€ for equipment rental. Snorkeling trips to two sites with Octopus Diving cost $40 (including all equipment).

TENNIS   You can try the courts at most of the large resorts, but you must call first for a reservation. Preference, of course, is given to hotel guests.

WATER-SKIING & PARASAILING   Most of French St. Martin's large beachfront hotels maintain facilities for water-skiing and parasailing, often from kiosks that operate on the beach.

Club Caraïbes at the Hôtel Mercure Simson Beach in Nettle Bay (© 690/33-30-01; www.skicaraibes.net) provides wakeboard and jet ski rentals, as well as water-skiing instruction with Laurent Guy and Brigitte Lethem (the 2004 U.S. Master Champion). You can learn slalom or tricks for 40€ per set; 5-day intensive water-skiing and wakeboard courses cost 350€ to 720€, depending on the season.

WINDSURFING   Most windsurfers gravitate to the eastern part of the island, most notably Coconut Grove/Le Galion Beach, Orient Beach, and, to a lesser extent, Dawn Beach, all in French St. Martin. The top outfitter here, **Tropical Wave,** Le Galion Beach, Baie de l'Embouchure (© 590/87-37-25; www.sxm-orientbeach.com/chez pat), capitalizes on the near-ideal combination of wind and calm waters. Pat rents Mistrals for 20€ an hour, with instruction offered at 30€ an hour, and 45€ for a 2-hour beginner course. They also rent snorkeling gear, pedal boats, and kayaks (tours can be arranged).

Wind-Adventures (formerly Club Nathalie Simon), on Orient Beach (© 590/29-41-57; www.wind-adventures.com), is one of the Caribbean's premier windsurfing schools. Lessons cost 120€ for 1- to 3-hours of instruction. Kite trips for the experienced to Green Cay start at 95€. Wind-Adventures also rents windsurfers and Hobie Cats and offers both safaris and instruction (with excellent multi-lesson discounts).

Shopping on St. Maarten/St. Martin

The island teems with duty-free bargains in just about everything from linen to liquor, china to cameras, with prices as much as 20% to 40% lower than those in the U.S. and Canada. There's an energizing hubbub in **Philipsburg** every morning as cruise-ship passengers scatter eagerly in search of latter-day treasure: The goods displayed in the windows along Front Street are a mind-boggling display of conspicuous consumption, with an emphasis on high-end (gold, diamond, and platinum) jewelry and designer watches. Philipsburg's inviting French counterpart **Marigot** boasts smart boutiques with striped awnings and wrought-iron balconies that recall the Riviera, and galleries showcasing local artists' work. Philipsburg encourages you to "shop till you drop." Marigot murmurs seductively, "relax, the shops will still be open in an hour or two": It's the perfect place to savor the salt air, watch the ferries load for Anguilla, and enjoy a steaming cup of café au lait.

1 THE SHOPPING SCENE

DUTCH ST. MAARTEN

Not only is Dutch St. Maarten a free port, but it has no local sales taxes. Prices are sometimes lower here than anywhere else in the Caribbean, except possibly St. Thomas. Many well-known shops from Curaçao have branches here. Except for the boutiques at resort hotels, the main shopping area is in the center of **Philipsburg. Maho Plaza** (surrounding the glitzy Sonesta Maho Beach Resort) is another area for name-brand offerings (and outlets), including branches of Philipsburg's Front Street stalwarts.

In general, the prices marked on merchandise are firm, though at some small, personally run shops, where the owner is on-site, some bargaining might be in order.

Philipsburg

Most of the leading shops—from Tiffany to Tommy Hilfiger—line **Voorstraat (Front Street),** which stretches for about 2km (1¼ miles).

> ⓘ **Tips** **Off-Season Bargains**
>
> I've found big discounts at clothing and shoe stores (including designer boutiques) on the French side during the off-season, with prices slashed by half by the mid-May doldrums.

The **Sint Rose Shopping Mall,** on the beachside boardwalk off Front Street, has such big names as Cartier, Lalique, and Façonnable. The best buys are in electronics, jewelry, watches, and cameras.

Just off Front Street, **Old Street** lives up to its name, with 19th-century houses that today contain specialty stores. More shops and souvenir kiosks sit along the little lanes, known as *steegjes,* that connect Front Street with **Achterstraat (Back Street),** another shoppers' haven.

In general, Dutch side shops stay open from 9am to 6pm.

FRENCH ST. MARTIN
Marigot

Many day-trippers head to Marigot from the Dutch side just to browse the French-inspired boutiques and shopping arcades. Since St. Martin is also a duty-free port, you'll find some good buys here as well, even at the ultraluxe boutiques along **rue de la République, rue du Général de Gaulle,** and **rue de la Liberté,** where French luxury items such as Christofle tableware, Vuitton bags, Cartier accessories, and Chanel perfume are sold as well as well-priced prêt-a-porter.

The waterfront **Le West Indies Mall** (ⓒ **590/51-04-19**) is a marbled stone-wood-and-concrete structure with arches, skylights, curved staircases, and gazebos galore—a hushed, icily ornate contrast to the steamy, ramshackle market across the street. But it does concentrate 22 big-name boutiques, from Escada to Lacoste. You'll also find a branch of the venerable gourmet shop **Hédiard** (established in Paris in 1854), where you can purchase champagne, caviar, and foie gras; its aromatic tea room is a delightful stop for fresh pastries. Smaller complexes include **Galerie Périgourdine** and **Plaza Cara-ïbes,** which houses Cartier, Longchamp, and Hermès outposts.

At Marigot's harbor side, a lively **morning market** on Wednesday and Saturday hosts vendors selling clothing, spices, and handicrafts. There's a cookie-cutter quality to the crafts, with many of the vendors offering the same (imported) goods, but it's a good spot to pick up spices, colorful and inexpensive children's clothes, and the occasional good-quality craft.

At **Marina Port la Royale,** mornings are bustling: Boats board guests for picnics on deserted beaches, and a dozen little restaurants ready for the lunch crowd. Marina Royale is peppered with narrow warrens and alleyways where boutiques sell everything from designer clothes to jewelry.

Prices are quoted in euros or U.S. dollars, and most salespeople speak English. Credit cards and traveler's checks are generally accepted.

Tip: Keep in mind that although most French St. Martin stores open around 9am and close around 7pm, most shopkeepers close to take an extended lunch break from around 12:30 to 2pm, or later.

Grand Case

Several clothing boutiques and galleries fight for scraps of space between the bistros along the main drag of St. Martin's "second" city, **Grand Case,** nicknamed "Caribbean Restaurant Row." They keep unusual hours: Most are shuttered during the day, but fling their doors open come evening for pre- and post-dinner strollers.

2 SHOPPING A TO Z

CLOTHING
Dutch Side

Del Sol St. Maarten   This shop sells men's and women's sportswear. Embedded in the mostly black-and-white designs are organic crystals that react to ultraviolet light, which transforms the fabric into a rainbow of colors. Step back into the shadows, and your T-shirt will revert to its original black-and-white design. The same technology is applied to yo-yos, which shimmer psychedelically when you rock the baby or walk the dog. 55 Front St., Philipsburg. (C) **599/542-8784.** www. delsol.com.

Rima Beach World   Crave ticky-tack souvenirs and generic beach paraphernalia? Cut out the middleman by coming to what is essentially a resortwear factory outlet stocked to the rafters with any and every beach accessory you need, from peasant skirts to pareos, flip-flops to kids' beachwear, and shellacked shells to beach toys, much of it in electric tropical hues. 95 Nisbeth (Pondfill) Rd. just north of Philipsburg. (C) **599/542-1424.** www.rimabeachworld.com.

French Side

Act III   Act III prides itself on its designer evening gowns and chic cocktail dresses. If you've been invited to a reception aboard a private yacht, this is the place to outfit yourself. Designers include Christian Lacroix, Cavalli, Armani, Lanvin, Versace, and Gaultier. The bilingual staff is accommodating, tactful, and charming. 3 rue du Général de Gaulle, Marigot. ✆ 590/29-28-43.

Havane Boutique This boutique is a hyper-stylish clothing store for men and women, selling designer clothes from Armani to Zegna. 50 Marina Royale, Marigot. ✆ 590/87-70-39.

L'Atelier ★ L'Atelier showcases clothing and accessories (shoes, belts, and bags) from well-known European designers, with the store stocked with the latest Paris fashions. 28 Marina Royale, Marigot. ✆ 590/87-13-71.

MaxMara This, the first Caribbean franchise for the Italian Maramotti empire, carries every line from the more casual, lower-priced SportMax and Weekend to the dressy Pianoforte. 33 rue du Président Kennedy, Marigot. ✆ 590/52-99-75.

Pomme Boutique ★ This children's clothing store has been selling top-quality kids' brands for more than 23 years. Look for darling frocks by Petit Bateau, Lili Gaufrette, Sucre d'Org, and Berlingot; expect slashed prices during the off season. 6 rue du l'Anguille, Marigot. ✆ 590/87-87-20.

Serge Blanco "15" Boutique Although a relatively unknown name in North America, in France Blanco is revered as one of the most successful rugby players of all time. His menswear is sporty, fun, and elegant. Clothes include polo shirts, shorts, shoes, and latex jackets. Marina Royale, Marigot. ✆ 590/29-65-49.

Vie Privée This shop offers belts in leather and various exotic skins from ostrich to crocodile with elaborate buckles. It also sells bags and luggage. Marina Royale, Marigot. ✆ 590/87-80-69.

CONTEMPORARY ART

The island's charming local scenes and resplendent light have inspired such renowned artists as Romare Bearden over the years. I generally find the galleries more sophisticated on the French side; curious shoppers can also visit various ateliers.

Dutch Side

Axum Art Cafe This airy, woody upstairs space houses an Internet cafe, a jazz, blues, and reggae club, a coffeehouse for poetry readings, and a smoothie bar—oh, and an art gallery with a rotating collection of artworks. You can see local artists' work on the walls and on the computers' screensavers. 7L Front St. ✆ 599/542-0662.

Planet Paradise   Also known as Island Arts of That Yoda Guy, this is the playpen of the wildly creative Nick Maley, an artist/SFX designer who was instrumental in fashioning *Star Wars*'s resident gnomic gnome and contributed to other blockbusters from *Superman* to *Highlander.* John Williams' iconic theme music wafts through the air as you examine rare Lucasfilm prints, posters signed by the director himself, and Nick's own island-themed artworks. If you're lucky, he'll be around, relating cinematic anecdotes. He's slowly creating a museum in back holding his own considerable collection of film memorabilia. There's a second location at 106 Old St. 19A Front St. *C* 599/542-4009. www.yodaguy.com.

French Side

Antoine Chapon ★   Painter Andrew Wyeth once lauded this Bordeaux-born painter's ethereal watercolors of serene island scenes. Chapon's watercolors are bathed in light and the interplay of blue sky and blue seas; his oils have a denser, earthier feel. Chapon, who has lived in St. Martin since 1995, offers limited-edition high-definition archival prints—*giclees*—at excellent prices. 1 Les Terrasses de Cul de Sac. *C* 590/87-40-87. www.chaponartgallery.com.

Atelier des Tropismes   With a studio in back, Atelier des Tropismes is run by several artists. Among them, Patrick Poivre de la Fréta studied in Paris with Salvador Dalí and creates playful, witty still-life paintings, genre scenes in Fauvist hues, and *objets* such as screens. Paul Elliott Thuleau faithfully reproduces Caribbean architecture in hyper-realist fashion and richly saturated hues. Nathalie Lepine's contemplative portraits of women bring to mind Modigliani and Giacometti. 107 Boulevard de Grand Case, Grand Case. *C* 590/29-10-60.

Dona Bryhiel   Dona Bryhiel brings a whimsical Fauvist sensibility to her decorative paintings of St. Maarten and her native Provence. You'll also find hand-painted T-shirts, beach towels, and textiles; stunning jewelry incorporating local materials from shells to banana wood; and the delicate enameled ceramics of fellow Provençal Martine Azéma. 9 Residence Lou Castel, Oyster Pond. *C* 590/87-43-93. www. donabryhiel.com.

Escale des îles   This art gallery opposite the Marigot Market features paintings, ceramics, handicrafts, and jewelry inside a colorfully painted vintage Creole *maison.* A recent exhibition showcased the stunning wood marquetry of Jean-Pierre Straub. 23 Boulevard De France, Marigot. *C* 590/87-26-08. www.donabryhiel.com.

Francis Eck ★   Francis Eck commands high prices for his intense, color-saturated abstract landscapes and seascapes. Their jazzy, Rothko-esque riffs of primary color and bold impasto (combined with knife and trowel) enable him "to explore the intersection of figurative and abstract." His atelier is open by appointment only. You can also see his work on display on the walls of Bistro Nu and Mario's Bistro in Marigot, and Restaurant Le Soleil and Bistro Caraîbes in Grand Case. Hotel Le Flamboyant, Baie Nettlé. ✆ 690/59-79-27. www.francis-eck.com.

Gingerbread Gallery ★ Gingerbread Gallery exhibits vivid, powerful Haitian art, including works by such modern masters as Françoise Jean and Profil Jonas. *Note:* The gallery building was up for sale at press time; call before you head out. BP 20, Marigot. ✆ 590/51-94-95. www.gingerbread-gallery.com.

Minguet Gallery ★ Another highly regarded French expat, Alexandre Minguet (1937–1996) was an accomplished painter and watercolorist whose vibrantly colorful canvases recall Matisse and Dufy; his gallery lies 2 minutes west of Grand Case. Another Minguet gallery is located in Maho on the Dutch side. Rambaud Hill btwn. Marigot and Grand Case. ✆ 590/87-76-06.

NOCOart Studio ★ NOCOart was founded in 2004 by German sisters Norma and Corinne Trimborn, whose work couldn't be more different. Norma's paintings are figurative with abstract expressionist elements; her delightful Impressionistic still lifes call to mind Cezanne. Corinne paints unsettling neo-surrealist works in striking color fields. 39 Falaise des Oiseaux, Terres Basses near Plum Bay. ✆ 590/87-55-29. www.nocoart.com.

Roland Richardson Paintings and Prints ★ Known for luminous landscapes, portraits, and still lifes, Roland Richardson's clearest influence is the 19th-century Barbizon School of Impressionists. A native of St. Martin and one of the Caribbean's premier artists, he works in numerous media—oil, watercolors, pastels, charcoal, even batik and stained glass. His work has been exhibited in nearly 100 one-man and group shows in museums and galleries around the world. Celebrity collectors have ranged from Martha Graham to Jackie Kennedy Onassis, Harry Belafonte to Ivan Lendl, the Getty family to Queen Beatrix of the Netherlands. He and his wife, Laura, are gracious hosts in their carefully restored landmark West Indian home with concealed courtyard garden and gallery dating back to the 1700s. Richardson is also the resident artist at the resort **La Samanna** (p. 56), where he has a changing collection of works. 6 rue de la République, Marigot. ✆ 590/87-84-08. www.rolandrichardson.com.

ELECTRONICS

Boolchand's ★ Need a digital camera stat? Locals recommend this place on St. Maarten as the place to go for all your electronics needs, with an au courant (and competitively priced) array of cameras, binoculars, cellphones, computers, jewelry, and watches. 12 and 50 Front St. ☎ 599/542-2245. www.boolchand.com.

HANDICRAFTS & GIFTS
Dutch Side
Blooming Baskets by Lisa   Blooming Baskets showcases the talents of two sisters from Harrisburg, Pennsylvania. The baskets are actually straw-and-raffia handbags in various sizes adorned with silk flowers duplicating not just island blossoms but a virtual botanical garden, from irises to sunflowers. Their hand-mixed dyes ensure no two bags are ever quite alike. Note that Blooming Baskets has moved its stores to the Porto Cupecoy shopping/residential complex in Cupecoy Beach. Marina Village of Porto Cupecoy, Cupecoy Beach. ☎ 599/586-7055. www.bloomingbasketsbylisa.com.

Lalique   It is surprising that this store is found in Philipsburg, not Marigot. The fabulous and fabulously priced art glass and stemware (as well as authentic jewelry) should tempt any collector. 13 Sint Rose Arcade, Front St., Philipsburg. ☎ 599/542-0763.

Linen Galore ★   The beautiful tablecloths, napery, placemats, towels, fine lace, and runners on sale here are carefully sourced from Europe (Belgian tapestries, Battenburg lace) and Turkey. 45 and 97 Front St., Philipsburg. ☎ 599/542-2533.

Sint Maarten National Heritage Foundation Shop ★   Museum gift shops often have the most original gift items around, and this modest store, set amid generic jewelry shops between Front Street and the beachside boardwalk, is no exception. It has an array of interesting crafts by local artists, including Christmas ornaments, as well as books, maps, and helpful guides to historic Philipsburg. 7 Front St., Philipsburg. ☎ 599/542-4917. www.museumsintmaarten.org.

French Side
Les Exotiques ★   This is the workshop and showroom of Marie Moine, a ceramicist who fires charming local scenes onto plates: Creole houses, birds flying over Monet-like ponds, tiny Antillean figures in traditional dress. 76 rue de la Flibuste, Oyster Pond. ☎ 590/29-53-76. www.ceramexotic.com.

The Perfect Ti Pot ★   This charming little shop at the foot of the Hotel L'Esplanade showcases the handmade pottery of Cécile Petrelluzzi. Her lovely pieces deftly balance art and function. The shop is open at irregular hours; call Petrelluzzi to make an appointment to see her wares. Hotel L'Esplanade, Grand Case. ☎ 690/61-90-48.

JEWELRY

Front Street can seem like one jeweler after another (not unlike New York's West 47th St. Diamond Exchange). All sell loose stones as well as designer items. Many stores operate branches on both sides of the island. *Note:* Beware of unscrupulous hucksters selling loose "gems" like emeralds and diamonds on the street.

Dutch Side

Hans Meevis Jewelry   Hans Meevis is a master goldsmith who works brilliantly in miniature. He loves using inlays, such as larimar in ebony, or fashioning mosaics of tiny gems. Signature items include dolphin rings and pendants and remarkable keepsake blued titanium disks with intricate relief of the island in burnished white gold—right down to salt ponds and isthmuses. But Hans is also happy to customize all manner of decorative pieces (including bric-a-brac) on-site. 65 Airport Blvd., Simpson Bay. (𝄢 599/522-4433. www.meevis.com.

Shiva's Gold & Gems ★   This family business comes highly recommended by several locals. It sells designer and custom-made jewelry and has a fine collection of diamonds and diamond jewelry. The family also owns **Trident Jewelers** at 70 Front St. (𝄢 599/542-5946). 75 Front St. (𝄢 599/542-5946. www.trident-shivas.com.

Touch of Gold   This store actually sells liquor and various luxury items as well as baubles. Sapphires, rubies, diamonds, emeralds, tanzanite, and more are prettily mounted on platinum and gold. Brandname watches include Daniel Mink, Skagen, and Christian Bernard; top-flight jewelry designers range from Louis Feraud to Susy Mor. 38 Front St. (𝄢 599/542-4120. www.touchofgold.com.

Zhaveri Jewelers   Zhaveri carries the spectrum of certified loose gems, as well as genuine cultured pearls, brand-name watches, and handsomely designed necklaces, rings, bracelets, and brooches. Two locations are on Front Street. 53A and 103 Front St. (𝄢 599/542-5176. www.zhaveri.com.

French Side

Artistic Jewelers   This store carries extravagantly designed and priced jewelry and watches, ranging from garish to utterly ravishing. Featured individual designers and brands include David Yurman, Mikimoto, Fabergé, Scott Kay, Van Cleef & Arpels, Piguet, and Girard-Perregaux. Visitors to the Philipsburg store, 61 Front St. (𝄢 599/542-3456), find even more inventory. 8 rue du Général de Gaulle. (𝄢 590/52-24-80. www.artisticjewelers.com.

Goldfinger   Goldfinger is the island's official Rolex agent. But time-piece fanatics will find it's the ticket for designs by Tag Heur to Tissot. Other high-ticket items include designer jewelry, art glass (Kosta Boda, Orrefors, Waterford), tableware (Christofle, Daum), and porcelain (Herend, Lladró). They seem to open a new store annually: You can also stop by Rue de la République (② 590/87-55-70), Marina Royale (② 590/87-59-96), and Philipsburg at 79 Front St. (② 599/542-4661). Le West Indies Mall on the waterfront. ② 590/87-00-11.

EDIBLES, POTABLES & CIGARS

In addition to the usual upmarket single malt and stogie culprits (remember that Cubanos are illegal in the U.S.), the island produces its own concoctions. Though the base rums are imported from Gua-deloupe, local distillers blend or infuse them creatively. Look for Rum Jumbie, whose flavored varieties include coconut, mango, vanilla, and pineapple. But the trademark libation is Guavaberry liqueur (incor-porating citrus, spices, and passion fruit), the traditional Christmas drink of St. Maarten.

Dutch Side

The Belgian Chocolate Box ★   All ages will savor the delicious chocolates here, with such specialties as Grand Marnier butter-cream truffles. It's always bustling, especially when cruise ships are berthed at the nearby piers. 109 Old St. ② 599/542-8863.

Cigar Emporium   This place claims to stock the Caribbean's larg-est selection of Cuban cigars under one roof, and the walk-in humi-dor is certainly impressive. The smoking lounge is often filled with would-be CEOs practicing one-upmanship, puffing out their chests while puffing on Partagas. The shop also carries countless cigar and pipe accessories, cutters, and cases. 66 Front St. ② 599/542-2787. www. cigaremporium.biz.

Guavaberry Emporium ★   Guavaberry Emporium sells the rare "island folk liqueur" of St. Maarten, which for centuries was made only in private homes and is the island's traditional celebratory Christmas drink. Sold in square bottles, this rum-based liqueur is flavored with guavaberries, grown on the hills in the center of the island. (Don't confuse the yellow guavaberries with guavas—they're quite different.) The liqueur has a fruity, woody, smoky, bittersweet tang. Some people prefer it blended with coconut as a guavaberry colada or splashed in a glass of icy champagne. You can sample the line of liqueurs at the counter. The charming 18th-century Creole cottage also contains exotic natural perfumes and hot sauces (such as habanero-lime or creole chipotle). The elegant hand-crafted specialty

bottles and hand-carved wooden boxes make especially nice gifts.
8–10 Front St. ℂ **599/542-2965.** www.guavaberry.com.

French Side

Busco ★★   If the heavenly smells in this little shop don't seduce you, you may be olfactorily challenged. The company sells high-quality jams, condiments, spices, sugars, fruit punches, and rhum agricole—the agriculturally produced rum made from pure sugarcane juice with a deceptively elegant perfume and toe-curling 70-proof kick. Everything is made in Guadeloupe and is brilliantly packaged. The boutique was moving at press time, so call in advance to get the new address in Grand Case. 4 Route de L'Esperance. ℂ **590/87-78-89.**

Le Goût du Vin ★★   This is one of the island's top sources for wines (as well as brandies and rare aged rums). The inventory of 300,000 bottles showcases the best of France, but thoughtfully includes intriguing offerings from around the globe. Rue de l'Anguille. ℂ **590/87-25-03.**

Ma Doudou ★ ⟨**Finds**⟩   Ma Doudou occupies a tiny shack virtually obscured by overgrown foliage in the town of Cul-de-Sac. Call ahead unless you're in the neighborhood, as it keeps irregular hours. Ma Doudou means "my darling" in Creole patois. Darling certainly describes the collectible hand-painted bottles garnished with madras clippings. The products—rum-filled candies, spices, jams, and 20 flavored rums—practically overflow the shelves in the cramped space. The owners often throw in a free bottle with a minimum purchase. Cul-de-Sac. ℂ **590/87-30-43.**

Vinissimo   This wine boutique, which also has locations in Anguilla and St. Barts, is one of the island's top places to buy wines from around the world. 1 Rue de Low Town, Marigot. ℂ **590/87-70-78.** www.stmaarten.org/shops/vinissimo.html.

PERFUMES & COSMETICS

Lipstick   This is a Caribbean chain noted for its top-notch selection of scents and cosmetics, from Clarins to Clinique, Chanel to Shalimar. Stylists here do makeovers, touch-ups, skin care sessions, and even facials utilizing primarily Dior products. There's a Dutch side branch at 31 Front St. (ℂ **599/542-6051**). Rue de Président Kennedy, Philipsburg. ℂ **590/87-73-24.**

Pharmacie Centrale ★   I find browsing in French pharmacies a fascinating shopping experience in itself. The French are famous for the quality of their creams and potions, and even basic toiletries—deodorants, toothpastes—are fashioned with typical French flair and care. Here you can find highly touted French brands at duty-free (and tax-free) prices: La Roche-Posay, Vichy, Carita, and more. 10 Rue du Général de Gaulle, Marigot. (© 590/51-09-37.

Tijon Parfumerie & Boutique ★ Finds   Looking for that certain something you won't find anywhere else? This boutique *parfumerie* and skincare manufacturer makes all its wonderfully scented products right here at its headquarters in Grand Case. The creams are divine, never overpowering, and built around the natural scents of the Caribbean. 1 L'Esperance, Grand Case. (© 590/52-08-12.

St. Maarten/ St. Martin After Dark

It's been said that the French/Dutch border was established by an 18th-century drinking contest. How fitting, then, that St. Maarten/St. Martin arguably contains more bars per capita than any other Caribbean island. Or maybe it just seems that way, given the myriad sunset booze cruises to toast the elusive green flash (no, not a superhero but an atmospheric phenomenon caused by prismatic refraction of the sun's rays).

This is a friendly, good-time place, where after-dark activities begin early—usually a sundowner on one of the Caribbean's most beautiful beaches. Nightlife choices range from barefoot beach bars to salvaged scows to glitzy discos and, of course, casinos—all 14 of them located on the Dutch side of the island. In fact, the Dutch side at times resembles perpetual spring break, with rolling happy hours at sun-splashed beach bars. Free entertainment abounds. Most restaurants (notably at Simpson Bay; see chapter 4) and beach bars (especially on Orient Bay; see chapter 5) host live bands at least once a week, not to mention joyous happy hours. Hotels sponsor beachside barbecues with string bands.

Then there are the regular community jump-ups. Friday nights, the Philipsburg boardwalk along Front Street percolates with activity, as does Marigot's waterfront market Wednesdays and Sundays in season. Tuesdays from January to May, the "Mardi de Grand Case" (aka Harmony Night) explodes with color and sound: brass or steel drum bands, dancers, street performers, local crafts booths, and barbecue.

To find out what's on during your stay, get the **Thursday edition** of *The Daily Herald,* which runs an "Out and About" section and lists of upcoming events.

Look for appearances around the island by the "king of soca," **T-Mo** (full name: Timothy iKing T-Moi van Heyningen)—a six-time winner of the title of "Soca Monarch." Another popular local musician, calypso king **Beau Beau,** can be seen most nights singing and dancing with the Beaubettes at his eponymous seafood restaurant at the Oyster Bay Beach Resort (℃ **599/543-6049;** www.beaubeaus.com).

1 CLUBS & LOUNGES

Both sides of the island provide the endorphin rush of dancing to a great DJ's mix. The action usually starts at 10pm (though the beach-front discos throw afternoon theme parties). Most of the clubs charge a small cover (around $10 per person) after 10pm or 11pm, but look for flyers or free-admission coupons in local events magazines.

DUTCH SIDE

Bliss ★ Conveniently located within walking distance of the Maho "strip," Bliss is an open-air nightclub where Miami Beach–style disco chic rules. A giant Jumbotron trained on the dance floor lets you watch your own fancy footwork. Every afternoon features a different theme or promotion, usually revolving around the heated pool with the swim-up bar (4–6pm happy hours are ideal for sunset-watching). Try a "Blisstini"—designer martinis flavored with espresso, watermelon, passion peach, and more. 2 Beacon Hill Rd. ℂ 588/545-3996.

Tantra ★ Formerly the Q-Club, this is the island's hottest dance club. The closest thing to a big city disco, it features several bars, multilevel dance floors, wraparound catwalks, and go-go dancers. It's the haunt of visiting C-list celebrities and international DJs. The vast space pulsates not only with deep house, techno, and jungle trip-hop mixes (courtesy of state-of-the-art sound system and an impressive roster of local and international spin gurus), but a color wheel of fiber-optic lighting and videos. It's jammed and jamming weekends. Casino Royale, Sonesta Maho Beach Resort. ℂ 599/545-2861. www.tantra sxm.com.

FRENCH SIDE

Club One Formerly known as In's Club/L'Alibi, this *boîte* lies among the hotbed of cool joints peppering the marina that bop until dawn. The two main DJs, Léo and Antoine, have developed quite a following, especially for their sizzling house mixes. Saturday nights are ladies' nights. Alberge de la Mer, Marina Royale, Marigot. ℂ 590/27-13-11.

StarBar This club attracts Gallic youth (and a smattering of celebs) for funky house and techno music. The tiny club is gussied up to match the showgirl *manquées* in spangled stilettos, leopard and zebra skins, plumed headdresses, feather boas, and scarlet Fu Manchu nails. No wallflowers or shrinking violets: Everyone's a star among this exhibitionist crowd begging for reality-TV cameras. Nettle Bay. ℂ 590/29-65-22.

2 BEACH BARS & CLASSIC HANGOUTS

BEACH BARS & SHACKS

For many people, the best hangs on the island are those barefoot **beach shacks** right on the beach, where you can sit under a palm tree or a shady awning, listening to music, sipping a drink, and dining on fresh grilled fish or ribs. Some, like the Sunset Bar, have gone on to semi-fame (or semi-notoriety), but others have remained blessedly low-tech and laidback. Here are a few I recommend.

Dutch Side

At **Dawn Beach, Mr. Busby's Beach Bar ★** (© 599/543-6828), is a favorite place to kick back and even take a dip in the sea during the day; it turns into Daniel's by the Sea at night. **Beau Beaus's at Oyster Bay** (© 599/543-6040) is the Oyster Bay Beach Resort's beachfront bar, which offers tropical drinks, music, and food, and nightly cabarets starring local calypso King Beau Beau.

French Side

At **Baie Rouge (Red Beach)** you have two beach bars to sample: **Gus'** (no phone) and **Chez Raymond** (© 690/30-70-49). The latter cooks up blistering barbecue and delivers a knockout punch with Raymond's Special, a blend of six rums; hear reggae on weekends. On **Baie Nettlé (Nettle Bay),** Laurent Maudert's **Ma Ti Beach Bar** (© 590/87-01-30) and **Layla's** (© 590/51-00-93) are lively beach bars with French and Creole specialties, respectively.

On isolated **Anse des Pères (Friar's Bay Beach), Friar's Bay Beach Café** (no phone) sells Laurent's sublime stuffed mussels. The competitor is **Kali's Beach Bar** (© 590/49-06-81), a thatched bamboo hut splashed in Rasta colors, where Kali serves some of the island's best barbecue. Kali hosts Full Moon parties, featuring reggae bands on the beach, a bonfire, and plenty of drinks.

Happening (and clothing-optional) **Baie Orientale (Orient Beach)** has full-service beach bars that offer not only food, but also beach chairs and umbrellas, live music, boutiques, massages, parasailing, jet ski rentals, kiteboard instruction, and more. **Waïkiki Beach** (© 590/87-43-19; www.waikikibeachxm.com) has fabulous parties and beach lounges, plus a restaurant and snack bar—on New Year's eve, it features one of the biggest fireworks displays in the Caribbean. **Kontiki** (© 590/87-43-27) has two sections: the main eatery and the Tiki Hut, serving a mix of dishes from jerk chicken to sushi; it's famous for its Sunday-night parties. **Kakao beach bar** (© 590/87-43-26; www.kakaobeachsxm.com) is an all-pupose beach bar that has watersports rentals, beach chairs and umbrellas, a boutique selling Kakao-labeled T-shirts, towels, and more, and a menu of grilled meats, pizzas, and fresh lobster. **Bikini Beach** (© 590/87-43-25; www.sxm-orientbeach.com/bikinibeach) is a beachside tapas bar and grill that also sells fresh fruit smoothies (along with more hardcore drinks). It has a full watersports facility, a boutique, and even a children's playground.

At **Baie de l'Embouchure,** embracing **Le Galion** and **Coconut Grove beaches,** tiki carvings and blue umbrellas mark the appealing **Le Galion Restaurant** (aka Chez Pat after owner Pat Turner; © 590/87-37-25; www.sxm-orientbeach.com/chezpat). Locals love this laid-back spot; many families make charcoal pits in the sand for impromptu barbecues.

CLASSIC HANGOUTS
Dutch Side

Axum Art Café ★   This cafe's woody treehouse decor (sponge-painted apricot walls, artfully rust-colored furnishings) reinforces its college-town coffeehouse feel. With rotating art exhibits (some are displayed on the computer screens; it's also an Internet cafe), reggae and jazz parties, poetry recitals, storytelling, open-mic nights, and more, it's actually quite fun, and that *could* be the next Sartre brooding one table over. This is synergistic multitasking: While you're yammering over coffee or beer, you can also check your e-mail, make international calls, and scan or print documents. Upstairs 7-L Front St. © 599/542-0547.

Bamboo Bernies ★   On the second floor at Sonesta Maho Beach Resort, Bernies remains an updated homage to the Trader Vic's tiki bar: a United Nations of Buddhas, African masks, Chinese paper lanterns, totem poles, Indian tapestries, torches, painted wood barrels, and transparent glowing tiki gods. The menu—and clientele—is almost as eclectic, with good sushi to tapas to house-smoked barbecued ribs. Inside sushi restaurant Bamboo Bernies, the **Buddha Lounge,** as the owners say, "may very well be the only place in St. Maarten where one can relax, chill out, and actually have a conversation and hear the other person while conversing." It serves food and drinks into the wee hours. Sonesta Maho Beach Resort, Rhine Rd. © 599/545-3622. www.bamboobernies.net.

Buccaneer Beach Bar   Head here any time of day or night for a sublimely mellow setting and kick back over pizzas or burgers and knockout rum punches. Under new ownership, the Triple B is less frenzied than other many of the other Simpson Bay and Maho beach bars, with an open-air bar and picnic tables under thatched umbrellas and palm trees, but it occupies a nice perch above the beach for sunset-watching. Kim Sha Beach next to Atrium Hotel and Simpson Bay Bridge. (℃) 599/544-5876. http://sxmbuccaneerbar.com.

The Greenhouse ★   This big, breezy, plant-filled, open-air eatery at the end of the Philipsburg boardwalk has views of the marina, Great Bay, and the massive cruise ships that dock nearby. It's a favorite among locals and island regulars who swarm the place during happy hours (4:30–7pm), downing two-for-one drinks and discounted appetizers from conch fritters to jalapeño poppers. Wednesday's Crab-a-ganza and Friday's Lobster Mania sate anyone's crustacean cravings. But the food at the Greenhouse is a great value at any time (especially the certified Angus steaks, mango chicken, and such seafood specials as baked stuffed swordfish). A second Greenhouse opened in the Simpson Bay area in 2009 (℃) **599/544-4173**). Bobby's Marina, Front St. (℃) **599/542-2941**. www.thegreenhouserestaurant. com.

Lady C Floating Bar   Although the rickety 1938 craft barely seems seaworthy, *Lady C* cruises Simpson Bay lagoon Wednesday and Sunday afternoons. The deceptively decorous-sounding *Lady Carola* remains berthed otherwise. It's basically a bar on a docked boat. It's the kind of spot that posts Wall of Shame photos of inebriated customers (all in good fun). Airport Rd. (℃) **599/544-4710**. www.ladycfloating bar.com.

Sunset Beach Bar ★   This legendary beach bar is back in business after being demolished by Hurricane Omar in 2008. Set directly on the beach and mobbed most afternoons and evenings, it has a new dance floor. No one seems to mind the roar of airplane engines from aircraft that seem to fly just a few dozen feet overhead (so close that the planes' exhaust perfumes the air, while management broadcasts radio transmissions between the pilots and air traffic controllers). A live band plays reggae or calypso music every Sunday—expect a good-time party atmosphere. The ultimate all-purpose, something-for-everyone, anything-goes venue, Sunset offers decent pub grub, a huge screen for sporting events, a tiny dance floor swept by laser lights, live music daily from acoustic guitar to hardcore reggae, sunset variety shows, and DJs. It's noisy, crowded, silly—and beers that not so long ago were $6 are now $10—but where else can you get buzzed by 757s and kamikazes? 2 Beacon Hill Rd. (℃) **599/545-3998**. www.sunsetsxm.com or www.sunsetbeachbar.com.

Taloula Mango's Caribbean Café ★ Facing Great Bay Beach, Taloula Mango's offers magnificent views of the harbor. The handsome colonial room (with ceiling fans and plantation shutters) is a fine place to sample creative cocktails and delicious pub grub (burgers, pizza, tapas, salads) as well as island specialties, such as fish prepared Creole style and Caribbean conch and dumplings. Weekends welcome jazz, blues, and funk artists such as saxophonist Sapphron Obois. On the Boardwalk, Great Bay Beach, Front St., Philipsburg. ✆ 599/542-1645. www.talmangos.com.

French Side

Bali Bar ★ A bohemian crowd bellies up to Bali's bar for cocktails and global tapas—grilled chorizo, shrimp tempura, chicken Chinese rolls, sautéed mushrooms—costing 4€ to 9€ a plate. It's a fun, sexy spot, with mauve drapes, Indian embroidered silk wall hangings, and carved teak chairs. Smoky soca and jazz chanteuses occasionally animate the proceedings. Marina Royale, Marigot. ✆ 590/51-13-16.

Calmos Café ★ This place defines the laidback beach shack ethos (a sign near the entrance warns NO SNOBS). Calmos Café is splashed in sunset colors, with lots of chaises on the sand; at a little front library, you can borrow beach reading. Young slicksters come to flirt, gossip, and drink (terrific frozen concoctions and homemade infused rums—try the banana). In winter, there's sometimes live jazz or blues to accompany the sublime, affordable food. 40 bd. de Grand Case, Grand Case. ✆ 590/29-01-85.

Le Shore At Le Shore, the Grand Case beach bar veers into Miami Beach/Euro jetset territory (one blogger called the look "modern French yuppie"), with chic monochromatic furnishings, a small pool, a dining terrace, and lounge chairs facing the beach. The owners are Baie Orient hospitality pros, and this spot already has a certain understated sizzle. It has a full menu. 28 bd. de Grand Case, Grand Case. ✆ 590/51-96-17.

The Tree Lounge ★ This lounge high up in the trees at Loterie Farm is a thoroughly pleasant place to relax over a drink and some delicious tapas with fellow grownups and is a switch from the beach-bar scene—you'll be nestled in greenery. It's perched atop the farm's original 19th-century milk shed. 103 Rt. De Pic Paradis, Loterie Farm. ✆ 590/87-86-16.

Zen It This and neighboring Calmos Café share a similar beach-bar philosophy: It's all about casual and laidback. While Calmos Café is firmly rooted in the beach sand, however, Zen It's sunset vantage point is from a raised wooden porch that feels more Cape Cod than

Caribbean. It's a wonderfully breezy spot to have a beer and a bite at the day's end. 49 bd. de Grand Case, Grand Case. ⓒ 590/29-01-85.

---

3 LIVE MUSIC

DUTCH SIDE

Cheri's Café ★   American expat Cheri Batson opened this cherished institution in 1988. The rare tourist trap that even appeals to locals, this great place to meet people is outfitted in an irrepressible color scheme of scarlet, hot pink, and white. Everybody from rock bands to movie stars, casino high rollers to beach bums, makes a pit stop at this open-air pavilion. The surprisingly good, relatively cheap food (think burgers, steaks, pastas, and fresh fish) is a bonus, but most come for flirting and dancing to an assortment of live acts 6 nights a week. Don't miss such regulars as Sweet Chocolate Band, if only to watch the guys don wigs and falsies. Rhine Rd. #45, Maho Village, Maho. ⓒ 599/545-3361. www.cheriscafe.com.

Pineapple Pete ★   Pete co-opts most of an alley between the lagoon and the main drag. T-shirts dangle from the rafters in the main room (with five pool tables and dart boards), where yachters, local businesspeople, and timeshare owners marinate and get chummy. The fairly priced fare is quite good—signature dishes include crab-stuffed shrimp, lobster thermidor, and dark rum crème brûlée. Infectious, if ear-splitting, live music keeps things rocking half the week, including live classic rock, pop, and blues Wednesdays through Sundays with local stalwart Ronny Santana. Airport Rd., Simpson Bay. ⓒ 599/544-6030. www.pineapplepete.com.

Red Piano Bar   This joint attracts 40-something singles looking for romance and couples looking to rekindle sparks. The grand piano is indeed quite red, and patrons are often red-faced from the killer cocktails. The performers, professional or otherwise, are variable, but the place is comparatively refined and quiet. Pelican Resort, Billy Folly Rd. ⓒ 599/544-6008.

Sopranos Piano Bar   Mobbed by 30-somethings in the mood for romance, the piano bar (replete with a small area for old-fashioned touch dancing) delivers a soigné ambience without thematic overkill (other than the signature Bada Bing merchandise for sale). The photos of musicians posed as Mafiosi and giant poster of James Gandolfini (aka Tony Soprano) glaring down at the grand piano are witty; the dim lighting, intimate dark wood banquettes, and red-and-black color scheme set the right tone. Sit back and enjoy the good martinis, superb cognac selection, and fine collection of Cuban cigars. Sonesta Maho Beach Resort & Casino. ✆ **599/580-1560.** www.sopranospianobar. com/stmaarten.

FRENCH SIDE

Blue Martini Although it doesn't have beach access, this place more than compensates for it with an enchanting garden, the perfect place to savor specialty cocktails, intriguing international beers like Abbé Leffe on tap, and tasty tapas. It stirs things up with live bands Tuesdays and Thursday through Saturday. 63 blvd. de Grand Case, Grand Case. ✆ **590/29-27-93.** www.bluemartinisxm.com.

Gecko Café Although nominally an Italian eatery, Gecko Café serves tapas and emulates Japanese decorative simplicity right down to tatami mats and low tables on the polished wood floor. It's an ideal place to zone out, except perhaps at sunset, when an invigorating mix of yachters and local yupsters cruise by for happy hours and late-night live acoustic jams Thursday through Saturday. Marina Royale. ✆ **590/ 52-21-25.**

La Chapelle ★ This restaurant/disco is where savvy locals head when they tire of the nonstop action at the "sand" bars on Orient Beach—but still want to drink, dine, dance, or shoot pool and the breeze in congenial surroundings. Orient Village. ✆ **590/52-38-90.**

4 FOR ADULTS ONLY

Dutch St. Maarten has its share of adults-only entertainment, from topless lounges to gentlemen's clubs.

Golden Eyes Calling itself a topless "ultra-lounge" with "American management and European dancers," Golden Eyes gives the Platinum Room a run for its (and your) money. In an effort to be inclusive, it welcomes couples and women. The club itself is handsomely appointed and the balcony offers lovely marina views. 12 Airport Rd., Simpson Bay. ✆ **599/527-1079.** www.goldeneyesclub.com.

Platinum Room The gold standard of gentlemen's clubs, this place cultivates an air of class: neo-colonial arches and colonnades, inlaid woods, knockoffs of Michelangelo's David and Grecian urns, sequined curtains, and cheery turquoise banquettes. It crowds up quickly, with everyone from suits to bikers to cyber-geeks, and stays open till 5am. Maho Village. ✆ **599/557-0055.** www.theplatinumroom. com.

St. Maarten's Red-Lights

The Dutch are notoriously liberal and have cultivated a permissive attitude regarding prostitution on St. Maarten. This review is neither endorsement nor encouragement; it merely offers some enlightenment on a major element of St. Maarten nightlife. Brothels operate around the island and must purchase a permit and supply affidavits on their employees (mostly Dominican, Venezuelan, Guyanese, and Jamaican immigrants who must submit to monthly medical checkups). Several brothels are situated just outside Philipsburg (if this is your thing, ask the security guards at your hotel for advice on where to go).

It all started with the **Seaman's Club** (79 Sucker Garden Rd.; © **599/542-2978**), known to the locals as the "Japanese club." It was founded in the 1940s to service Japanese tuna fishermen who'd been to sea for months at a time. These single men needed a place to carouse, and the government didn't want them hassling local girls, so a tradition was born.

Note: One big difference from Amsterdam's red-light district is that possession of marijuana is not tolerated here. An infraction could lead to stiff fines or even imprisonment.

5 CASINOS

Gaming is currently only legal on the Dutch side. This is no Caribbean Vegas, but that's not necessarily a bad thing. Think low-key, laidback gaming, played to a lilting calypso beat. The 14 casinos offer free live theater, with everyone from blue-haired fanny packers to dreadlocked Rastas robotically feeding the maw of the machines. If you indulge, just remember there's no such thing as a sure system (or, Lord help us, ESP)—and the odds always favor the house, especially in games like Keno. Hours vary, but most casinos are open from 1pm to 6am. Here is a sampling.

Atlantis World Casino ★ This is St. Maarten's most Vegas-style venue, if only for adopting that destination's gourmet aspirations. The owner/developer cleverly attracted top restaurateurs by offering competitive rents. The interior is fairly posh if you don't look too closely:

mirrored ceilings, Christmas lights, faux plants, lipstick red accents, and murals and frescoes, mostly depicting cherubs cavorting in azure skies or surreal encounters between Renaissance figures and islanders. Atlantis features all the major table games, as well as more than 500 slot and video poker machines. It tends to attract a more mature, settled crowd: guys chomping on cigars and tan women who look like aging Lakers Girls, as well as junior corporate sharks in the Texas Hold 'Em poker room. Rhine Road 106, Cupecoy. (*€* 599/545-4601. www. atlantisworld.com.

Casino Royale ★ St. Maarten's largest, glitziest, and supposedly ritziest gaming emporium, Casino Royale's splashy exterior of illuminated fountains and its huge multihued neon sign spitting lasers almost approximates the gaudy best (and worst) of Vegas. Despite the upscale pretensions, most people ignore the rarely enforced dress code (no shorts or tank tops). The casino offers games from blackjack to baccarat and more than 400 slot machines. The 800-seat **Showroom Royale** is the island's largest, most technologically sophisticated theater; its glittery shows change every few months, but generally follow the same pattern. Like a poor man's *Ed Sullivan Show/Star Search,* the evening might include acrobatics, jugglers tossing bowling pins and bad jokes with equal aplomb, and/or magicians with the usual large-scale tricks up their sleeves. Upstairs is the island's loudest dance spot, **Tantra** (see "The Club Scene," earlier in this chapter). Sonesta Maho Beach Resort. (*€* 599/545-2590 or 599/544-2115. www.mahobeach.com.

Hollywood Casino The Hollywood Casino does make some half-hearted stabs at playing up its name: How about "Oscar" door handles, movie stills (*Pulp Fiction* and *Planet of the Apes*), fake stars in the ceiling, klieg lights, Rodin-like statues, and a wall devoted to Marilyn Monroe? It offers a panoramic view of the bay, roulette, blackjack, stud-poker, Let It Ride, progressive jackpot bingo, 150 slot machines, bingo, and a high-tech Sports Book with nine screens broadcasting major events via satellite, plus nightly dancing on the Pelican Reef Terrace and island shows featuring Caribbean bands. Pelican Resort, 37 Billy Folly Rd., Simpson Bay. (*€* 599/544-2503 or 599/544-4463. http://mostelegant.com/hollywood.

Jump Up Casino A Carnival-themed casino, Jump Up has several ornate costumes on display. Live late weekend shows (11pm–2am) showcasing the island's hottest bands (Playstation, Jump Up Stars, Explosion, Impact) are the best reason to visit. Emmaplein 1, end of Front St., Philipsburg. (*€* 599/542-0862. www.jumpupcasino.com.

Princess Casino ★ This place wins the prize for overall elegance, as evidenced by the dressier crowd and handsome neoclassical design (columns, arches, domes, and frescoes galore). Princess has more than 650 one-armed bandits and 20 table games from craps to blackjack. Dining options include the Peg Leg Pub, a fine buffet, and a sushi bar. The live shows are spectacularly mounted (by island standards). Princess Port de Plaisance Resort, Cole Bay. (℃ **599/544-4311.** www.princess portdeplaisance.com/casino/casino.htm.

Rouge et Noir   This joint is all red and black inside, just like a roulette wheel, with a vaguely futuristic design. It offers slot machines, roulette, blackjack, bingo, and Antillean and 3-card poker. 66 Front St., Philipsburg (℃ **599/542-3222** or 599/542-2952.

Anguilla

by Alexis Lipsitz Flippin & Sherry Marker

Once upon a time Anguilla was one of the Caribbean's best-kept secrets. Then, in the 1980s, this small, serene, secluded island embarked on a careful plan of marketing itself as a top-end destination with a handful of resorts. Quite deliberately, Anguilla (rhymes with "vanilla") turned its back on the package tours, the casinos and cruise ships, the glitzy shopping and nightlife of neighboring Dutch St. Maarten.

Just like Anguilla itself, the island's first resorts were (and remain) boutique gems, serene and secluded. The island has also emerged as the Caribbean's top dining spot, with Anguillan chefs running away with top prizes in annual regional competitions. You will dine superbly here, and you will pay dearly to do so.

Prepare yourself for two guaranteed pleasures: the breathtaking beauty of the island's 30-odd beaches and the genial hospitality of Anguilla's 12,000 inhabitants. Even though Anguilla is one of the Caribbean's most upscale destinations, the island has remained laid-back and unaffected. It's an egalitarian society, where politicians and taxi drivers rub shoulders at their favorite beach bars. If you're looking to rest, unwind, and be pampered without pomp or snobbery, then this is the place for you.

Anguilla has no large commercial harbor or bustling international airport, a la St. Maarten. The beaches here are all public, and although some resorts make non-guests park some distance away from their manicured beaches, many of the best beaches are ones you'll discover yourself—long, liquid strands of tawny sand and bottle-green surf. In addition to the island's justly famous first-class resorts, Anguilla also has a number of affordable small inns and guesthouses. Stay at one of Anguilla's more modest places and you'll still have those famous beaches to enjoy. The budget-minded will also find plenty of dining choices that won't cost an arm and a leg. Simply head to one of Anguilla's many local beach bars and barbecue shacks, where the ambience is barefoot casual.

The northernmost of the British Leeward Islands in the eastern Caribbean, 8km (5 miles) north of St. Maarten, Anguilla is only 26km (16 miles) long, with 91 sq. km (35 sq. miles) in land area.

Anguilla: A Love Affair

The first time we went to Anguilla, in 1989, my husband and I were fleeing Puerto Rico after 2 waterless and powerless weeks following Hurricane Hugo. When Anne Edwards of Sydans Villas met us at the airport and asked if we had some bottled water, I thought, *What have I gotten into! Have I fled an island disaster only to land on an island where you're expected to have your own water?* (Turns out, in those days some people *did* bring bottled water with them to Anguilla. The local water has a sea-tang, and bottled water was still expensive in those days on Anguilla.) When we arrived that first time, there were no lights between the airport and Sandy Ground. Really. I had no idea where we were going or if there was any *there* there. We woke up in the morning to find a small goat staring at us through the screen door and nibbling my towel, which I had left as an inadvertent snack on a chair outside the room. And, I admit, this may not sound like an intro to why I have been going back to Anguilla (and Anne Edwards' Sydans) for 20 years, but it sure turned out that way.

—Sherry Marker

Once part of the federation with St. Kitts and Nevis, Anguilla gained its independence in 1980 and has since been a self-governing British possession.

For years, many Anguillan men were forced to leave the island to find work in shipping, fishing, and trade. Today, the tourist and hospitality industries employ a number of islanders. In fact, in the last few years, Anguilla has seen more building activity than in the last several decades, but at press time the global recession had put the brakes on most large-scale development. On (perhaps permanent) hold is the ambitious Temenos resort/villa complex, which ran out of funds after building the island's first 18-hole golf course, now managed by Cap Juluca. The homey old Rendezvous Bay Hotel had high hopes of reinventing itself as a an upscale hotel and condo complex, but the entire project stalled—will a smaller-scaled boutique hotel land on Rendezvous Bay in the future? It took the Viceroy Anguilla 3 years to open, but it did, and it's quite a monumental undertaking. A new government has been installed, and among its major mandates is sustainability of the island's precious resources. The one thing that hasn't changed? The truth of Anguilla's slogan: "Tranquillity Wrapped in Blue."

VISITOR INFORMATION

The **Anguilla Tourist Board,** Coronation Avenue, The Valley, Anguilla, B.W.I. (© **264/497-2759** or 800/553-4939; fax 264/497-2710; www.anguilla-vacation.com), is open Monday to Friday from 8am to 5pm.

In the United States, contact Ms. Marie Walker, 246 Central Ave., White Plains, NY 10606 (© **877/426-4845** or 914/287-2400; mturnstyle@aol.com), or log onto www.anguilla-vacation.com. For U.S. travelers who need quick answers to questions about Anguilla, contact the toll-free **Anguilla Hotline** (© **800/418-4620**).

In Canada, contact Ms. Dale Pusching, SRM Marketing, 20–225 Dundas St. E., Suite 411, Waterdown, Ontario, Canada L0R2H6 (© **866-348-7447**; dpusching@anguillacanada.ca).

In the United Kingdom, contact Ms. Caroline Brown, c/o CSB Communications, Ltc., Suite 11, Parsons Green House, 21–37 Parsons Green Lane, London SW64HH (© **207/736-6030**; info@ anguilla-tourism.com).

USEFUL WEBSITES   In addition to the websites above, other helpful Internet sites include **www.gov.ai** (Anguilla government), and **www.ahta.ai** or **www.anguillahta.com** (Anguilla Hotel and Tourism Association) and the *Anguillian* **newspaper** (www.anguillian.com). The **Anguilla Guide** (www.anguillaguide.com) and the **Anguilla Forum** (www.anguillaforum.com) are very helpful, and the message boards often contain invaluable travel tips. *Anguilla Life* magazine comes out three times a year (www.anguillalife.com).

USEFUL READING   In the Valley, the **Anguilla Arts and Crafts Center** (© 264/497-2200) and the **National Trust Office** (© 264/497-5297; www.axanationaltrust.org) stock books on Anguilla, including guides to the local flora and fauna and Brenda Carty and Colville Petty's *Anguilla, an Introduction and Guide,* which is usually also available at Mr. Petty's **Heritage Collection Museum ★** in the island's East End (see "Exploring Anguilla," below).

GETTING THERE

BY PLANE   During high season, Anguilla's Clayton J. Lloyd International Airport is abuzz with private Gulfstreams and Fortune 500 executive jets purring on the runway. There are no nonstop flights from mainland North America into Anguilla, so visitors either transfer through San Juan, Puerto Rico, or the Princess Juliana International

A Little History

In 1980 Anguilla gained its independence from an awkward federation with St. Kitts and Nevis and has since been a self-governing British Dependent Territory. The British government is represented by the governor, who is responsible for a good deal, including foreign policy. There is an elected House of Assembly and the chief Anguillan elected official is the chief minister. Public holidays, including Anguilla Day (May 30), the Queen's Birthday (June 18), and Separation Day (Dec 19) honor both Anguilla's ties to Britain and its independence from St. Kitts and Nevis. Most government offices are in the Valley, Anguilla's capital, where most of the island's banks, groceries, and shops are also located. While you're in the Valley, be sure to drive up Crocus Hill and see some of the island's oldest and most charming Caribbean gingerbread cottages.

ANGUILLA

8

ESSENTIALS

Airport, St. Martin's main airport, on nearby Dutch St. Maarten, or fly in by private charter.

Clayton J. Lloyd International Airport, located just outside the Valley, can only accommodate small- to medium-size aircraft. Currently, the two commercial airlines with connecting flights into Clayton J. Lloyd International are **American Eagle** (© 800/433-7300 in the U.S. and Canada; www.aa.com), the commuter partner of American Airlines, with one nonstop daily flight to Anguilla's Clayton J. Lloyd International Airport from American's San Juan hub; and **LIAT** (© 888/844-5428 or 264/497-5002; www.liatairline.com), which in 2007 merged with the now-defunct Caribbean Star and now offers daily flights from Antigua, St. Kitts, Nevis, and St. Thomas. *Note:* At press time **Winair** (Windward Islands Airways International; © 888/255-6889 in the U.S. and Canada; www.fly-winair.com) had suspended daily flights to Anguilla from Dutch St. Maarten.

A fast and convenient option is to hop on one of the handful of private regional airlines that offer chartered plane service from St. Maarten/St. Martin or other nearby islands directly to Anguilla. At press time, **Anguilla Air Services** (© 264/498-5922; www.anguilla airservices.com) was offering one-way flights at rates of $80, a very reasonably priced alternative to a private boat charter (which can cost $50–$85). Offering comparable fares is the other Anguillan airline,

0   2 mi
0   2 km

ANGUILLA

ESSENTIALS

Prickly Pear Cay

C A R I B B E A N

S E A

Flat Cap P

Sandy Island

20 Nor
Hill
17 **16** *Road Salt*
Road Bay *Pd.*
Sandy Ground **15** **19**
Long Lower South Hill **14** **18**
Bay South Hill
13
Meads Bay *Rendezvous*
Bay Salt Pd.
12
10 **11** *Meads Bay*
8 **9** *Pond* **Blowing Point**
Barnes Bay **2** **1**
7 *Cove*
Pond ↘ **Rendezvous**
Bay *Blowing Point*
3 *Harbour*
5
6 **4**
↖ **Maundays Bay**
Shoal Bay West
Anguillita
◊ *Blowing Rock*

Anguilla Channel

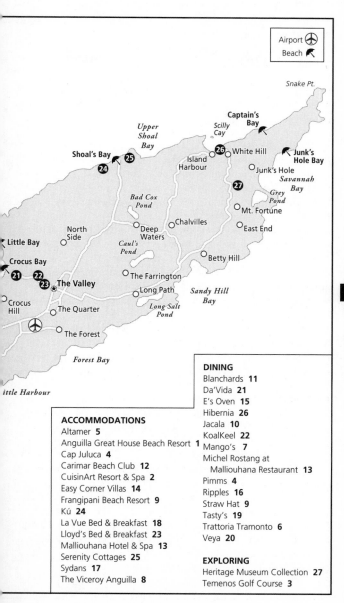

Airport ✈
Beach 🏖

Snake Pt.

Captain's Bay

Scilly Cay ○

㉖ ○ White Hill

🏖 **Junk's Hole Bay**

Upper Shoal Bay

Shoal's Bay ㉕

Island Harbour

○ Junk's Hole

Savannah Bay

㉔

㉗

Grey Pond

Bad Cox Pond

○ Chalvilles

○ Mt. Fortune

North Side ○

○ **Deep Waters**

○ East End

Caul's Pond

○ The Farrington

○ Betty Hill

🏖 **Little Bay**

Crocus Bay

㉑ ㉒

㉓ **The Valley** ✈

○ Long Path

Sandy Hill Bay

○ Crocus Hill

○ The Quarter

Long Salt Pond

✈

○ The Forest

Forest Bay

ittle Harbour

ANGUILLA

8

ESSENTIALS

Trans Anguilla Airways (© 264/497-8690; www.transanguilla. com). **Rainbow International Airlines** (www.rainbowinternational airlines.com) flies out of San Juan.

BY FERRY   The majority of people coming in to Anguilla arrive via the Blowing Point ferry port. Public ferries run between Marigot Bay, St. Martin, and Anguilla (© 264/497-6070), every 30 minutes. The trip takes 20 to 25 minutes, making day trips a snap. Usually, the first ferry leaves St. Martin at 8am and the last at 7pm; from Blowing Point, the first ferry leaves at 7:30am and the last at 6:15pm. The one-way fare is $15 ($10 children 2–18) plus a $3 departure tax. A departure tax of $20 (children $10) is charged on your return trip to St. Martin; day-trippers and visiting yachts pay a $5 departure tax. No reservations are necessary. Ferries vary in size, and none takes passenger vehicles. *Tip:* Keep in mind that if you have a late-arriving flight, you may quite literally miss the (ferry) boat. You can either spend the night in St. Maarten/St. Martin or arrange a charter plane connection (see above) into Anguilla.

A convenient option is to take one of the **privately run charter boats and ferries** that shuttle passengers between Anguilla and the airport in St. Maarten. Anguilla-based charter boats will pick you up at the Princess Juliana airport in St. Maarten and transport you and your luggage to Blowing Point or a hotel on the south side of Anguilla. These boats are more expensive than the public ferries, but let you avoid having to travel from the airport to the ferry port in Marigot by taxi (a 10- to 15-min. trip)—a smart option for travelers with a lot of luggage or a lot of kids. Plus, the privately run boats are smaller and have fewer passengers and can even arrange full-boat charters for groups or families. Keep in mind that these boats do not run as frequently as the government-run ferry, but most do include ground transportation. *Good news:* In 2010, an agreement between the St. Maarten/Anguilla governments is designed to greatly facilitate the ease of private boat transfers (and passing through immigration) from the airport—which means that ideally you will be able to get off the plane and jump on a boat straight to Anguilla in under 30 minutes.

Check out the *GB Express* (© 264/235-6205 in Anguilla; 599/ 581-3568 on St. Maarten; www.anguillaferryandcharter; $55 one way, $90 round-trip); the **MV *Shauna VI*** (© 264/476-0975 or 264/772-2031 in Anguilla; 599/580-6275 on St. Maarten; myshauna6@hotmail.com; round-trip fare $60 adults, $40 children 2–12); or **Funtime Charters** (© 866/334-0047 or 264/497-6511; www.funtime-charters.com; $55 per person one-way; half-price for children 11 and under). Reservations required.

ANGUILLA

8

ESSENTIALS

Taxi Zones: Decoding Anguilla Taxi Fares

If you feel taxi fares are expensive on Anguilla (and if you do, you aren't alone), consider this: Not only does each driver has to pay costly insurance to insure you, the passenger, but gas is astronomically expensive, at press time nearly $5 a gallon, and most drivers have vans—which can cost $75 to fill up. Plus, Anguilla taxis don't have meters, so if a customer is dragging his feet, drivers are not compensated for the wait. But the main reason a taxi ride costs what it does is that the government has parceled the island into 10 strictly delineated taxi zones, with a set fee schedule based on travel within and out of each zone. So, for example, Zone 1 covers the West End, where many of the top resorts and restaurants are located. Within that zone, a taxi ride will cost $10 (plus an additional $4 after 6pm). But from Zone 1 to Zone 2—another busy resort area 5 minutes away—the fare jumps to $14 (plus $4 after 6pm).

Tipping is at the discretion of the customer. You can check out the latest rate schedules by going to the **Anguilla Hotel & Tourism Association** website (www.ahta.ai/Taxi_Service.html).

Most Anguilla hotels will also arrange (for a fee) private boat charters between the airport in St. Maarten and the ferry dock at Blowing Point, Anguilla, with door-to-door ground transportation.

Tip: If you'd like to do some shopping and have lunch in Marigot before you take your ferry to Anguilla, simply store your bags at the ferry landing. The Port de Marigot has a small baggage storage area ($5, plus tip).

GETTING AROUND

BY RENTAL CAR   To explore the island in any depth, I highly recommend you rent a car, though be prepared for some badly paved roads. Four-wheel-drive vehicles are a real bonus for exploring the island's unpaved and pitted back roads, but not necessary elsewhere. Car rental agencies on the island can issue the mandatory Anguillan driver's license, which is valid for 3 months. You can also get a license at police headquarters in the island's administrative center, the Valley,

Festivals & Sailboat Races

Anguilla's most colorful annual festival is **Carnival,** held jointly under the auspices of the Ministries of Culture and Tourism. The festival begins on the Thursday before the first Monday in August and lasts 10 days. The festival also features spectacular parades with floats, elaborately costumed dancers, terrific bands, and lots of competitions, including the very popular Miss Anguilla contest. Carnival harks back to Emancipation Day, or "August Monday," in 1834, when enslaved Africans all throughout the British colonies were freed. **Boat races** are Anguilla's national sport, and the distinctive swift, high-masted, brightly painted open boats—many of them crafted here on the island—stage a number of exciting races during Carnival. In early May, the **Anguilla Regatta** (www.anguillaregatta.com) features competitive races over a 3-day weekend, with free entertainment and barbecues every night. Anguilla's other major festivals are the 4-day late-March **Moonsplash Music Festival** (www.bankiebanx.net/moonsplash), founded by Anguilla's best-known musician, Bankie Banx, and **Tranquility Jazz Festival** (www.anguillajazz.org), held in the second week of November. On an early April weekend, Island Harbor celebrates fishing and the sea in the **Festival del Mar.**

and at ports of entry. You'll need to present a valid driver's license from your home country and pay a one-time fee of $20.

Remember: Drive on the left side of the road!

Most visitors take a taxi from the airport to their hotel and arrange, at no extra charge, for a rental agency to deliver a car there the following day. All rental companies offer small discounts for rentals of 7 days or more. Car hire is not cheap on Anguilla, and begins at about $40 a day, plus insurance and taxes, which can be steep.

Avis, which is represented by **Apex** in the Valley (*©* **800/331-1212** in the U.S. and Canada, or 264/497-2642; www.avis.com; avisaxa@anguillanet.com), offers regular cars and some four-wheel-drive vehicles as does **Hertz**'s representative, **Triple K Car Rental,** Airport Road (*©* **800/654-3131** in the U.S. and Canada, or 264/497-2934; www.hertz.com; hertzatriplek@anguillanet.com). Local firms include **Connor's Car Rental,** c/o Maurice Connor, South Hill

(© 264/497-6433), **Island Car Rentals,** Airport Road (© 264/497-2723; islandcar@anguillanet.com), and **Carib Rent A Car** (© 264/498-6020; caribcarrental@anguillanet.com).

Note: It's worth pricing a car rental with one of the larger agencies and then checking with your hotel to see what price they can get for you. Many hotels and inns on Anguilla rent all their customers' cars from one or more small local agencies. Your car may not be as new and shiny as some of the other rentals available, but your savings may be considerable.

BY TAXI Taxi fares are posted at Walblake Airport, at the Blowing Point ferry, and in most taxis. Taxis can be pricey, for numerous reasons—so don't take it out on your driver if you think your fare is, well, unfair. For the lowdown on how taxi fares are determined, see "Taxi Zones: Decoding Anguilla Taxi Fares," above. And if you find a taxi driver you like, ask for his card and cellphone number for future rides. You can also get a cab through the **Airport Taxi Stand** at © 264/497-5054 or **Blowing Point Ferry Taxi Stand** at © 264/497-6089. A $4 surcharge goes into effect between 6pm and 6am.

I highly recommend **Accelyn Connor** (© 264/497-0515 or 264/235-8931; premiertaxiandtour@hotmail.com). I also highly recommend the taxi service of **Malcolm Hodge** (© 264/235-7384 or 264/235-7381), a gentleman and a stickler for good service (I once saw him ream out the GM of a big resort for dawdling and possibly keeping a guest from making her ferry on time).

Taxi drivers also make great tour guides; check out "Exploring Anguilla," later in this chapter.

---

2 ACCOMMODATIONS

Anguilla has some of the most desirable high-end properties in the Caribbean—no wonder it's a hot honeymoon destination. But it also has charming small hotels, inns, and guesthouses, many just steps from a gorgeous beach. Villas, another increasingly popular lodging option, range from breathtakingly sumptuous to serviceable; for help in choosing your villa, see "Renting a Villa on Anguilla," below.

At press time, construction had stalled on the island. The ambitious recreation of the homey old **Rendezvous Bay Hotel** into a mega resort/hotel/condo complex was dead, as was the **Fairmont Anguilla** hotel complex development. Most famously, the **Temenos** hotel, villa, and condo complex went bust, but not before the **Greg Norman–designed golf course** opened (Bill Clinton played here in 2007). Today, the course is managed by the team at Cap Juluca.

| (Tips) | **Baby-Equipment Rentals** |

Many resorts on Anguilla are happy to provide cribs and other baby and toddler essentials. If you're renting a villa or condo, however, a convenient, hassle-free option to dragging everything with you (and paying extra-baggage costs) is to rent the kids' stuff you need. **Travel Lite** delivers premium-brand baby- and toddler-equipment rentals (cribs, strollers, car seats, highchairs, and playpens) to your villa door, as well as swings, safety gates, baby monitors, even DVDs. Travel Lite will also help you plan children's parties, holiday celebrations, and activities for the kids. Contact Travel Lite (© **264/476-9990** or 264/476-0999 or go to www.travelliteanguilla.com).

If you're looking for ways to cut costs, consider visiting in the shoulder or low seasons, when rates plummet. Be sure to get on a resort's e-mail list: Many offer terrific money-saving packages (*especially* during the low seasons) advertised via e-mail or Twitter.

Keep in mind that the government imposes a mandatory 10% room tax, and resorts tack on an additional service charge of 10%.

RENTING A VILLA ON ANGUILLA   Anguilla has some of the most stunning and luxurious villas (beach houses) in the Caribbean, but it also offers reasonably priced options. For a list of Anguilla Hotel & Tourism Association–affiliated villas, apartments, and villa rental agents, head to the AHTA website at **www.ahta.ai** (look under "AHTA Members"). Keep in mind that "villa" is used on Anguilla to mean either a separate unit *or* a self-contained unit in a building with several other self-contained units. That's a big difference, so check which kind of villa your rental is before you send off your deposit!

VERY EXPENSIVE

If your idea of a Caribbean getaway includes being waited on by a personal butler and staff of eight, you may want to make one of architect Myron Goldfinger's three beachside villas at **Altamer** (Shoal Bay West, the Valley; © **264/498-4000;** www.altamer.com) your "private palace," as its website suggests. The five- to six-bedroom villas go for prices that nudge upward towards a whopping $50,000 a week in high season, but tumble to a mere $27,500 to $30,000 off season. Creature comforts at all the villas include a private swimming pool, an elaborate game room (with pool table), and entertainment center (including a home theater).

Cap Juluca ★★★ Things are percolating at Cap Juluca. New ownership, new management, and a savvy refashioning of the public spaces have given this much-loved resort a fresh vigor. The newly renovated lobby and the Maundays Club bar have become the beating heart of the resort. This is one of the premier properties on the island, and its name appears over and over again at or near the top of everyone's list of the Caribbean's best. Encircling Maundays Bay's lovely white-sand beach and nestled in luxuriantly landscaped 179-acre grounds, Cap Juluca defines excellence: It employs 375 employees for 98 rooms. A $29-million renovation in 2009 completely repositioned the Main House, capped by a soaring domed ceiling and a glorious Moroccan chandelier. The lobby has two libraries containing 2,000 books and 1,000 DVDs.

Of course, having one of the best beaches on the island doesn't hurt; here, beachside pampering is a daylong affair, with three massage cabanas and five mini beach bars. As you lie in your custom-made beach lounger, you can enjoy lunch, served on the beach from noon to 5. Get there early and you can enjoy Beach Cardio at 8:30am. On Wednesday nights the classics are on tap at Movies on the Beach. The architectural style throughout is quasi-Moorish, with sun-blasted exteriors, white domes, arched doorways, and walled courtyards. All of the spacious rooms and villas are undergoing a "reenvisioning," with luxurious Frette-sheathed beds, ceramic-tile floors, and colonial-style louvered doors opening onto patios, many with pathways leading directly to the sea. All have been outfitted with the essential modcons of 21st-century life—flat-screen TVs, Wi-Fi, iPod docks, Bose Wave music systems—and a number of villas have private plunge pools. Bathrooms are enormous and sheathed in marble. And plans are underway for the building of five new villas.

A 31-year-old chef is hitting his stride at **Pimm's,** which features what it calls "Eurobbean" cuisine—a marriage of European and Caribbean styles and flavors. **Blue** replaces George's as the casual alfresco beachfront spot that's open for breakfast and lunch and dinner drinks (and the twice-weekly barbecue buffet), and the pan-Asian **Spice** has replaced Kemia. In late 2009, Cap Juluca took over management of the Greg Norman–designed **Temenos Golf Course,** just minutes away and the island's first and only golf course. Now open year-round, the resort has taken an aggressive tack in offering well-priced packages and off-season deals; get on the Cap Juluca e-mail list so you can get in on the action. The Cap Juluca is open year-round.

Maundays Bay (P.O. Box 240), Anguilla, B.W.I. ℂ **888/858-5822** in the U.S., or 264/497-6666. Fax 264/497-6617. www.capjuluca.com. 71 units. Winter/spring $995–$1,195 double, from $1,595 suite; off season $425–$695 double, from $695 suite. Children 11 and under stay free in parent's room. Airport boat/taxi transfers: $75 one-way per person semi-private boat; $425 (1–4 persons) private boat. AE, MC, V. **Amenities:** 3 restaurants; 2 bars; babysitting; children's programs (in summer only); fitness center; driving range; golf course; outdoor pool; room service; spa; 3 tennis courts; watersports equipment (extensive). *In room:* A/C, TV/DVD, CD player, hair dryer, minibar, MP3 docking station, Wi-Fi (free).

CuisinArt Resort & Spa ★★★ (Kids) Pillowed in the sand dunes that line a lovely stretch of Rendezvous Bay beach, CuisinArt's whitewashed villas seem transplanted from some sunny Greek isle. This handsomely landscaped resort has an infinity pool that flows all the way to the beach—its long stretches of shallow water are perfect for toddling kids. CuisinArt has a happy, comfortable vibe, with roosters crowing in the morning and lizards skittering in the underbrush and a palm-fringed patio that faces the gleaming pool. And, yes, it is owned by CuisinArt (of blender fame), and yes, it takes its food seriously, with Anguilla's first and only hydroponic farm, an herb garden, and twice-weekly **barbecue buffets ★**, laden with grilled lobster, spit-roasted chicken, ribs, homemade desserts, and sides and salads made with hydroponic-farm-fresh produce.

The rooms are sun-splashed and cheerful, with comfy wicker and dark wood furniture and bright Haitian paintings on the walls. Bathrooms are luxuriously spacious, with lots of marble and fluffy towels. Patios have spectacular ocean views. Six new luxurious villas have been built on the resort's east flank.

The onsite restaurants are very good indeed; you can tack on full and modified meal plans during your stay. The resort's formal main dining room, **Santorini,** serves dinner only. The poolside **Mediterraneo** has more casual fare, with great breakfasts that include delicious corn pancakes and fresh fruit smoothies. The newly renovated and expanded **Venus Spa** features 16 treatment rooms, a Thalasso pool of heated seawater, and an oceanfront relaxation room. CuisinArt frequently has excellent on-and-off season specials with seriously reduced rates.

Rendezvous Bay (P.O. Box 2000), Anguilla, B.W.I. © **800/943-3210** or 264/498-2000. Fax 264/498-2010. www.cuisinartresort.com. 93 units. Winter/spring $740 double, $920–$2,270 suite, $3,150–$3,670 penthouse; off season $400–$495 double, $495–$1,500 suite, $1,700–$2,550 penthouse. Children 11 and under stay free in parent's room. Airport boat/taxi transfers: $65 one-way per person semi-private boat; $350 (1–4 persons) private boat; additional person $25. AE, MC, V. Closed Sept–Oct. **Amenities:** 3 restaurants; 3 bars; babysitting; mountain bikes; bocce court; croquet; billiards room; children's playground; fitness center; Jacuzzi; outdoor pool; room service; spa; 3 tennis courts; watersports equipment (extensive); Wi-Fi (free, in lobby). *In room:* A/C, TV/VCR (DVD in some), CD player, minibar, hair dryer, high-speed Internet ($15/day).

ANGUILLA

8

ACCOMMODATIONS

Down on the (Hydroponic) Farm

It's the world's only hydroponic farm in a greenhouse setting, where hundreds of ripe red tomatoes, foot-long cucumbers, dewy lettuces, and fragrant herbs ripen spectacularly with little more than water and a sprinkling of plant nutrients. There's no soil, no weeds, no bugs. To help feed guests and staff in a country where much of the soil is non-arable and most of the fresh produce must be flown in, CuisinArt hired plant scientist and horticulturist Dr. Howard Resh, Ph.D., to devise a greenhouse that could produce vegetables year-round and withstand strong winds. Today the farm supplies both resort restaurants and the employee cafeteria with an average harvest of 128 heads of lettuce a day. Call ✆ **264/498-2000** to join one of the regularly scheduled free tours with Dr. Resh, who is passionate about every aspect of the farm. You'll even get to sample sweet cherry tomatoes right off the vine.

Malliouhana Hotel & Spa ★★★ (Kids) The island's oldest and most celebrated resort, which in 2010 celebrated its 25th year on the island, resides over a magical setting, its sun-blasted limestone villas terraced on a rocky bluff overlooking the broad sweep of Meads Bay. Pillowed in lush cliffside gardens between two crescent beaches, Malliouhana's 10 hectares (25 acres) hold pools, tiled walkways and open arches, and fountains in a carefully tended landscape of palms, seagrape, agave, and banks of flowers. A sturdy Bismarck palm stands guard in the curving drive up to the hotel, and a Golden Shower tree *(Cassia fistula)* rains buttery-yellow petals on the lawn. The Meads Bay **beaches** at the foot of the resort are some of the island's best, with terrific off-the-beach snorkeling around the rocks. Equally fine is the **Michel Rostang at Malliouhana** restaurant, which garnered a top spot on *Condé Nast Traveler's* Gold List in 2010 as one of the best hotels for food in the Americas and the Caribbean. The world-class **wine cellar** is the largest in the Caribbean, capable of holding 25,000 to 35,000 bottles. If you're traveling with a child, a terrific supervised **playground** surrounds a faux pirate ship (nonguests pay $25 per person per day for access). The **spa ★** is world-class, 15,000 square feet of oceanfront pampering. The terraced public spaces provide privacy-seeking guests with utter discretion.

In spite of all this wonderfulness, some say the resort has gotten a little tired. Yes, amenities could use updating. Hair dryers are circa

1985, and the air-conditioning kicks in and out with a burlesque wheeze. The rooms have no TVs and no clocks. But after spending a few days here, you're so locked in to the circadian rhythms going on around you that these issues seem insignificant. You can tell the time by the pelicans that swoop in languidly every afternoon to roost in the treetops. The week before I arrived, a 6-foot-long leatherback turtle crawled up on the beach here and laid her eggs. Six-foot-long turtle? TV? No contest. And who can deny the pleasure of living amidst walls hung with Haitian art, the incomparable collection of owners Nigel and Leon Roydon?

Truth is, Malliouhana may be a dowager, but she's got stupendous bones and rattling good jewelry. And a new management team is smartly connecting the dots between new and old (and hopefully eliminating that chintzy $10-a-day room Wi-Fi charge, when everyone else—even bare-bones guesthouses—is giving it away for free). All 55 rooms have sea or garden views—sometimes both—and spacious marbled bathrooms. Rooms are decadently large, with closet space designed for steamer trunks and entourages. The day my ship comes in, I plan to book a stay in the sumptuous **Pool Suite,** the size of a small airplane hangar with a bathroom big enough to hold an entire football team. I'll dine on the grand terrace, enveloped in that vast ocean of turquoise, as the pelicans swoop in for the night.

Meads Bay (P.O. Box 173), Anguilla, B.W.I. ⓒ **800/835-0796** in the U.S., or 264/497-6111. Fax 264/497-6011. www.malliouhana.com. 55 units. Winter $860–$1,220 double, $1,175–$3,660 suite; off season $430–$670 double, $660–$2,360 suite. AE, MC, V. Airport boat/taxi transfers: $70 one-way per person. Closed Sept–Oct. **Amenities:** 2 restaurants; 2 bars; babysitting; basketball court; children's playground; concierge; fitness center/gym; Jacuzzi; 3 freshwater outdoor pools; private boat; room service; 4 lighted tennis courts; spa; watersports equipment (extensive). *In room:* A/C and ceiling fan, minibar, hair dryer, Wi-Fi ($10/day).

The Viceroy Anguilla ★★★ It's jaw-droppingly impressive, and it's bringing a new level of luxurious modernity to Anguilla. The crisp white lines and Kelly Wearstler's hyperdesigned interiors may not be your cuppa, but you can't deny the property's "wow" factor. The Viceroy delivers what it promises. And what it promises is a lifestyle immersion in 21st-century high chic. From afar, the 35-acre resort, which opened in December 2009, looks like a small city landed on the promontory between Meads Bay and Barnes Bay. The architecture comes into focus up close, the sleek white structures smartly juxtaposed against the blue Anguillan sea and sky—the layout has good feng shui. Rooms and suites are outfitted with every 21st-century toy, furnished in a palette of cream, sand, and brown punctuated with golden sunbursts (the Viceroy logo). Every suite (except for the Viceroy King) has its own plunge pool; six "rooftop" suites are duplexes with the plunge pool situated on the second-story terrace, with dizzying sea views. The four- and five-bedroom villas are luxe dialed to 11—in the parlance of one very astute fellow, they're "sick." Each villa—more like an exquisite mini-mansion, really—comes with a ridiculously fabulous kitchen, master baths with deep-soaking tubs and outdoor showers, a pool and outdoor cabana, grill, and hot tub.

Coba, the main restaurant, is encased in glass for seamless sea and sky views. The **Sunset Bar** feels like the heart of the resort, but an entire second, self-contained family-friendly section has at its center a sprawling pool and restaurant, **Aleta.**

I love the Viceroy's community spirit: Its employee base is 90% Anguillan. One minor issue: The beach around the resort has had some erosion from storms (it's expected to build up again); the best beach is a short walk (or shuttle) away on Meads Bay, where the Viceroy lounges and umbrellas have been set up. The Viceroy is open year-round.

Barnes Bay (P.O. Box 8028), Anguilla, B.W.I. ⓒ **888/622-4567** in the U.S., or 264/497-7000. Fax 264/497-7001. www.viceroyhotelsandresorts.com/anguilla. 166 units. Winter $695–$995 double, $1,095–$1,195 1-bedroom suite, $2,295–$2,695 2-bedroom suite, $4,750–$6,500 3-bedroom suite, $7,500–$9,500 villa; off season $495–$795 double, $895–$995 1-bedroom suite, $1,095–$1,295 2-bedroom suite, $1,795–$2,095 3-bedroom suite, $2,500–$4,500 villa. Airport boat/taxi transfers: $85 one-way per person. AE, DC, MC, V. Closed Sept–Oct. **Amenities:** 3 restaurants; 2 bars; babysitting; children's programs; concierge; fitness center/gym/spinning room; 3 outdoor pools; room service; spa; watersports equipment (extensive). *In room:* A/C and ceiling fan, TV, kitchen or kitchenette (in 2-bedroom deluxe suites, 3-bedroom suites, and villas), hair dryer, minibar, plunge pools (except in Viceroy King rooms), Wi-Fi (free).

EXPENSIVE

Frangipani Beach Resort ★★ Set directly on a spectacular stretch of Meads Bay beach, this appealing pink-hued resort continues to upgrade its rooms and public spaces to stay competitive in an increasingly competitive market. The Spanish Mediterranean–style buildings feature one-, two-, and three-bedroom configurations. The one-bedroom suites are the best, with gleaming stainless-steel kitchens, ocean views, and spacious living quarters. (All junior suites, one-bedroom suites, and two-bedroom suites have full kitchens and washer/dryers.) It has a nice big infinity pool, and the **Straw Hat** restaurant (which moved here in 2009) is an island favorite.

Meads Bay (P.O. Box 1378), Anguilla, B.W.I. ⓒ **866/780-5165** in the U.S., or 264/497-6442. Fax 264/497-6440. www.frangipaniresort.com. 18 units. Winter $385–$525 double, from $685 suite; off season $325–$425 double, from $525 suite. Rates include continental breakfast. AE, MC, V. Closed Sept–Nov. **Amenities:** Restaurant; bar; babysitting; 2 pools; tennis court; watersports equipment. *In room:* A/C and ceiling fans, TV/DVD, CD player, hair dryer, full kitchen (in suites only), washer/dryer (in suites only), Wi-Fi (free).

At press time, **La Sirena Resort** (www.sirenaresort.com) was being refurbished under new ownership (Caribbean hoteliers Robin and Sue Ricketts) and management. It's expected to open in October 2010 as the **Anacaona Boutique Hotel,** a stylish, good-value, 27-room hotel steps away from Meads Bay. Stay tuned.

Anguilla Great House Beach Resort (Value) This old-time, low-key resort sits on a delicious stretch of beach along Rendezvous Bay. This particular patch of sand has what many do not: a shaded grove of trees, under which you can park yourself in a beach chair for hours of breezy bliss. You may be joined by a handful of guests and a couple of playful dogs—or you may have this paradise to yourself. Unfortunately, that may be because the resort is not so great these days, with unkempt lawns and rooms in need of a revamp. Worse, hotel detritus is often piled up behind the cottages. Some of the staff, too, seems to have given up. On the plus side, the pool is nicely maintained, and the gingerbread-trimmed cottages are just steps from the beach. Many (especially 111–125) boast water views from their back and front porches—ask for one of these. Rooms in each cottage are cheek-by-jowl, but guests seem respectful of their neighbors' close proximity. Most rooms have pitched ceilings and bright local artworks, and the shower-only bathrooms are clean and well-kept. The alfresco restaurant, **Old Carib,** serves food that often is much better than the sad-sack ambience warrants: savory shrimp in garlic butter and wine, say, or Creole ratatouille. If you'd like a self-catering unit, and don't mind being a few minutes from the beach, ask about the rates for nearby **Kerwin Kottages**—four self-catering one-, two-, and three-bedroom units that enjoy hotel privileges and represent excellent value.

Rendezvous Bay, Anguilla, B.W.I. (C) **264/497-6061.** Fax 264/497-6019. www. anguillagreathouse.com. 35 units. Winter $310–$340 double; off season $210– $240 double. AE, MC, V. **Amenities:** Restaurant; bar; outdoor pool; room service; watersports equipment. *In room:* A/C and ceiling fan, TV, fridge, hair dryer, Wi-Fi (in some, free).

Carimar Beach Club ★ (Kids) This 24-apartment resort is sitting pretty on one of the loveliest stretches of beach on the island. It's a small, folksy place, broken into six villas surrounding a flower-filled courtyard. It has no pool or restaurant, but Blanchards and Jacala are just next door; and the restaurants at Malliouhana and Frangipani are within easy walking distance. Villas 1 and 6 are oceanfront, with the priciest rates. The suites are simply but comfortably furnished one- or two-bedroom apartments with fully equipped kitchens; the two-bedroom apartments have two baths, which makes them great for

families. Guests get together on their patios or balconies for drinks or
else stay glued to their beach lounges for the fabulous sunsets.

Meads Bay (P.O. Box 65, the Valley), Anguilla, B.W.I. ✆ **264/497-6881.** Fax 264/497-6071. www.carimar.com. 24 units. Winter $390–$470 1-bedroom suite, $515–$600 2-bedroom suite; off season $200–$295 1-bedroom suite, $295–$395 2-bedroom suite. Extra person $75. AE, DISC, MC, V. **Amenities:** Babysitting; bikes; concierge; 2 tennis courts; watersports equipment. *In room:* A/C (in bedrooms only) and ceiling fan, TV/VCR, hair dryer, full kitchen, Wi-Fi (free).

Easy Corner Villas (Value)   On a bluff overlooking Sandy Ground (aka Road Bay), this place is a good 15-minute drive from the best beaches, so you'll definitely want a car. No problem: The owner is Anguillan Maurice Connor, the same entrepreneur who rents many of the cars on the island. Easy Corner's one-, two-, and three-bedroom apartments (known as villas) are set on modestly landscaped grounds with beach views from some of the private porches. Each comes with kitchen facilities, an airy combination living/dining room, good storage space, and simple furnishings. Some guests have complained about the size of the bathrooms here—but I'm not sure why, especially at these prices. Maid service is available for an extra charge, except on Sunday. Note that new buildings below partially obstruct the views of Sandy Ground and the sea from a number of units—but even with less of a view, this is still a good-value spot.

South Hill (P.O. Box 65, the Valley), Anguilla, B.W.I. ✆ **264/497-6433.** Fax 264/497-6410. www.easycornervilla.com. 12 units. Winter $210 suite, $190 1-bedroom villa, $230 2-bedroom villa, $295 3-bedroom villa; off season $175 suite, $155 1-bedroom villa, $195 2-bedroom villa, $255 3-bedroom villa. AE, MC, V. *In room:* A/C and ceiling fan, TV/VCR, kitchen.

Kú (Value)   Many of the most famous of the island's resorts hide themselves away in acres of landscaped privacy. Kú, on the other hand, is happily in the heart of things at Shoal Bay. It's an easy barefoot back-and-forth walk from the island's most popular beach to good-value quarters on stratospherically priced Anguilla. At press time, renovations (much-needed, some say) were scheduled for all the suites, each with a living/dining room and full kitchen, a good-size bedroom and bathroom, and an oceanfront terrace or ocean-view balcony. Kú's beach bar and pool is a daylong gathering place for guests, who range in age from 30-something to AARP members of long standing. **Uncle Ernie's,** one of Anguilla's best-known beach bars and grills, is just next door, as is the Shoal Bay Scuba Center. Other restaurants and bars are strung out for a good mile or so along the beach, which is increasingly chock-a-block with rental umbrellas, beach chairs, and day-trippers from St. Martin. In short, Shoal Bay is Anguilla's only crowded beach, which makes Kú a great place for action and people watching—but not necessarily for blissed-out Caribbean tranquility.

Shoal Bay East (P.O. Box 51), Anguilla, B.W.I. ℂ **800/869-5827** or 264/497-2011. Fax 264/497-3355. www.ku-anguilla.com. 27 units. Winter $315–$475 double; off season $180–$220 double. AE, MC, V. **Amenities:** Restaurant; bar; babysitting; dive shop; gym; outdoor pool; spa. *In room:* A/C and ceiling fan, TV/DVD, CD player, Internet ($8/day), kitchen.

Serenity Cottages ★ (Finds) With a great location at the quiet end of Shoal Bay Beach, Serenity is one place that lives up to its name. The crowds at Uncle Ernie's and Kú are a brisk 15-minute stroll away along the beach. Anguillan owner Kenneth Rogers keeps his eye on every detail here, and it all runs smoothly. The two cottages are surrounded by lovingly tended flowers and trees (at least one unit's shower has a glass wall brushed by palm fronds). The furnishings have a solid, understated elegance, with a good deal of dark wood furniture offset by cheerful floral fabrics, and the views from the rooms and their balconies through the gardens to the sea are marvelous. The bar in the open-air restaurant functions as a meeting place. Serenity also has a toes-in-the-sand beach hut bar and restaurant, and Gwen's Reggae Grill is just steps away down the beach. One thing to keep in mind: There are coral reefs in the sea here, and the waters can be rough; a short walk will take you past the reefs to Shoal's usually calmer waters.

Shoal Bay East (P.O. Box 309, the Valley), Anguilla, B.W.I. ℂ **264/497-3328.** Fax 264/497-3867. www.serenity.ai. 18 units. Winter $325–$350 studio, $425–$450 1-bedroom suite; $525–$550 2-bedroom suite; off season $195–$225 studio, $295–$325 1-bedroom suite; $395–$425 2-bedroom suite. Extra person $100. MC, V. **Amenities:** Two restaurants; beach bar; babysitting; limited room service; Wi-Fi (lobby). *In room:* Ceiling fan, TV, fridge, hair dryer (in some), kitchen (in suites only).

INEXPENSIVE

La Vue Bed & Breakfast (Value) This very nice addition to the inexpensive priced lodging scene in Anguilla is set on a bluff high above Sandy Ground and represents great value. Its rooms are sprawling and comfortably furnished—all have king-size beds and fully equipped kitchens—and some have patios with splendid views of the harbor below. The upstairs rooms in back are bigger but lack full ocean views, and the units on the first floor are bigger still. Room #201 has a nice living-room area and great harbor views; #204 has a handsome bed and a bigger patio. A "Caribbean continental" breakfast is included, Wi-Fi is free throughout, and you're minutes from the action at Sandy Ground—La Vue looks like a winner.

Back St., above Sandy Ground (P.O. Box 52), Anguilla, B.W.I. ℂ **264/497-6623.** Fax 264/497-6410. www.lavueanguilla.com. 17 units. Studio $90–$130, 1-bedroom

suite $165, 2-bedroom suite $265. Children 11 and under free in parent's room.
Extra person $50. Rates include continental breakfast. MC, V. *In room:* A/C and ceiling fan, TV/VCR, hair dryer, kitchen, Wi-Fi (free).

Lloyd's Bed and Breakfast (Value)

The island's oldest inn opened in 1959 on the crest of Crocus Hill in the Valley. This family-owned B&B is the sort of place that makes you feel at home the moment you walk through the door. The bright yellow exterior, with lime green shutters and a wide, inviting veranda, is exuberantly Caribbean. Inside, the smallish rooms have filmy curtains at the windows and hand-crocheted bedspreads. Lloyd's main room—part dining room, part lounge—with its traditional wood and cane furniture, old prints, and small library, is the perfect place for island travelers (many are repeat guests) to trade tall tales. There's only one drawback here: Lloyd's is not on a beach. Still, there's an excellent beach down the hill at Crocus Bay (site of the jumping hot spot **Da'Vida;** see below), and since nothing is very far away on Anguilla, the island's other beaches are just a short drive. A full, family-style breakfast is included in the price, which makes Lloyd's one of the most charming bargains in the Caribbean.

Crocus Hill (P.O. Box 52, the Valley), Anguilla, B.W.I. (C) **264/497-2351.** Fax 264/497-3028. www.lloyds.ai. 9 units. $135 double. Rates include breakfast. MC, V. **Amenities:** Restaurant (breakfast only); bar; Internet. *In room:* A/C and ceiling fan, TV.

Sydans (Value)

Anguillan Anne Edwards is the tirelessly helpful proprietor of Sydans, a hospitable family-run inn that overlooks Sandy Ground's large salt pond and is only steps from the sea. Some guests from the States and Europe have been coming here every year for 20 years; others use this as a long-term home-away-from-home. All rooms have kitchens (some stoves have burners, but not ovens), bathrooms with tub/shower combinations, and homey bed- and sitting rooms. The second-floor units overlooking the salt pond are a birder's delight, with spottings of pelicans, cranes, herons, and seasonal birds; ground-floor rooms open into a central courtyard, lack the pond view, and are less quiet. Sydans is very much part of the Sandy Ground neighborhood: You'll hear roosters at sunrise, see the school bus drop off neighborhood children in the afternoon, and know when Johnno's or the Pumphouse has live music until the wee hours. Things are casual here (water outages are not unknown), but if you ask Ms. Edwards for an extra reading lamp or towels, they'll be in your room by the time you're back from the beach.

Sandy Ground, Anguilla, B.W.I. (C) **264/497-3180** or 264/235-7740. www.inna.ai/sydans. From $100 double. MC, V. *In room:* A/C, ceiling fan, TV, kitchen.

3 DINING

To many discerning diners, Anguilla is the Caribbean's premier dining destination, and native Anguillan chefs like Dale Carty (Tasty's and Dune Preserve) and Glendon Carty (Ripple's and Cap Juluca) are essential elements in the island's effervescent food-and-drink scene.

Eating on Anguilla is not cheap, however—a high percentage of what ends up on your plate has been imported. Fortunately, many local chefs are increasingly packing their menus with sustainable choices: **local seafood** and **Anguilla-grown produce and grains.** Fresh, locally caught fish—red snapper, yellowtail snapper, yellowfin tuna, grouper, mahimahi, red hein, bass, bonito—gets plenty of play on restaurant menus, as does Anguillan lobster and local crayfish, big and sweet and at the other end of the size spectrum from its mudbug cousin, the crawfish. *Note:* At many restaurants, prices for fish, lobster, and crayfish rise and fall depending on availability.

A forward-thinking government agricultural initiative to **farm vegetables** on a large swath of land in Central (with a bit of a heavy-handed slogan in "Farm Today or Starve Tomorrow") is putting fresh sweet potatoes, peppers, corn, squash, tomatoes, lettuces, and pigeon peas into the marketplace. Old farmers are rediscovering the pleasure of growing food, and new farmers (and future chefs) are being initiated into this agricultural renaissance.

Most restaurants include a service charge in the menu pricing. The menu should state whether service is included, but always confirm whether gratuities are added. In many instances tips are pooled among the staff (including the back of the house), so it never hurts to add a little extra if you feel your server warrants it.

You won't want to miss the all-you-can-eat **barbecue buffets** at **CuisinArt Resort & Spa** (© 264/498-2000; www.cuisinartresort. com), with grilled lobster, chicken, and ribs; homemade desserts; and delicious sides and salads made with hydroponic-farm-fresh produce; a string band provides the entertainment.

EXPENSIVE

Michel Rostang at Malliouhana Restaurant ★★★ FRENCH
MEDITERRANEAN   You dine ever so dramatically in a sweeping open-sided pavilion set on a cliffside promontory over the sea; down below big bass float, mesmerized by the lights illuminating the rocks. It makes for a truly memorable night—and the food lives up to the magical setting. The menu—classic Mediterranean infused with Caribbean accents—is supervised by the Parisian two-star Michelin chef Michel Rostang and prepared by head chef Fred Cougnon and a staff

Resources for Self-Catering

Anguilla is pricey enough as it is without having to pay marked-up hotel prices for basics like milk, soft drinks, snacks, and beer. For groceries, drinks, and kitchen staples, stock up at **Albert's Supermarket** (📞 **264/497-2240**), in the Valley, a large, full-service grocery store. In Anguilla's West End, you can get a full complement of groceries and other sundries at **Foods Ninety-Five** (📞 **264/497-6196**), just after the entrance to Cap Juluca. **Ashley & Sons** (📞 **264/497-2641; www.ashleyandsons.com**), in the South Valley, has a wide selection of beverages, snacks, fruit, and toiletries. Monday through Saturday, don't miss stopping at the **Fat Cat Gourmet** (📞 **264/497-2307; www.fatcat.ai**) by Albert's supermarket in the Valley; hands down, this place has the tastiest take-out goodies (from entire meals to cakes) on Anguilla. This is also a great place to pick up snacks for a picnic on the beach.

of 26. Many of the Malliouhana classics remain on the menu, but the house specialty is a whole snapper baked in a case of salt with vegetables in papilotte (for two). Equally good is the pan-seared scallops on a bed of buttery sautéed leeks. Start with lobster and sweetpea soup under a golden crust of pastry or the marinated snapper and scallop tartar. Kids dine on a special children's menu from 6 to 7pm and then are whisked away so the grownups can have some fun. The extraordinary wine cellar—overseen by sommelier Albert Lake for the past 20 years—holds some 25,000 to 35,000 bottles, many rare vintages.

Meads Bay. 📞 **264/497-6111**. www.malliouhana.com. Reservations required. Main courses $36–$44. AE, MC, V. Daily 7–11:30am, 12:30–3pm, and 7:30–10:30pm.

Blanchards ★★★ INTERNATIONAL   In 1994, when Anguilla was just beginning to attract high-spending foodies, Bob and Melinda Blanchard opened a restaurant at the end of a dirt track to the sea. It was elegantly casual and offered a fresh and inventive haute cuisine. Frankly, many wondered how long Blanchard's would survive. Since then, this place with indoor-outdoor dining on the beach (now reached by a good road) has become *the* place to eat for many foodies. It's not uncommon to see dinner guests arrive here clutching copies of the Blanchards' book *A Trip to the Beach*, a charming account of how they created their restaurant. Now Blanchards' only problem is how to live up to its reputation. No problem: The crackerjack staff keeps the engine humming night after night. Behind tall teal shutters (open to the sea breezes), diners enjoy sophisticated but unfussy food with a spirited Caribbean flair. Among the perpetual favorites are sublime lobster-and-shrimp cakes—worth the trip alone. The Caribbean sampler features oven-crisped mahimahi with coconut, lime, and ginger; roasted Anguilla lobster; and jerk chicken with cinnamon-rum bananas. You can buy one of the Blanchards' newest tomes on the way out; oh, and those are son Jesse's colorful paintings on the walls. At press time, Blanchards was serving a recession-friendly three-course prix fixe meal.

Meads Bay. ✆ **264/497-6100.** www.blanchardsrestaurant.com. Reservations required. Main courses $38–$58. AE, MC, V. Mon–Sat 6:30–10pm. Closed Sept 1–Nov 1 and Sun and Mon in off season.

Hibernia ★★ (Finds) FRENCH/INDOCHINESE Anguillan residents since 1987, Chef Raoul Rodriguez and his wife, hostess Mary Pat O'Hanlon, have converted a traditional West Indian cottage at the east end of Anguilla into an inventive restaurant decorated with French- and Indonesian-inspired *objets d'art* collected from their annual world travels. The food here is equally international, with touches of the West Indies, Thailand, and France. This is a place where it's tempting to make a meal of starters, perhaps the Caribbean fish soup and a terrine of foie gras with aged rum, cashews, and dates. Main courses include tender duck breast, classic beef tenderloin, and Caribbean seafood prepared Thai style. Save room for the homemade ice cream in a dreamy selection of flavors that includes mint, lavender, and chestnut. Be sure to make a reservation: Hibernia has only 11 tables.

Island Harbour. ✆ **264/497-4290.** www.hiberniarestaurant.com. Reservations recommended. Main courses $32–$45. AE, MC, V. Tues–Sat noon–2pm and 7–9pm; Sun 7–9pm. Closed Aug–Sept and Mon–Tues during low season.

Jacala ★★ (Finds) FRENCH At press time everybody was fever-ishly talking up the new boy on the Meads Bay block. Jacala was opened by two veterans of the local restaurant scene, Jacques Borderon and Alain Laurent, who worked at Malliouhana, practically next door, for 24 years. It's right on Meads Bay beach, and you can almost reach out and grasp the last rays of sun melting into the sea. It's a fairly simple menu, from a modest fettuccine with sautéed fresh tomato, garlic, and basil to a steak tartar to grilled lobster or whole snapper; the brilliance is in the execution.

Meads Bay. ✆ **264/498-5888.** Reservations recommended. Main courses $16–$44. MC, V. Tues–Sat noon–2pm and 7–9pm.

KoalKeel ★★ CARIBBEAN/ASIAN This handsome restaurant is housed in one of the island's oldest stone houses, a former sugar plantation "Great House" from the 1790s. (The oldest dwelling on the island, originally a building sheltering slaves, is just across the street.) Executive chef Gwendolyn Smith and chef Leonard "Smoke" Sharplis prepare an eclectic menu of local specialties with Asian-inspired flavors and techniques, including island pigeon-pea soup and homemade dumplings, and "rice paper" snapper in a lemon-soya sauce. Meats are slow-cooked in the 200-year-old "Old Rock Oven." Oenophiles will appreciate the 15,000-bottle wine cellar; there's also a lounge for aged rums and cigars. Pastries here are terrific; be sure to stop by the KoalKeel Patisserie one morning between 6 and 9am to get some of the French bread, croissants, or other treats available for takeout. KoalKeel offers complimentary shuttle service to and from a number of Anguilla resorts. With the exception of the delicious pastries, some feel the quality of the food here is inconsistent; that said, the pleasure of dining in this historic house is considerable.

The Valley. ✆ 264/497-2930. www.koalkeel.com. Reservations required. Main courses $28–$75. AE, MC, V. Mon–Sat 6:30–8:30pm.

Mango's ★★ CARIBBEAN   This pavilion a few steps from the edge of the sea, on the northwestern part of the island, fulfills anyone's fantasies of a relaxed but classy beachfront eatery; its doors open to the breezes and its walls are brightened by local murals. All the breads and desserts, including ice cream and sorbet, are made fresh daily on the premises. You might start with Barnes Bay lobster cakes and homemade tomato tartar sauce, or creamy conch chowder flavored with smoked bacon and chockfull of onions and potatoes. Grilled local crayfish is splashed with lime, curry, and coconut; chicken is barbecued with rum, and snapper filet is marinated in a soy-sesame-tahini mix, but the simple grilled fish with lemon-and-herb butter shines.

Seaside Grill, Barnes Bay. ✆ 264/497-6479. Reservations required for dinner. Main courses $26–$45. AE, MC, V. Wed–Mon 6:30–9pm. Closed Aug–Oct.

Pimms ★★ CARIBBEAN/CONTINENTAL   I've never, ever had a bad meal at a Cap Juluca restaurant but I've rarely had a memorable "wow" meal either. Until now. Johnny Clero, the 31-year-old chef of Pimms, is hitting his stride as the resort's star rises once again. They call the food here (a little too cutely) "Eurobbean" cuisine. Start with the signature lobster bisque with creamy cognac or a sprightly asparagus and summer bean salad. Follow with grilled Anguillan crayfish, West Indian lobster ravioli, or a deftly cooked Black Angus beef tenderloin. The setting alongside Maundays Bay is high romance; here's hoping Pimms and Clero can keep serving food that measures up to the ambience.

Cap Juluca, Maundays Bay. ✆ 264/497-6666. www.capjuluca.com. Reservations recommended. Main courses $23–$49. AE, DC, MC, V. Tues–Sun 7:30–10am.

Straw Hat ★ CARIBBEAN/INTERNATIONAL   In its new location at the Frangipani Beach Resort, the Straw Hat has barely missed a beat as one of the island's most satisfying culinary experiences. Perched on a deck overlooking Meads Bay, the Straw Hat does a very brisk business indeed, packing 'em in with consistently good food and that sizzling setting. The indoor dining area is light, bright, open to the beach and sea, with paintings by local artist Lynn Bernbaum (see "Shopping," below). The menu shies away from the more contrived touches of some local fusion menus: sauces may be drizzled, but, as yet, no foam. The Straw Hat Seafood Stew (shrimp, crayfish, fresh local fish simmered with ginger, coconut milk, cilantro, and tomatoes, served over coconut rice) is a very reasonable $36. Smart buys include snapper, tuna, chicken, or shrimp "plain grilled" with two sides (fried plantains, Caesar salad, garlic mashed potatoes, Anguillan rice and peas).

Frangipani Beach Resort, Meads Bay. ℂ **264/497-8300.** www.strawhat.com. Reservations recommended. Main courses $23–$48. AE, DC, MC, V. Daily 7:30–10am, noon–3pm, and 6:30–9pm.

Trattoria Tramonto ★ (Kids) NORTHERN ITALIAN   This favorite of many, serving solid Italian food, is on the West End tip of the island. There's even a Bellini, to make Italiphiles remember the ones they drank at Harry's Bar in Venice. The chef takes special care with his appetizers, including sautéed shrimp with saffron and a porcini-mushroom sauce, and spicy hot penne with a garlic, tomato, and red-pepper sauce. The house specialty is a sublime lobster-filled ravioli in a heart-stopping cream sauce. Kids are treated like celebrities here.

Shoal Bay West. ℂ **264/497-8819.** www.trattoriatramonto.com. Reservations required. Main courses lunch $16–$36, dinner $24–$38. MC, V. Tues–Sun noon–3pm and 6:30–9pm. Closed Sept–Oct.

Veya ★★ CARIBBEAN/ASIAN   With a transporting ambience that one writer likened to an "Indonesian treehouse," Veya is perched on the hillside above Sandy Ground and enveloped in bamboo, date and coconut palms, and flowering frangipani trees. Veya's fans—and there are lots of them—love the feeling of looking out into tropical greenery and prize the consistently excellent food and service. Detractors find the setting more memorable than the food. Veya's extensive wine list earned it a 2009 *Wine Spectator* Award of Excellence. The restaurant serves what owners Carrie and Jerry Bogar call the "cuisine of the sun," with ingredients and styles of preparation taken from a wide range of sunny countries straddling the equator. You might start with the grilled watermelon and poached shrimp appetizer, sprinkled with spiced pecans and mint. Favorite entrees include local crayfish with a ginger beurre blanc, vanilla-cured duck breast, and five-spiced pork tenderloin. Veya's Tasting Menu ($85), a five-course medley of the chef's current favorites, is a good way to sample the offerings. **Veya's Café** (② **264/498-2233;** Mon–Sat 9am–5pm), a cluster of shaded outdoor tables downstairs, serves great panini and salads ($8–$14) and freshly baked johnnycakes and does a brisk take-out business (whole jerk, tandoori, or garlic-herb rotisserie chicken).

Sandy Ground. ② **264/498-8392.** www.veya-axa.com Reservations required. Main courses $28–$46. AE, MC, V. Mon–Sat 6–10pm.

MODERATE

If you find yourself in the Valley at lunchtime, remember two tasty, good-value spots. Longtime favorite **English Rose** (② **264/497-5353**) serves up generous portions of stews and grills. A newcomer, the **Valley Bistro** (② **264/497-8300**) is the place to head if you are longing for pasta, pizza, or delicious French onion soup and a croque-monsieur. Both have daily specials, and you could eat at either for less than $20 (both closed Sun).

Da'Vida ★★ CARIBBEAN   Does it really matter that this place is slicker and more uptown than other island beach bars? Nah, not with this sunny vibe, beautiful setting, and delicious food—and admirable efforts at cooking sustainably with local ingredients. After Roy's casual beachside restaurant moved from Crocus Bay to Sandy Ground a few years ago, Crocus Bay had no restaurant and fell into decline—until the Da'Vida complex opened in 2009 on the beach at Crocus Bay. Anguillan Chef Guy Gumbs' restaurant quickly became one of the island's favorite places for celebratory dinners. Da'Vida—whose motto is "Celebrate Life"—comprises an upscale restaurant (with a happening bar/special-events space upstairs) and the more casual **Bayside Grill.** Everything is just steps from shimmering Crocus Bay. The main restaurant is open to the sea on three sides, but the dark wood tables and crisp linen and crystal make the mood more elegant than casual. The menu draws heavily on local seafood (crayfish, snapper, grouper) and does creative, often Asian-inspired twists on traditional island cuisine. Start with lobster bisque with corn fritters and cinnamon cream or try the sweet potato gnocchi with sweet basil and tomato coulis. Mains include coconut-crusted scallops and grilled local fish (snapper, grouper, lobster, crayfish). Ask for an order of johnnycakes. The more casual Bayside Grill has that same brilliant seaside setting, with picnic tables under the palms, clusters of tables under umbrellas, and a menu of grilled favorites (barbecued chicken or ribs, with rice and peas and salad). Beach chairs and umbrellas mean that guests here can alternate dining with dipping into the sea.

Crocus Bay. (② **264/498-5433.** www.davidaanguilla.com. Main courses (restaurant) $32–$39. Barbecued ribs or chicken (Bayside Grill) $18–$20. Da'Vida: Tues–Sun 11am–3pm and 6:30–9pm; Bayside Grill 11am–5pm.

Sun, Sand, Music & Barbecue

Anguilla has no casinos or other gambling spots—the local Church Council, which has its say in matters such as this, ensures that the island stays that way. If you feel the need for some casino action, St. Maarten and its 14 casinos are just a 20-minute ferry ride (and a short cab ride from there) away.

In high season, various hotels host barbecues or hire calypso groups and string bands, both local and imported, for entertainment. But you should really get out and sample the island's wonderful **beach bars and grills,** which serve great food and drink and feature live music at least 1 day a week. (You can have a light meal and a drink for around $20.) These places are about as casual as casual can be, but remember, this is modest Anguilla; if you've been swimming, cover up before you sit down to eat.

At Upper Shoal Bay, check out **Gwen's Reggae Bar & Grill** (© 264/497-2120), which features Gwen Webster's barbecue daily into the early evening; on Sunday it showcases live reggae performances. Ask for a side order of Gwen's special slaw. The palm grove here is one of the few naturally shady seaside spots on the island, and it comes with hammocks. At the more populated end of Shoal, island institution **Uncle Ernie's** (© 264/497-3907) is open from morning 'til at least sunset, serving up generous plates of chicken and ribs, fresh fish, fries, slaw, and cold beer.

At the west end of the island, a sign points off the main road down a bumpy road to Nat Richardson's **Palm Grove Bar & Grill** (© 264/497-4224) at Junk's Hole. Islanders and visitors flock here for what many think are Anguilla's most succulent grilled lobsters and lightest johnnycakes. Bring your swimming gear and snorkel until your lobster comes off the grill.

Over at Sandy Ground, the **SandBar** (© 264/498-0171; sandbar.anguilla@email.com) is the first—and currently the only—place to get tapas at Sandy Ground. Opened in late 2009 by Anguillan husband-and-wife Joash Proctor and Denise Carr, this indoor/outdoor beachbar is the island hot spot for a sundowner and a wide range of tapas (including grilled shrimp, conch fritters with payaya chutney, chicken or beef satay with peanut curry), priced from $6 to $12. The Sandbar is open from around 4pm to at least 10pm and at least midnight on nights when there is live music. Another island favorite, **Johnno's** (© 264/497-2728; closed Mon), has live music most Wednesday evenings (reggae and soca) and Sunday afternoons (jazz). Burgers and grills are available all day, or you can just order a rum punch, plop down at one of the picnic tables on the beach, and watch the spectacular Sandy Ground sunset. A few minutes' stroll down the beach, **Elvis** (© 264/461-0101) opened in 2007 and gives Johnno's some sunset competition. Elvis's bar occupies an Anguillan boat beached on the sand, with tables and chairs nearby. There's great rum punch and nibbles (sometimes barbeque) and live music several times a week.

Halfway between Johnno's and Elvis, overlooking the Salt Pond, the **Pumphouse** (© 264/497-5154; www.pumphouse-anguilla.com; closed Sun) has rafter-shaking live music almost every night, enormous cheeseburgers, and crisp Caesar salads. *Warning:* One Pumphouse rum punch is equivalent to at least two anywhere else! This former rock-salt factory, with some of its original machinery still in place, is the funkiest bar on the island—unless that award should go to Bankie Banx's **Dune Preserve** (© 264/497-2660; www.dunepreserve.com) at Rendezvous Bay, with its own salvaged boats and the island's most seriously relaxed musician. Reggae star Bankie Banx is usually in attendance and joins in the live music performances here several times a week. Heading from Bankie's toward the east end of the island, keep an eye out for the small sign that points from the main road to **Smokey's** (© 264/497-6582; wwwsmokeysatthecove.com) at Cove Bay. Delicious crayfish, lobster, ribs, and spicy wings are served up most days—this is one of the island's top spots to chill. Smokey's has live music Saturday afternoons and Sunday evenings.

Tasty's ★★ CARIBBEAN/AMERICAN   Set inside a Creole cottage painted in teals, blues, and lavenders is Dale Carty's uplifting hymn to the local cuisine. It's located on the right as you head through South Hill along the main road toward the East End. Colorful island murals by artist Susan Croft line the walls. Trained in international cuisine in the kitchen in Malliouhana, the award-winning chef prepares food that is consistently, well, *tasty*. In Carty's hands, local specialties sing with flavor. Conch Creole is paired with coconut dumplings; grilled snapper is elevated with a savory onion-pepper-tomato herb sauce. Tasty's shrimp are sautéed in coconut curry sauce and served with a sweet potato puree. Among the delicious breakfast entrees is a Caribbean sampler breakfast: fried and salt fish, johnnycakes, fried plantains, and bush tea. Okay, you're not on the sea—you're on a main road with the sounds of passing traffic, in fact—but the interior's bright pastels are welcoming nonetheless.

South Hill. ✆ **264/497-2737.** www.tastysrestaurant.com. Dinner reservations recommended. Main courses $18–$30 (lobster $36–$40). AE, MC, V. Daily 7:30am–3pm and 7–10pm.

INEXPENSIVE

Delicious, affordable food is served at Anguilla's fabulous beachside bars and barbecue shacks. See the sidebar "Sun, Sand, Music & Barbecue," above, for details.

E's Oven ★ (Finds) CARIBBEAN/INTERNATIONAL   Darting from beach to beach, it's easy to neglect some of Anguilla's inland restaurants. This place at South Hill (by the big curve in the main road) is very popular with locals, and when you eat here, you'll know why. The coconut-flavored pumpkin soup and garlic-crusted crayfish

---

(Tips)   Roadside Eats

Especially on the weekends, you'll notice a number of **roadside food stalls** in the Valley near the outdoor People's Market (a great place to get fresh fruit and veggies) and around the roundabout by the school and library. Out on the island, you may see other food stalls, often doing barbeque in grills fashioned out of oil drums. This is a great way to sample such local delicacies as bull foot soup, pigtail soup, goat water, roti, and fungi. Keep an eye out for **Hungry's,** the mobile food van that is usually parked near the Post Office in the Valley. You can eat yourself silly on sandwiches, wraps, curries, or stews, usually for a good deal less than $10.

ANGUILLA

DINING

tails are yummy, and the seafood pasta is one of the main reasons some friends of mine say they keep coming back to Anguilla! The dining room is simple, with tables and chairs, nothing fancy, but perfectly pleasant.

South Hill. ☎ **264/498-8258.** Main courses $10–$20. MC, V. Wed–Mon 11am–midnight.

Ripples ★ (**Value**) CARIBBEAN/INTERNATIONAL   Set in a restored clapboard house, Ripples has a raised deck, comfy wicker chairs, a casual West Indian decor, and a nightly crowd of regulars and drop-ins (including Brad Pitt and Jennifer Aniston the night before they announced their separation). No wonder: Caribbean Chef of the Year Glendon Carty is behind the stove. You can get anything from a burger to fresh local fish—mahimahi, snapper, tuna, and grouper—prepared any way you like. The weekly early-bird special offering a choice of three entrees (usually one veggie, one seafood, and one traditional English roast) for $15 is one of the island's best bargains. The bar scene gets increasingly lively as the night wears on.

Sandy Ground. ☎ **264/497-3380.** Dinner reservations recommended. Main courses $15–$25. MC, V. Daily noon–midnight.

---

4 BEACHES

We love Anguilla's limestone and scrub interior, its roaming goats, salt ponds teeming with birds, and the wildflowers that spring up after rain showers. Still, let's face it, it's the beaches that bring us here. Superb beaches are what put Anguilla on the tourist map. There are some 33 of them, plus another handful of idyllic offshore islets, like Sandy Island and Prickly Pear; see "A Trip to an Offshore Cay," below. As new roads are built, fewer beaches are reached via the bone-jarring dirt paths that make some of us nostalgic for the old days of, well, 10 or 20 years ago. For now, keep in mind that all beaches—even those of the fanciest resorts—are open to the public. (That said, many locals and old-timers are increasingly unhappy at how many beaches are becoming the *de facto* preserve of new resorts.)

Most of the best beaches (Barnes, Maundays, Meads, Rendezvous Bay, Shoal Bay West) are on the island's West End, site of the most expensive hotels. **Rendezvous Bay** ★★ is a long, curving ribbon of satiny, pale gold sand that stretches along the bay for 4km (2½ miles). For now, you will probably have to enter the beach from the public access near the Anguilla Great House or Bankie Banx's Dune Preserve—and pray that future construction does not ruin this beach forever. **Meads Bay** ★★★ is lined with a number of resorts and

A Trip to an Offshore Cay ★★★

As beautiful as Anguilla's beaches are, there's something about boating off to a desert island that is both exhilarating and liberating. (Cruising along in that clear turquoise sea is certainly a big part of it.) Visiting one of Anguilla's tiny off-shore gems is a must-do during your visit—and none is more than 20 minutes from shore. Here you can snorkel in gin-clear waters, beachcomb for shells and other treasures, and generally putter about a spit of sand in the castaway spirit. A handful even have ramshackle beach restaurants, where fresh lobster and fish are always on the grill. Some resorts, like Malliouhana, have their own powerboats to get you out to the cays. Otherwise, book an offshore excursion with **Shoal Bay Scuba** ✆ 264/235-1482; www.shoalbayscuba. com) or **Gotcha! Garfield's Sea Tours** (✆ 264/235-7902; www.gotcha-garfields-sea-tours-anguilla.com).

The most westerly cay is the privately owned **Dog Island,** truly a deserted isle, 500 acres of sugary-sand beaches, salt ponds, and limestone cliffs. **Prickly Pear** is perhaps the most popular offshore cay, with great snorkeling and two beach restaurants, an offshoot of **Johnnos** (on Sandy Ground), and the **Prickly Pear Restaurant & Bar** (✆ 264/235-5864; www. pricklypearanguilla.com), where the drinks are made in a

beachside restaurants—Malliouhana, Frangipani, Carimar, the Vice-roy, Blanchards, Jacala—but it never feels crowded. We've been here on May mornings when fishermen in colorful wooden skiffs with boat bottoms filled with bonito are the only souls on the beach. This is one sweet stretch of beach, with surprisingly good snorkeling off the beach around the rocks of Malliouhana.

In the northeast, 3km (2-mile) **Shoal Bay ★★★** is Anguilla's most popular beach, a Caribbean classic, with silver-white, powder-soft sands and a backdrop of sea-grapes. This beach is often called Shoal Bay East to distinguish it from Shoal Bay West (see below). The waters are luminous, brilliantly blue, and populated by enough fish to make most casual snorkelers happy. At noon the sands are blindingly white, but at sunrise and sunset they turn a pink to rival any beach in Bermuda. Rental umbrellas, beach chairs, and other equipment are available just behind Uncle Ernie's at the long-established, amazingly helpful **Skyline Beach Rentals** (✆ 264/497-8644) from brothers solar-powered blender. Both Shoal Bay Scuba and Gotcha! Garfield's Sea Tours offer twice-weekly trips to Prickly Pear for $55 to $65 per person (including lunch).

Sandy Island, on the northwest coast, is a tiny islet with a few palms surrounded by a coral reef, a dilapidated (and seasonally abandoned) beach bar and restaurant. During the high season, a $5 speedboat from **Sandy Ground** takes visitors back and forth to Sandy Island almost hourly from around 9am to 4pm. Of course, the closest cay lies just 150m (500 ft.) off the pier at Island Harbour. To get to tiny **Scilly Cay** (pronounced "silly key"), just go out on the pier and wave your arms (or dial ✆ **264/497-5123**) and a boatman will pick you up. Five minutes later you're at Eudoxie and Sandra Wallace's glorified tiki hut, **Gorgeous Scilly Cay** (✆ **264/497-5123**; www.scillycayanguilla.com), picking out a fresh spiny lobster or crayfish (or chicken or veggies). You can snorkel around the reef or just relax over one of Eudoxie's Rhum Punches and watch the pelicans dive for fish. Lunch is daily Tuesday to Sunday from noon to 3pm, with live music Wednesdays and Sundays. This is a place to laze away the day; by the time you leave, you may have spent $100 per person—but what a day.

Calvin, Raymond, and Solomon. And, no trip to Anguilla is really complete without at least one order of ribs (washed down with a Ting or a Red Stripe) at Uncle Ernie's.

Shoal Bay West ★ has pristine white sands tinged with pink opening onto the southwest coast. Visitors find deluxe accommodations, including Covecastles, and superior snorkeling at its western tip. Adjoining it is 1.5km-long (1-mile), white-sand **Maundays Bay** ★★, site of Cap Juluca and justifiably one of the island's most popular shorelines, with gentle surf for good snorkeling and swimming. Though the waters are luminescent and usually calm, sometimes the wind blows enough to attract windsurfers and sailboats. Most days, you see St. Martin across the way; some days, you see the pointy peak of Saba in the distance.

The northwest coast has a number of other beaches worth seeking out, notably the glittering white stretch of **Barnes Bay** beneath a bullying bluff. You can admire the offshore islands silhouetted against the horizon or join the windsurfers and snorkelers.

Little Bay Beach ★ lies at the foot of Anguilla's steepest cliffs. The sands are not the characteristic Anguillan white but, well, *sandy*. That said, none of us who have been there, including serious bird-watchers, snorkelers, and scuba divers, seems to mind. (We do mind when day-trippers from St. Martin come over and occupy the beach.) You can get a boat here most days from about 9am to 4pm from Crocus Bay for around $10 round-trip. You can also climb down (and back up) the cliff at Little Bay, holding onto a knotted rope that is bolted into the cliff. The little cove is a terrific spot for snorkeling; thousands of silver jacks have been spotted swirling about the rocks. The restaurant and beach bar Da'Vida is set on the beach here.

Sandy Ground (aka **Road Bay**), also on the northwest coast, paints an idyllic old-time Caribbean scene, right down to meandering goats, spectacular sunsets, and clear blue waters, often dotted with yachts coming from St. Martin and beyond. You can watch fishermen and lobstermen set out in fishing boats as brightly colored as children's finger paints. **Johnno's** is arguably the archetypal beach bar, serving burgers and grilled fish and rocking at night. Indeed, many of the weathered wooden Antillean houses around here, shaded by turpentine trees and oleander, hold casual bars, making Sandy Ground Party Central on Friday nights. **Island Harbor** is still a working fishing port, with island-made boats bobbing by the pier. For centuries Anguillans have set out from these shores to haul in spiny lobster, which are still cooked up here at **Smitty's** (© 264/497-4300). It was Smitty who set up generators and started the tradition of live music and grilled lobster at his toes-in-the-water restaurant back in the 1970s before Anguilla had electricity. Islanders of a certain age remember walking for hours to get to Smitty's on the weekend to hear the music—and then walking back home after dark by the light of the moon.

Savannah Bay (aka **Junk's Hole**) ★ offers a long stretch of uncrowded white sand and offshore reefs full of eels, squid, and manta rays. The only attraction here is Nat Richardson's **Palm Grove Bar & Grill** ★ (and seemingly the only building for miles), with its perfectly boiled or grilled lobster, crayfish, or shrimp and barbecued ribs. Chances are you'll have **Captain's Bay** ★ all to yourself. Here's why: There's no shade and the undertow is very dangerous. The rock formations are starkly beautiful, but this is a spot for a stroll, *not* a swim.

5 EXPLORING ANGUILLA

The best way to get an overview of the island (if you don't have local friends) is on a **taxi tour.** In about 2 hours, a local driver (all of them are guides) will show you everything for around $60 (tip expected).

The driver will also arrange to let you off at your favorite beach after a look around, and then pick you up and return you to your hotel or the airport. I highly recommend **Accelyn Connor** (© **264/497-0515** or 264/235-8931; premiertaxiandtour@hotmail.com), whose personable and informative tours make him a sought-after guide. His Premier Property Tour accounts for drinks (including beer), snacks, and admission to the museum ($70 single or double; $10 each additional person). Be sure to ask Accelyn about his new **Medicinal Tours.** Before the arrival of modern grocery stores, Anguillans used native plants and shrubs for all sorts of medicinal and dietary purposes (the balsam bush was used for scouring pots, for example, and pepper cilament and candlebark were natural insecticides). Accelyn has planted a native garden filled with medicinal and dietary plants, shrubs, and trees where he discusses Anguillan folk medicine and provides refreshing beverages made with indigenous fruit.

It's easy to combine a great lunch at the Palm Grove Bar & Grill at Junk's Hole with a visit to the **Heritage Museum Collection ★**, East End at Pond Ground (© **264/497-4092**), open Monday to Saturday 10am to 5pm, charging $5 admission ($3 children 11 and under). The modest look of the museum belies the range of fascinating artifacts inside, which include Arawak Indian tools, slave shackles, and household items belonging to 19th-century settlers. If Mr. Colville Petty, who founded the museum, is here when you visit, you will have an especially memorable visit—he collected many of these artifacts himself and has even been awarded an OBE from Queen Elizabeth II.

The **Anguilla National Trust** offers daily **wildlife and eco tours ★** to places like Big Spring, with 1,000-year-old rock carvings and an underwater spring; and East End Pond, a richly inhabited wildlife conservation site. Call © **264/497-5297** to book a spot ($25 adults, $10 children 2–12). Also ask locally whether former chief minister Sir Emile Gumbs, an Anguilla National Trust volunteer, has resumed his delightful **eco-tours** (© **264/497-2711**) spiked with wonderful, often wry historical and political anecdotes.

6 SPORTS & OTHER OUTDOOR PURSUITS

Although sailing, fishing, and watersports are integral parts of the Anguillan culture, some water-borne playthings are not—namely **jet skis,** which are not allowed on the island. Spear fishing is also not allowed on Anguilla.

BICYCLE TOURS   Accelyn Conner's **Premier Tour Service** (© 264/497-0515 or cellphone 264/235-8931) offers a 1½-hour bike tour that travels the scenic route overlooking the harbor and down to Shoal Bay with a professional cyclist as your guide. Helmets and bikes are provided. Tours start at your hotel ($60/couple).

CRUISES & BOATING   At Sandy Ground, **Sandy Island Enterprises** (© 264/476-6534), **Shoal Bay Scuba** (© 264/497-4101; www.shoalbayscuba.com), and **Gotcha! Garfield's Sea Tours** (© 264/235-7902; www.gotcha-garfields-sea-tours-anguilla.com) all arrange excursions and offer boat charters. Private charters run about $125 an hour; sunset cruises cost around $350.

FISHING   Shoal Bay Scuba (© 264/497-4101; www.shoalbay scuba.com) offers offshore fishing charters in a fully equipped Panga Classic; rates are $125 an hour, four persons maximum. Your hotel can also arrange for a local fisherman to take you out; bareboating without a local captain is not allowed.

GOLF   The 18-hole, par-72 Greg Norman–designed **Temenos Golf Course,** between Long and Rendezvous bays (© 264/498-5602; www.capjuluca.com), sits on a sprawling 111-hectare (274-acre) site that sputtered as a mega-resort but is now under the management of Cap Juluca. Bill Clinton has played here, and so can you, for green fees of around $225 per person during peak hours. Check with your hotel desk or the tourist office for the latest details on this development.

HORSEBACK RIDING   First-time and advanced riders can go horseback riding on the beach or "through the bush" with **Seaside Stables,** located at Paradise Drive (next to Paradise Cove in western Anguilla), Cove Bay (© 264/235-3667; www.seaside-stables-anguilla.com). Per-person rates for scheduled beach rides are $70 to $80; kids' half-hour pony rides to the beach are $35; moonlight rides are $90; rides including a swim on horseback are $90.

SAILING   Sailing is the island's national sport, and local kids learn the ropes from a young age. **The Anguilla Sailing Association** (© 264/584-7245; www.sailanguilla.com) is the force behind the Anguilla Regatta in early May and offers sailing lessons for kids and adults at its Optimist Sailing School on Sandy Ground; four lessons cost from $100 to $125.

SCUBA DIVING & SNORKELING   Most of the coastline is fringed by coral reefs, and the crystalline waters are rich in marine life, with coral gardens, brilliantly colored fish, caves, miniwalls, greenback turtles, and stingrays. Conditions for scuba diving and snorkeling are ideal (check out www.scuba.ai for some helpful information). Over the years, the government of Anguilla has artificially enlarged the existing reef system, a first for the Caribbean. Battered and outmoded ships, deliberately sunk in carefully designated places, act as nurseries for fish and lobster populations and provide new dive sites. At **Stoney Ground Marine Park,** off the northeast coast, you can explore the ruins of a Spanish galleon that sank in 1772. Offshore cays **(Anguillita, Prickley Pear, Sandy Island, Dog Island)** offer pristine conditions.

Shoal Bay Scuba (© 264/497-4101; www.shoalbayscuba.com) has a custom-built, state-of-the-art boat. A two-tank dive costs $90, plus $10 for equipment. They also provide snorkel trips, fishing charters, sunset cruises, and windsurfer rentals and lessons. At Sandy Ground, ask around for PADI-trained **Doug Carty** (© 264/235-8438 or 264/497-4567; www.dougcarty.com), who with his company **Special D** takes visitors on scuba excursions; a single tank dive costs from $50. At Meads Bay, **Anguillian Divers** (© 264/497-4750; www.anguilliandiver.com), is a one-stop dive shop that answers most diving needs. PADI instructors are on hand, with a two-tank dive costing $85, plus another $10 for equipment.

Most hotels provide snorkeling gear. Several places, such as long-established **Skyline Beach Rentals** (© 264/497-8644) at Shoal Bay, rent snorkeling gear, if your hotel doesn't provide it. The snorkeling's great off the beach at Shoal Bay, Maundays Bay, Barnes Bay, Little Bay, Road Bay, and Mead Bay beneath the rocks at the Malliouhana resort.

TENNIS Most of the resorts have their own tennis courts (see "Accommodations," earlier in this chapter). **Malliouhana,** Meads Bay (© 264/497-6111), has a pro shop and four championship Laykold tennis courts. All courts are lit for night games.

7 SHOPPING

For serious shopping (Gucci, Louis Vuitton, and the like), take the ferry (see earlier in this chapter) and visit the shops in Marigot on French St. Martin. St. Martin is also a good place to stock up on French wines and cheeses if you're planning a long stay on Anguilla.

Clothes are not cheap on Anguilla, and the hotel boutiques do not go out of their way to stock bargains. Stocked to the rafters with everything you need to be a stylin' Anguillan—silky kurtas, bejeweled caftans, scads of fine and costume jewelry, slinky bathing suits—is **ZaZAA ★** (© 264/497-0460) in Shoal Bay East at the Ku resort. If you need a bathing suit, T-shirt, stylish sandals, or any beach gear, you'll find it in the colorful cottage at **Irie Life** (© 264/498-6526) on the cliff-side road at South Hill. ("Irie" is Rastafarian for "cool.")

Anguilla Art

Anguilla has a thriving local arts and crafts scene and a surprising number of small art galleries featuring the works of talented resident artists both native-born and from around the world. In the Valley, the **Anguilla Arts and Crafts Center** (© 264/497-2200) has paintings and ceramics by local artists, as well as embroidery and lovely cloth dolls. If you're looking for collectibles, or just looking for good art, head to the following:

- **Alak Gallery,** Shoal Bay East Rd. (© 264/497-7270). Accomplished Anguillan artist Louise Brooks paints genre island scenes and Caribbean flora and fauna in vivid, saturated hues. Roosters hold a particular charm for Brooks.
- **Art Café,** Coconut Paradise Building, Island Harbour (© 264/497-8595) has intriguing rotating art exhibits and also doubles as a restaurant serving breakfast and lunch (chicken roti, burgers, local fish, and lobster).
- **Bartlett Collections,** by the roundabout at South Hill (© 264/497-6625), has island crafts (as well as terrific smoothies at its outdoor cafe).
- **Lynne Bernbaum** (© 264/497-5211; www.lynne bernbaum.com), is an American painter whose George Hill studio features her bold images of Anguilla, the

Even if you don't buy anything, you'll get a fantastic view down to Sandy Ground.

8 ANGUILLA AFTER DARK

Many visitors to Anguilla never leave the confines of their hotels for nighttime entertainment, especially in high season when the resorts host barbecues, West Indian parties, and calypso groups and string bands, both local and imported. But who wants to miss out on an essential part of Anguillan culture? For an immersion in the island's lively music scene and a chance to hang with the easy-going, music-loving locals, check the listings in the latest *Anguilla Life* magazine or ask around—much of the action is down at the bars in Sandy

Caribbean, and France. In addition to paintings, Ms. Bernbaum sells prints of her works, including some very Anguillan cactuses and goats.

- **Cheddie's Carving Studio,** West End Road, the Cove (© **264/497-2949;** www.cheddieonline.com), is the domain of self-taught Cheddie Richardson, who sculpts intricate, whimsical figures from driftwood, stone, and coral.
- **Devonish Art Gallery,** in Long Bay opposite CuisinArt Road (© **264/497-2949**), features the work of Courtney Devonish, the well-known Anguillan potter and sculptor, as well as a good collection of paintings from local artists.
- **Savannah Gallery,** Coronation Street, Lower Valley (© **264/497-2263;** www.savannahgallery.com), on the road to Crocus Bay, has a fine selection of paintings by Anguillan and Caribbean artists.
- **Stone Cellar Art Gallery,** Government Corner, the Valley (© **264/498-0123;** www.oldfactory-anguilla.ai): This 1868 former cotton gin has rough-hewn limestone walls and wood-beam ceilings. It's the home of rotating art exhibits (on the second floor) and Sir Roland Richardson's Caribbean Impressionistic paintings on the first.

Ground, and things don't really get cooking until after 11pm. Look for such popular soca/reggae/calypso entertainers as the Musical Brothers, Darvin & his DC Band, and the British Dependency. Dancing the night away—well, until around 2am, when things wind down—is absolutely de rigueur.

The island's wonderful beach bars and grills serve great food and drink and feature live music at least 1 day a week. For a rundown on the perpetual favorites, see "Sun, Sand, Music & Barbecue," earlier in this chapter.

Keep in mind that Anguilla has no casinos or other gambling spots—the local Church Council, which has its say in matters such as this, ensures that the island stays that way. If you feel the need for some casino action, St. Maarten and its 14 casinos are just a 20-minute ferry ride (and a short cab ride from there) away.

St. Barthélemy

It's been called the French Riviera in the Caribbean. St. Barts is a place where mega-yachts preen for other mega-yachts, where the well-heeled come to chase eternal youth under the tropical sun. In addition to historic architecture and thrilling aquatic activities, St. Barts offers pampering without pomp, inimitable French flair and a congenial Caribbean vibe, world-class beaches, and the promise of eternal sun and blue skies (it rarely rains).

Despite its reputation as a playground for the rich, a friendly, laid-back attitude prevails, as does casual dress—sandals, flowing kurtas, tousled hair, bangles, little else—though the sandals are likely Manolo and the bangles 24-karat gold. Yes, St. Barts can be prohibitively pricey, from the upscale resorts and tony French restaurants to the luxury brands and couture fashions. But it doesn't have to cost a fortune to stay here: You can rent a villa or private home (half the visitors who come here do), cook your own meals, and beach-hop with the rest of the islanders—all the beaches are public and free. And yes, you may spot a celebrity living it up, but then again, you may be too busy living it up yourself to care.

New friends call it "St. Barts," while old-time visitors prefer "St. Barths." Either way, it's short for St. Barthélemy (San Bar-te-le-*mee*), named by its discoverer Columbus in 1493. For the most part, St. Bartians are descendants of Breton and Norman fisherfolk. Many are of French and Swedish ancestry, the latter evident in their fair skin, blond hair, and blue eyes. The year-round population is small, about 8,000 people living on 41 sq. km (16 sq. miles) of land, just 24km (15 miles) southeast of St. Martin and 225km (140 miles) north of Guadeloupe.

Despite the constant influx of young arrivals, old ways endure. A few locals still speak 18th-century Norman, Breton, or Poitevin dialect. In little **Corossol,** you might glimpse wizened *grand-mères* wearing the traditional starched white bonnets known as *quichenottes* (a corruption of "kiss-me-not"), which discouraged the close attentions of English or Swedish men on the island.

For a long time, the island was a paradise for a handful of millionaires, such as David Rockefeller. It still caters to an ultra-affluent crowd with European-style discos and flashy yachts elbowing their way into the little seaport of **Gustavia,** the island's enchanting capital. Old and new money feed a vibrant (and duty-free) luxury-goods market. Yet the island diligently maintains a quaintness, a natural warmth, and a generous bonhomie. It has an almost old-fashioned storybook quality, with gaily painted Creole cottages tucked into hillsides and flower boxes spilling over with colorful blooms. Picturesque cemeteries are dotted with simple white crosses draped in blooms and ringed by picket fences.

St. Barts has retained its quaint character for a number of reasons. The island has no clanging casinos, and cruise ships are discouraged (the natural harbor is too small to handle big cruise ships anyway). The airport and its comically short runway are too small to handle big jets. Local authorities, keenly sensitive to the perils of overdevelopment, have placed style and size restrictions on new resorts; most are tastefully tucked into the glorious landscape. For many people, just getting here can be daunting. Unless you're a passenger on a zillionaire's yacht, you'll have to fly in on a tiny plane that makes a heart-stopping landing on a tiny airstrip lined up between two mountains. Those who go by boat or high-speed ferry have the unpredictable, sometimes stomach-churning seas to contend with.

St. Barts' terrain is vastly different than that of its neighbor, Anguilla, where flat, sandy scrubland is the prevailing topography. St. Barts is a volcanic island, where roads carved into the creases and folds of the landscape have Monte Carlo–style curves and rollercoaster dips and rises. Driving these roads in a zippy little European number, hair tousled and kurta flowing, is almost like flying—one minute you're cruising past meadows where baby goats graze and the next you're rounding a corkscrew cliff, with nothing between you and the crashing sea below but a rocky promontory and that witchy Caribbean air. Add a French-inflected reggae soundtrack, and that, more than Manolos and 24-carat gold, is St. Barts.

1 ESSENTIALS

VISITOR INFORMATION

Comité du Tourisme de Saint-Barthélemy, St. Barts' official tourism agency, was founded in 2008 when the island became a French overseas collectivity in its own right (no longer a French *commune* under the administration of Guadeloupe). Its website is **www.saintbarthtourisme.com** (or www.cttsb.org). In St. Barts, the tourist office is located in Gustavia adjacent to La Capitanerie (the Port Authority Headquarters) on the pier, quai du Général-de-Gaulle, Gustavia (℃ **590/27-87-27;** www.cttsb.org).

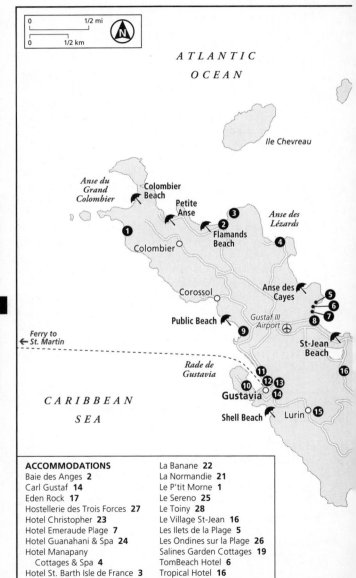

ATLANTIC
OCEAN

Ile Chevreau

Anse du
Grand
Colombier

Colombier
Beach

Petite
Anse

Anse des
Lézards

Flamands
Beach

Colombier

Anse des
Cayes

Corossol

Public Beach

Gustaf III
Airport

Ferry to
← St. Martin

St-Jean
Beach

Rade de
Gustavia

Gustavia

CARIBBEAN
SEA

Shell Beach

Lurin

ACCOMMODATIONS

Baie des Anges **2**
Carl Gustaf **14**
Eden Rock **17**
Hostellerie des Trois Forces **27**
Hotel Christopher **23**
Hotel Emeraude Plage **7**
Hotel Guanahani & Spa **24**
Hotel Manapany
  Cottages & Spa **4**
Hotel St. Barth Isle de France **3**

La Banane **22**
La Normandie **21**
Le P'tit Morne **1**
Le Sereno **25**
Le Toiny **28**
Le Village St-Jean **16**
Les Ilets de la Plage **5**
Les Ondines sur la Plage **26**
Salines Garden Cottages **19**
TomBeach Hotel **6**
Tropical Hotel **16**

DINING
The B4 **12**
Bartoloméo **24**
Bonito Saint Barth **13**
Eddy's **11**
The Hideaway **8**
La Plage **6**
La Route des
  Boucaniers **11**
Le Gaïac **28**

Le Grain de Sel **20**
Le Restaurant
  des Pêcheurs **25**
Le Tamarin **18**
Maya's **9**
O'Corail Restaurant **26**
Pipiri Palace **10**
Santa Fe **15**
Taino/Mango **23**
Wall House **10**

Ile Toc Vers

Ile Frégate

Les Grenadines

*Pointe
Mangin*

Ile Tortue

Pointe Milou

23

*Baie de
St-Jean*

Marigot Beach

**Grand Cul-de-Sac
Beach**

24
25
26

L'Orient
Marigot

L'Orient
22
21

17

La Petit
Saline

Vitet **27**   Devet

Mt. Lurin **18** **19**
20

Grand
Fond

28 Toiny

*Anse
Toiny*

*Anse du
Grand Fond*

**Grande Saline
Beach**

**Gouverneur
Beach**

Fourmis

Ile Coco

Airport ✈
Beach ◤
Mountain ▲▲
Ferry Route - - -

On the island, pick up a copy of *Ti Gourmet;* this solid little guide is packed with invaluable information on absolutely everything. (See info under "Read All About It," below.) Online, the **Insiders' Guide to St. Barthélemy** (www.sbhonline.com) offers very instructive read-ers' forums and trip reports. The Web-only *St. Barths Online* (www.st-barths.com) offers details on arts, dining, shopping, and nightlife listings.

ISLAND LAYOUT & NEIGHBORHOODS

St. Barts lies 24km (15 miles) southeast of St. Martin and 225km (140 miles) north of Guadeloupe. The island's capital and only sea-port is enchanting **Gustavia,** named for a Swedish king. This doll-house-scale port rings a splendid harbor where little fishing boats bob alongside sleek yachts. Its narrow streets—lined with 18th-century Swedish or French stone buildings housing gourmet eateries, galleries, chic boutiques, and an excellent **Municipal Museum**—are easily explored on foot. Traveling northwest from Gustavia, you reach the typical villages of **Corossol** and **Colombier,** where a handful of women still weave lantana straw handicrafts from hats to handbags in cotton-candy-colored *cazes* (traditional wooden houses) garlanded with flowerpots and fishing nets.

Right by the airport, **St-Jean** is the closest thing to a resort town: a tropic St-Tropez, brimming with smart boutiques and beachfront bistros. A few minutes' drive east is serene **Lorient,** site of the first French settlement with a popular locals' beach; beautifully adorned graveyards; 19th-century Catholic church, convent, and bell tower; and reconstructed 17th-century Norman manor. Farther east, **Grand Cul-de-Sac** (Point Milou) is the island's second major resort center, its wide curve of sand surveyed by resorts and top-notch eateries.

GETTING THERE

BY PLANE   The flight from St. Maarten is just 10 minutes long, but for many people, landing on a tiny airstrip between two volcanic hills and braking mere feet from sunbathers on the beach is 10 min-utes of terror. The makeshift landing strip at St-Jean airport on St. Barts is just 651m (2,170 ft.) long and accommodates only STOL (short takeoff and landing) aircrafts no bigger than 19-seaters. Even on these small planes, landing on St. Barts has often been compared (and not favorably) to touching down on an aircraft carrier. The pilot must divebomb between two mountains (one with a giant white Swedish cross), then pull up abruptly: no extra charge for the thrill ride. (In fact, any pilot who plans to land in St. Barts is required to qualify for a special permit first.) No landings or departures are per-mitted after dark.

There are no nonstop flights to St. Barts from North America. From the United States, the principal gateways are St. Maarten, St. Thomas, and Guadeloupe. Most people from the U.S. or Canada first fly to St. Maarten; for details on getting to St. Maarten, see chapter 2. From St. Maarten, **Windward Islands Airways International** (known by everybody as **Winair;** ℰ **866/466-0410** in the U.S. and Canada, or 590/27-61-01; www.fly-winair.com) offers 10 to 20 daily flights to St. Barts. One-way passage costs around 64€—but that figure excludes taxes and surcharges, which can double the cost (including inflated fees for credit-card charges). Flight duration is a mere 10 minutes.

Our favorite carrier is **St. Barth Commuter** (ℰ **590/27-54-54;** www.stbarthcommuter.com), which flies four flights Monday through Saturday (two Sun) from little L'Espérance Airport in Grand Case, St. Martin (one-way fares 60€ adults, 45€ children 2–11). It flies once daily from St. Maarten's Princess Juliana Airport (one-way fares 65€ adults, 50€ children 2–11).

Air Caraïbes (ℰ **877/772-1005** in the U.S. and Canada, or 590/82-47-00 and 590/27-71-90; www.aircaraibes.com) flights depart four or five times a day from Pointe-à-Pitre's Pôle Caraïbes Aéroport in Guadeloupe. Round-trip passage to St. Barts starts at 236€; trip time is 45 minutes.

Tradewind Aviation (ℰ **800/376-7922;** www.tradewindaviation. com) offers two daily first-class charter flights to St. Barts from San Juan; the flight is an hour long and round-trip cost (including taxes and surcharges) is $395 per person Monday through Thursday and $495 per person Friday through Sunday.

ⓘ Tips   Airline Advice

Always reconfirm your return flight from St. Barts with your interisland airline. If you don't, your reservation will be canceled. *Note:* On rare occasions, a flight will be rescheduled if the booking doesn't meet its fuel quota. Also, don't check your luggage all the way through to St. Barts, or you may not see it for a few days. Instead, check your bags to your gateway connecting destination (usually St. Maarten), then take your luggage to your interisland carrier and recheck it to St. Barts. Just in case, pack a change of clothes, any required medicine, and a bathing suit in your carry-on.

BY BOAT The **Voyager** vessels (© **590/87-10-68;** www.voy12. com or www.voyager-st-barths.com) make frequent (usually twice daily, sometimes more) runs between St. Barts and either side of St. Maarten/St. Martin. The schedule varies according to the season (and the seas), but the **MV *Voyager II*** usually departs Marigot Harbor for St. Barts every morning and evening. **MV *Voyager I*** travels from Oyster Pond to Gustavia two to four times daily. Advance reservations are a good idea; fares run around 50€ to 58€ adults, 30€ children 2 to 12 one-way (plus taxes). The trip can take around 45 minutes and can be rough; it's recommended that those with weak tummies take seasickness medication before the trip.

The technologically advanced, speedy, more luxurious and stable 20m (65-ft.) aluminum mono-hull *Great Bay Express* (© **590/27-60-33;** www.sbhferry.com) offers daily 20- to 40-minute crossings between St. Maarten's Bobby's Marina in Philipsburg and Gustavia. The boat can carry 130 passengers. Reservations are essential; the round-trip fare is 56€ to 95€ adults, 40€ to 50€ children 2 to 11 years (plus taxes).

GETTING AROUND

BY TAXI Taxis meet all flights and are not very expensive, mostly because destinations aren't far from one another. Dial © **590/27-75-81** or 590/27-66-31 for taxi service. A typical rate, from the airport to Cul-de-Sac, is 20€. Fares between 8pm and 6am, and on Sundays and holidays, are 50% higher. Taxi service must be arranged between midnight and 6am—call ahead. There are taxi stands at the St-Jean airport and in Gustavia.

The government imposes official fares on tours by taxi. Many travelers simply approach a taxi driver and ask him to show them around. The official rates for one to three passengers are 45€ for 45 minutes, 44€ for 60 minutes, and 60€ for 90 minutes. For four or more passengers, add 8€ to each of the above-mentioned prices.

BY RENTAL CAR A rental car is an essential in St. Barts; it's really the best way to come and go as you please. You can reserve one yourself or have your hotel rent one for you. A number of rental agencies are located at the airport, although most rental agencies are happy to deliver cars straight to your hotel or villa (many resorts keep an assortment of rental cars on-site, ready to go; others, like Le Sereno, include a rental car in your resort rates). All valid foreign driver's licenses are honored.

Star Location Car Rentals (© **690-42-28-42;** www.star-loc.com) offers rates with a 1€=$1 equivalency—still a good deal for Americans at press time. It's located right at St-Jean Airport, with a wide range of rental cars, from automatic-drive Suzuki SUVs and four-wheel-drives to stick shift vans. Rates run from 38€ to 130€ a day, depending on the season. Also at the airport is **Gumbs Car Rental** (© 590/27-75-32), a longtime island car-rental company with a fleet of 65 cars; the reasonable rates start at around 20€ a day. Those with an itch to drive a Mini Cooper convertible around the island can rent one for around 120€ a day from **Pure Rental,** on Rue du Roi Oscar II, in Gustavia (© 590/27-64-76).

Budget (© 800/472-3325 in the U.S., or 590/29-62-40; www.budget.com) rents various 4WD Suzukis and automatic Daihatsus for 60€ a day, with unlimited mileage. Be sure to reserve at least 3 business days before your arrival.

Hertz (© 800/654-3131 in the U.S. and Canada; www.hertz.com) operates on St. Barts through a local dealership, **Henry's Car Rental,** with branches at the airport and in St-Jean (© 590/27-71-14). It offers open-sided Suzuki Samurais for 65€ a day, and more substantial Suzuki Sidekicks for 70€ to 90€ per day.

At **Avis** (© 800/331-1212 in the U.S. and Canada, or 590/27-71-43; www.avis.com or www.avis-stbarth.com), you'll need a reservation a full month in advance during high season. In the winter, cars range from 68€ to 98€ a day. In the off season, rentals are 44€ to 90€ a day.

Note: For Budget, Hertz, and Avis, if you reserve your car in the U.S. you will be charged in dollars, not euros.

DRIVING ST. BARTS   Driving is on the right and maximum speed is 50kph; seatbelts are required. Never drive with less than half a tank of gas on St. Barts. There are only two gas stations on the island, and both are closed on Sunday: one near the airport (open only 7:30am–noon and 2–7pm—with an all-night automatic pump that usually accepts MasterCard and Visa), the other in Lorient (open 7:30am–noon and 2–5pm).

Driving on St. Barts is an interesting experience, with corkscrewing roller-coaster roads (all 2-lane) and blind corners announced by signage of no words, just an exclamation point. Unless you're comfortable driving up and down steep hills with ease in a standard four-on-the-floor, I say opt for an automatic car. Slow down as you maneuver 90-degree curves, and don't let tailgating motorbikes and scooters push you into speeding up. Also: If you plan to park on the road, say, in St-Jean, amid tight traffic, be sure to pull in your driver's side rear-view mirror, or you might find it shorn off when you return. Happy driving!

BY MOTORBIKE & SCOOTER   **Denis Dufau** operates two affiliates (© 590/27-70-59 and 590/27-54-83). A helmet is provided (helmets are required), and renters must either leave an imprint of a valid credit card or pay a deposit. Rental fees vary from 24€ to 35€

per day, depending on the size of the bike. For all but the smallest models, presentation of a valid driver's license is required and you must be 21 or older.

JOGGING/BY BICYCLE   St. Barts is not the ideal place to ride a bike or go for a run along the roadside. The two-lane roads have few sidewalks and narrow-to-nonexistent shoulders, traffic can be heavy, and the topography consists largely of steep hills and curving roadways with few flat stretches. Serious joggers can use their resort fitness rooms or head to the newly resurfaced **track around the soccer field** in St-Jean Carrenage (behind the St-Jean firehouse). Gustavia is also a good place to run when the traffic is light.

2 ACCOMMODATIONS

St. Barts has some 30 hotels, most of which trend toward boutique—the largest property on the island has only 65 rooms. Hotels and resorts throughout the island, with some exceptions, tend to be expensive, and a service charge of between 10% and 15% is usually added to your bill. Tack on a weak dollar, and St. Barts becomes quite the pricey proposition for North Americans. If you're looking for ways to cut costs, consider visiting in the shoulder or low seasons. Off-season rates plummet and often include a rental car for stays of a week or more. In March, it's difficult to find a place to stay on St. Barts unless you've made reservations far in advance, but check in during May and you'll have the run of the place. Be sure to get on a resort's e-mail list: Many offer terrific money-saving packages (especially during the off season) advertised via e-mail or Twitter. Note that a number of properties close between August and October.

VERY EXPENSIVE

Carl Gustaf ★★★   The "Goose," as it's affectionately known, has always been *the* spot for sunset cocktails. Gustavia's most glamorous

Renting a Villa in St. Barts

If you choose to rent a villa in St. Barts instead of going the hotel route, you won't be alone. St. Barts has some 450 **villas, beach houses, and apartments** for rent by the week or month. Villas are dotted in and around the island's hills—very few are on the beach. Instead of an oceanfront bedroom, you get a panoramic view. Rentals, priced in U.S. dollars, can range from a one-room "studio" villa away from the beach for $980 per week in off season, up to $40,000 per week for a minipalace at Christmas. Most rentals average between $2,500 and $4,000 a week in the high season between mid-December and mid-April, with discounts of 30% to 50% the rest of the year. One of the best agencies to contact for villa, apartment, or condo rentals is **St. Barth Properties,** 12 Washington St., Ste. 201, Franklin, MA 02038 (© **800/421-3396** or 508/528-7727 in the U.S. and Canada; www.stbarth.com). Peg Walsh, a longtime aficionado of St. Barts, and her capable son, Tom Smyth, will let you know what's available. She can also make arrangements for car rentals and air travel to St. Barts and can book babysitters and restaurant reservations. Another excellent option with similar rates and services is **Wimco** (P.O. Box 1481, Newport, RI 02840; © **800/449-1553** or 401/847-6290; www.wimco.com), which has some 250 villa properties to rent.

hotel has ratcheted up the glam factor, with a modern restaurant and bar, a state-of-the-art spa, and a four-bedroom suite, the 2,600-square-foot Royale Suite. The hotel oversees the town's harbor from a steep hillside. Each of the hotel's 14 suites is in one of a dozen pink or green, red-roofed villas. Access to each building is via a central staircase, which tests the stamina of even the most active guests. The wood-frame units are angled for maximum views of the boats bobbing far below in the bay and panoramic sunsets, best enjoyed from the plunge pool on the private patio bisecting each suite. Bedrooms are exceedingly well furnished: You'll feel like a pasha as you walk across Italian marble floors under a pitched ceiling to reach your luxurious bed. Beaches are a 10-minute walk away. In the newly redesigned restaurant **Victoria's,** Chef Emmanuel Motte has revitalized the classic French kitchen.

ST. BARTHÉLEMY

9

ACCOMMODATIONS

Rue des Normands, 97099 Gustavia, St. Barthélemy, F.W.I. © **800/322-2223** in the U.S., or 590/29-79-00. Fax 590/27-82-37. www.hotelcarlgustaf.com. 14 units. Winter 1,150€–3,550€ suite; off season 750€–2,600€ suite. Rates include continental breakfast. AE, MC, V. **Amenities:** Restaurant; bar; outdoor pool; room service; sauna; spa; watersports equipment (extensive). *In room:* A/C, TV/DVD, CD player, fax, fridge, hair dryer, kitchen (in Royale Suite only), kitchenette (in 1- and 2-bedroom suites only), minibar (in spa suite only), MP3 docking station, private plunge pools, Wi-Fi (free).

Eden Rock ★★★   Greta Garbo checked in as Suzy Schmidt for a 3-day holiday but ended up staying 3 weeks. That was eons ago, but this legendary hotel still exerts a magnetic pull on the rich and fabulous.

Eden Rock occupies the most spectacular site on St. Barts, a quartzite promontory cleaving St-Jean Bay into two perfect white-sand crescents. When the island's former mayor, Remy de Haenen, paid $200 for the land some 60 years ago from an old woman, she ridiculed him for paying too much.

Owners David and Jane Spencer Matthews continue to reinvent Eden Rock into one of the Caribbean's most glamorous addresses, where even celebrities people-watch. The attention to detail is unparalleled. The individually decorated accommodations either climb the rock or are perched steps from the water on either side. The original "Rock" rooms are stuffed with antiques, family heirlooms, silver fixtures, steamer trunks, four-poster beds, and watercolors of local scenes by Jane (an accomplished artist herself) and her children. The newer units include eight suites with decks opening onto the beach as well as five one- to three-bedroom beach houses with outdoor Jacuzzis and plunge pools (two have full swimming pools). The 450-sq.-m (1,500-sq.-ft.) **Howard Hughes Suite,** atop the Main House on "the rock," features hardwood floors, three verandas offering 360-degree panoramas, and two bathrooms uniquely clad in welded copper. The newest luxury villa is **Villa Nina,** with two bedrooms and its very own art gallery, a private pool, and a beachside location. Opening in time for the 2010 season is the **Rockstar Suite,** a 1,486-sq.-m (16,000-sq.-ft.) stunner with four master suites, a screening room, a fully equipped recording studio, a pool table, a private pool, and a dedicated butler. Cost: $130,000 per week.

For lunch, head to the casual beachfront **Sand Bar.** Dinner (and people-watching) is served up at the swanky **On The Rocks Restaurant.** The **Eden Rock Gallery,** opened by Jane Matthews, showcases local and international artists.

Baiede, 97133 St-Jean, St. Barthélemy, F.W.I. © **877/563-7105** in the U.S., or 590/29-79-99. Fax 590/27-88-37. www.edenrockhotel.com. 33 units. Winter 685€–1,025€ double, from 1,295€ suite; off season 490€–645€ double, from 785€ suite. Extra person 6 and over: 125€. Rates include VIP airport transfers and buffet breakfast. AE, MC, V. Closed Aug 30–Oct 8. **Amenities:** 2 restaurants; bar; babysitting; fitness center; room service; watersports activities. *In room:* A/C, TV/DVD, hair dryer, kitchen (in some), MP3 docking station, minibar (in some), private plunge pools (in some), Wi-Fi (free).

Hôtel Manapany Cottages & Spa ★

This stylish resort climbs a steep, landscaped hillside on the northwest side of the island, a 10-minute taxi ride north of the airport. Manapany is intimate and accommodating; the name, translated from Malagese, means "small paradise." The gingerbread-trimmed Antillean cottages are set on the sloping hillside or inside the curve of Anse des Cayes. The rambling verandas and open-sided living rooms let in the trade winds. The decor is a mix of white rattan and Caribbean colonial pieces carved from mahogany. Mosquito netting covers most of the four-poster beds for a romantic touch.

Anse des Cayes, 97098 St. Barthélemy, F.W.I. ℂ **590/27-66-55.** Fax 590/27-75-28. www.lemanapany.com. 42 units. Winter 462€–525€ double, 630€–1,155€ junior suite, 910€–1,750€ suite; off season 277€–315€ double, 378€–693€ junior suite, 546€–1,050€ suite. AE, MC, V. **Amenities:** Restaurant; bar; fitness room; outdoor pool; room service; spa; tennis court. *In room:* A/C, TV/DVD, CD player, hair dryer, minibar, Wi-Fi (free).

Hôtel St. Barth Isle de France ★★

Effortless elegance distinguishes this family-run hotel, which continues to rack up awards for its luxurious lodging and excellent service. It opens right onto glorious Flamands beach. The architecture blends the richly saturated colors of Corsica with Caribbean and colonial New England influences. Guest rooms are unusually spacious for St. Barts. Each top-notch unit contains a private patio or terrace overlooking the pool, beach, or lavishly landscaped grounds. Beds are luxurious, fitted with fine linen. Commodious marble-clad bathrooms are equipped with dual basins, large tubs (some with whirlpool jets), and showers. For a sense of privacy, you might opt for the Hillside Bungalow, which overlooks the gardens and has a terrace; or the Fisherman's Cottage, with two en-suite bedrooms, a kitchenette, and its own interior courtyard. Four new 139 sq. m (1,500-sq.-ft.) one-bedroom suites open onto the beach and come with private infinity plunge pools, fully equipped kitchens, and stone bathtubs.

The on-site Spa at Isle de France, created by Molton Brown, and quintessential beachfront *boîte,* **La Case de l'Isle** (island-tinged French fare), complete the memorable experience.

97098 Baie des Flamands, St. Barthélemy, F.W.I. ℂ **800/810-4691** in the U.S., or 590/27-61-81. Fax 590/27-86-83. www.isle-de-france.com. 40 units. Winter 845€–1,280€ double, from 1,545€ suite; off season 525€–795€ double, from 1,055€ suite. Rates include continental breakfast. AE, MC, V. Closed Sept–Oct 15. **Amenities:** Restaurant; bar; babysitting; exercise room; 2 outdoor pools; room service; spa; tennis court. *In room:* A/C and ceiling fan, TV, fridge, hair dryer, minibar, MP3 docking station, Wi-Fi (free).

Le Sereno ★★ Opening onto Grand Cul-de-Sac Beach, this intimate, all-suites hotel is a chic and stylish retreat. It was designed by the fabled Parisian designer Christian Liaigre (who also did NYC's Mercer Hotel) and is the latest reincarnation of a much older (and much-beloved) hotel that many felt had grown stale. The suites are both relaxingly understated and exquisitely a la mode, with all those extra touches and modcons that make for luxe living (signature robes and linens from Porthault, plasma TVs, personal iPods)—but some are better than others. Definitely ask for the Grand Suite Plage rooms #20–35; they are the same category as the other Grand Suite Plage rooms (and a step up from the simple Garden Rooms) but much, much roomier. The pool and the **Restaurant des Pecheurs** (see "Dining," below) are the resort's social hubs. The three **three-bedroom villas** ★★★ above the hotel are absolutely spectacular, each with a pool, personal butler, and amazing views of Grand Cul de Sac (so high up you can even see whales passing by). Inside are sleek designer kitchens stocked with Le Creuset pots and pans; music is pumped into the pools. A complimentary rental car is included in the rates in low season.

Grand Cul-de-Sac, 97099 Barthélemy, F.W.I. ✆ **888/LESERENO** (537-3736) in the U.S., or 590/29-83-00. Fax 590/27-75-47. www.lesereno.com. 37 units. Winter 680€–1,190€ suite, 1,330€–2,330€ villa; off season 480€–780€ suite, 990€–1,930€ villa. Rates include breakfast and airport transfers. AE, MC, V. **Amenities:** Restaurant; 2 bars; gym and spa; outdoor pool; room service; watersports equipment. *In room:* A/C, TV, bar, fridge, hair dryer, MP3/MP3 docking station, Wi-Fi (free).

Le Toiny ★★★ One of the Caribbean's most glamorous resorts, this Relais & Châteaux enclave has but 15 villas, scattered among a half-dozen buildings clinging to a gently sloping hillside overlooking the windswept Toiny coast. Abundant flowering shrubs protect privacy-seekers from prying eyes, though Brad Pitt, on vacation with his then-girlfriend Gwyneth Paltrow, was supposedly so relaxed that he dropped inhibitions and more for the paparazzi. Each sumptuous suite features its own private plunge pool, tropical-wood floors, teak and mahogany furnishings, espresso machines, Villeroy & Boch tubs, and beds swaddled in Frette linens. Outside, the patio's plunge pool overlooks hills and sea, with bougainvillea spilling out of big blue pots. Giant bathrooms impress with impeccable hand-painted moldings and colorful tiles. Le Toiny now has direct beach access—a pleasant 5-minute path through a coconut grove, but the waters at Toiny Beach can be rough. In the **Serenity Spa Cottage,** you can get a spa treatment featuring spa products from Le Ligne of St. Barts. The outstanding restaurant, **Le Gaïac,** reviewed in "Dining," below, is still the island's gold standard. At Le Toiny, you don't have to see or be seen by anyone—even breakfast arrives in a hush, set out on a patio table sheathed in crisp linens and silver cutlery. From every vantage point—even reflected in your bathroom mirror—the sea/sky/mountain vista is soul-stirring.

Anse de Toiny, 97133 St. Barthélemy, F.W.I. ℂ **800/278-6469** in the U.S., or 590/27-88-88. Fax 590/27-89-30. www.hotelletoiny.com. 15 units. Winter 1,250€–1,680€ suite, 2,780€ villa; off season 520€–930€ 1-bedroom suite for 2 guests, 1,210€–1,800€ villa. Rates include breakfast and hotel transfers. AE, DC, MC, V. Closed Sept 1–Oct 25. **Amenities:** Restaurant; bar; babysitting; bikes; concierge; fitness center; outdoor pool; room service; spa; watersports equipment. *In room:* A/C, TV/DVD, hair dryer, kitchenette, minibar; MP3 docking station, private plunge pool, Wi-Fi (free).

EXPENSIVE

Baie des Anges ★ (**Value**) For beach lovers, it's hard to imagine a more appealing spot. Opening right onto the gorgeous white sands of Flamands beach, this retreat is cooled by trade winds and has a laid-back, carefree atmosphere, as opposed to some of the snootier spots on the island. Surrounded by gardens, the two-story, ocean-fronting property is relatively simple but has its own charm. If your sinks must be clad in cool marble and your beds in Porthault, this is not the place for you. The simple, spacious, and newly refreshed accommodations are attractive and comfortable, decorated in sea colors of blue and green and with handsome, king-size beds (some four-poster), kitchenettes, and private terraces. You can opt for a room opening onto the sea or the courtyard with its pool, where guests can be found when the Atlantic waves get too rough for swimming. For such a small place, the inn has a first-rate restaurant, **La Langouste,** where non-guests can dine for lunch and dinner on the Creole or French specialties. The hotel posts its rates in U.S. dollars.

Baie des Anges, Flamands, 97133 St. Barthélemy, FWI. ℂ **590/27-63-61.** Fax 590/27-83-44. www.hotelbaiedesanges.fr. 10 units. Winter $415–$565 double, $460–$625 triple; off season $230–$370 double, $265–$420 triple. MC, V. **Amenities:** Restaurant; bar; babysitting; pool; room service. *In room:* A/C and ceiling fan, TV, hair dryer, kitchenette, Wi-Fi (in some).

Hôtel Guanahani and Spa ★★★ (**Kids**) St. Barts' largest hotel would be a jewel of a small boutique hotel anywhere else. Don't let its casual good nature fool you: Guanahani defines excellence. Service is as good here as you'll get anywhere, with the warm, friendly staff knowing what you need before you know it yourself.

This hotel enjoys a spectacular situation on its own peninsula bracketed by two scenic beaches, one facing the Atlantic ocean, the other, the Grand Cul-de-Sac Bay, overlooking Marigot Bay. The intimately scaled resort spills down a lush hillside to the spacious beach. I don't know of many other resorts of this caliber going all out with such rich, saturated color. The lobby alone has teal green walls, pink/orange furniture, blue trim—all grounded by an earthy wooden floor. It's a boldly conceived tropical garden interior that manages to avoid tropical resort cliches.

Of the resort's 69 rooms, 36 are suites—and 14 of these have private pools. Guanahani has several unique free-standing villas that offer space, privacy, and a modern Creole cottage feel. The two restaurants, airy, alfresco **Indigo** and **Le Bartolemo** (see "Dining," later in this chapter), offer creative continental cuisine. Kids are welcomed throughout the resort, with children's programs and a big box of beach toys. Onsite, the **Clarins Spa ★** is first-rate, with its own good-size swimming pool. Up above the spa is the Caribbean equivalent of a charming Parisian garret: The **Wellness Suite** is a private, self-contained haven, with a terrace and views of Grand Cul-de-Sac from every window; it has an outdoor shower with a beautiful pebbled floor and a fabulous stone sink that's practically primal: You step on a button on the floor and water spills out as if from a hillside cataract. The occupant of the Wellness Suite has a private key to the spa; you can tiptoe in for a refreshing dip in the pool.

In 2010 Guanahani will undergo major renovations on 20 rooms down near the beach. Note that the resort is not for those with mobility problems; the sometimes steep and rambling layout is not particularly pedestrian-friendly.

Grand Cul-de-Sac, 97133 St. Barthélemy, F.W.I. *©* **800/223-6800** in the U.S., or 590/27-66-60. www.leguanahani.com. 69 units. Winter 595€–965€ double, from 1,090€ suite; off season 360€–600€ double, from 700€ suite. Rates include full American breakfast and round-trip airport transfers. AE, MC, V. **Amenities:** 2 restaurants; 3 bars; babysitting; butler services (villas only) horseback riding; children's programs (ages 2–6); concierge; fitness center; Jacuzzi; 2 outdoor pools; room service; spa; 2 tennis courts; watersports equipment; Wi-Fi (free). *In room:* A/C and ceiling fan, TV/DVD, hair dryer, minibar, MP3 docking station.

Hotel Emeraude Plage ★   Location, location, location: It doesn't get more central than this hotel, planted right on the St-Jean sands. The hotel has one villa, two cottages, four suites, and 21 bungalows, all connected by a maze of walkways. Rooms are drenched in white, with accents in brown (curtains) and beige (the tile floors), and all have fully equipped kitchens for maximum self-catering options. The only real public space is a book-filled reception and a small outdoor bar/restaurant on a deck facing the beach—oh, and that beach, with Eden Rock perched on one side and planes zooming in on the other. The **Club Eau de Mer** is open for breakfast, light lunch, and sunset cocktails.

Baie de St-Jean, 97133 St. Barthélemy, F.W.I. *©* **590/27-64-78.** Fax 590/27-83-08. www.emeraudeplage.com. 11 units. Winter 370€–910€ bungalow, 580€ cottage, 1,290€ villa; off season 275€–760€ bungalow, 470€ cottage, 1,080€ villa. Extra person 100€. AE, MC, V. **Amenities:** Babysitting; concierge; watersports equipment; Wi-Fi (free; in lobby). *In room:* A/C and ceiling fan, TV, CD player, hair dryer.

Les Ilets de la Plage ★ (Kids) Homey and warm, set on a serene, secluded stretch of St-Jean beach (even with the planes arriving and departing next door), Les Ilets is a charming departure from resort sleek and chic. In the lexicon of typical beach resort landscaping, Les Ilets is a sweet anomaly. Each cottage faces out toward curving beach and intensely blue sea, but the surrounding terrain is more like the sun-dappled and slightly overgrown summer backyards of a bygone past. Les Ilets has 11 cottage-style villas, with one-, two-, and three-bedroom units available (four are directly on the beach), all with room to spare and fully equipped kitchens. The villas are charmingly outfitted and very private—and in that location you're just minutes away from great St-Jean restaurants and shopping.

Baie de St-Jean, 97133 St. Barthélemy, F.W.I. ℭ **590/27-88-57.** Fax 590/27-88-58. www.lesilets.com. 11 units. Winter 440€–690€; off season 225€–370€. AE, MC, V. **Amenities:** Babysitting; concierge; outdoor pool; watersports equipment. *In room:* A/C and ceiling fan, TV/DVD/VCR (available on request), CD player, hair dryer, kitchen, Wi-Fi (free).

TomBeach Hotel This bustling boutique hotel opens onto a popular section of St-Jean Beach; next door are windsurfing and watersports rentals. A party atmosphere prevails, so if you're an early-to-bed type, check in elsewhere. The flamboyantly painted villas are enveloped by a Caribbean garden and painted in bright pastels. Bedrooms are spacious and rather stylish, each adorned with draped four-poster beds, opening onto terraces complete with wet bars. The hotel's popular **La Plage** restaurant is recommended separately (see below).

Baie de St. Jean, 97133 St-Barthélemy, F.W.I. ℭ **866/617-4578** or 590/27-53-13. www.tombeach.com. 12 units. Winter 450€–690€ double; off season 290€–480€ double. AE, MC, V. **Amenities:** Restaurant; bar; Internet; outdoor pool. *In room:* A/C, TV/DVD, hair dryer, minibar.

MODERATE

Hostellerie des Trois Forces ★ (Finds) Breton astrologer Hubert Delamotte (a Gemini) and his wife, Ginette, created this hilltop sanctuary dedicated to enriching the flow between life's primary three forces: mind, body, and spirit. Yet it's too special to be labeled just another New Age retreat; patrons of all persuasions—seers to CEOs, Meryl Streep to Ram Dass—seek refuge and refreshment here. Even the site was divined by the ancient eco-art of geomancy: organizing environments to optimize harmony between user and space. The inn occupies panoramic grounds in Vitet about a 10-minute drive from Cul-de-Sac and Lorient beaches. The gingerbread bungalows are staggered to maximize privacy and sweeping ocean vistas. Each is named for a sign of the zodiac and decorated with the appropriate color scheme. Holistic services include massage therapy, yoga, past-life regression therapy, and psychic readings. Hubert believes, "The stomach is a spiritual gate," and his on-site restaurant's French fare earned him membership in France's prestigious gastronomic order Confrérie de la Marmite d'Or.

Morne Viet, 97133 St. Barthélemy, F.W.I. © 590/27-61-25. Fax 590/27-81-38. www. 3forces.net. 7 cottages. Winter 270€ double; off season 170€ double. AE, MC, V. **Amenities:** Restaurant; bar; outdoor pool. *In room:* A/C, kitchenette (in 2 units), minibar.

Les Ondines Sur la Plage ★ **(Kids)** This postmodern all-suites-hotel, sequestered by a private garden lagoon opening onto Grand Cul-de-Sac beach, has a kid-pleasing fish-shaped freshwater pool. The five one-bedroom and two two-bedroom suites range from 60 to 139 sq. m (643–1,500 sq. ft.)—enormous by St. Barts standards. Most suites have glorious ocean views. All feature such necessities as fully equipped kitchens, high-speed Internet access, and fax (two-bedroom units even have a washer/dryer and dishwasher). Creative touches extend to modish kitchens and track-lit bathrooms (stunning bas-relief moldings and mosaics).

Grand Cul-de-Sac, 97133 St. Barthélemy, F.W.I. © **590/27-69-64.** Fax 590/52-24-41. www.stbarth-lesondineshotel.com. 7 units. Winter 350€–690€ double; off season 215€–450€ double. Rates include continental breakfast and airport transfers. AE, MC, V. Closed Sept–Oct. **Amenities:** Outdoor pool; room service; watersports equipment. *In room:* A/C, ceiling fan, TV/DVD, hair dryer, Internet (free), kitchen, Wi-Fi (free).

La Banane ★ This former disco is still a social nexus. La Banane is not on the beach; in fact, it's located just off a shopping-center parking lot on the outskirts of Lorient. But this intimate little gem manages to feel like a private hideaway. That's in large part because of the layout and dense, jungle landscaping; road traffic feels far, far away. It's all pillowed in richly planted gardens of banana trees, palms, frangipani, jasmine, and bougainvillea. Nine bungalows are scattered around the pool, much like cottages encircling a main villa. Guests gravitate to the resort nerve center—the handsome lobby, bar, and pool area—and become fast friends as they lounge amid the smart and smartly curated modernist furniture selection (including Le Corbusier–inspired pieces that look both snappy and irresistibly comfy). Rooms have pop-art floors, four-poster beds, and colorful mosaic tiles in the bathrooms. Bathrooms open onto patios or private gardens so that taking a shower becomes a perfumed ritual amid tropical flora. No kids under 13 are allowed.

Baie de L'Orient, 97133 St. Barthélemy, F.W.I. © **590/52-03-00.** Fax 590/27-68-44. www.labanane.com. 7 units. Winter 485€–585€ double; off season 385€–485€ double. Extra person/bed: 70€. No children under 13. Rates include breakfast and airport shuttle. Closed Sept and Oct. AE, MC, V. **Amenities:** Bar; 2 outdoor pools; room service; watersports equipment. *In room:* A/C, ceiling fan, TV/DVD, CD player, hair dryer, minibar, Wi-Fi (free).

Hotel Christopher ★★ (Value) Set on a dramatic, sun-splashed promontory above the sea, this Pointe Milou hotel has undergone a spectacular new renovation and reduced its prices in the process. Confused? With sensational views over the blue Atlantic and two very good restaurants, the Christopher represents real value on pricey St. Barts. A lifestyle hotel that's "contemporary but not intimidating," the Christopher serves up a supremely relaxed atmosphere against a background of precise service. The hotel is not adjacent to the beach (guests must drive about 10 minutes to reach Plage de Lorient) but it has the biggest pool on the island, a sprawling, lowslung pair of inter-connected ovals facing the sea. The Christopher is an exciting work in progress, under the guidance of Christian Langlade, an Orient-Express hotel pro involved in numerous hotel launches around the world, including Sandy Lane in Barbados. By press time, 30 out of the 42 rooms will be renovated, including 19 spacious new suites with rainforest showers built into ceilings, bleached louvered ceilings, and square tubs built for two. Everything is impeccably and sustainably sourced: Floors are a cool concrete composite laid with a trowel; tables and benches were made from recycled timber from Indonesia; and beds are swathed in organic Belgian coverlets. Turin-based Laura Tonnato created the soaps and shampoos.

Of the two on-site restaurants, **Taino** ★ (open for breakfast and dinner) sits right over the lip of the sea and serves a French-Caribbean "ingredients cuisine," using sustainably sourced local seafood whenever possible; croissants are homemade and the fish is smoked in-house. Lunch is served at **Mango** ★, a 60-seat spot where the tables are literally set down in the sand; it's the only official barefoot restaurant on the island. Mango serves a homey *"cuisine de bonne femme,"* where fresh local fish are sprinkled with fresh herbs and fire-roasted. The resort is largely a couples' retreat in the high season, but families are heartily welcomed the rest of the year. A **Christopher Day Pass** includes lunch at Mango (60€; 110€ with massage).

9 Pointe Milou (B.P. 571), 97133 St. Barthélemy, F.W.I. ✆ **590/27-63-63.** Fax 590/27-92-92. www.hotelchristopher.com. 42 units. Winter 300€–470€ double, 545€–900€ suite; off season 200€–300€ double, 350€–580€ suite. Rates include full American breakfast. Extra person/bed 100€. One child 2 and under can stay free in parent's room. AE, MC, V. Closed Sept–Nov 14. **Amenities:** 2 restaurants; 2 bars; babysitting; gym; outdoor pool; room service; watersports equipment. *In room:* A/C and ceiling fan, TV, hair dryer, minibar, Wi-Fi (free).

Le P'tit Morne ★ (Finds)   This is hardly the most luxurious or stylish lodging on an island that's legendary for its glamorous five-star hotels. But the hotel's government-rated three-star format, its moderate rates, and the warm welcome extended by its island-born owners, Mr. and Mrs. Felix and their daughter Marie-Joëlle, make it a worthy vacation site. It's a 10-minute drive from the beach. The colonial-style guest rooms are filled with completely unpretentious furniture and comfortable king-size beds. There's plenty of elbow room, and units were built to catch the trade winds.

Colombier (P.O. Box 14), 97095 St. Barthélemy, F.W.I. ✆ 590/52-95-50. Fax 590/27-84-63. www.timorne.com. 14 units. Winter 185€–230€ double; off season 95€–150€ double. AE, MC, V. Closed Sept. **Amenities:** Babysitting; room service. *In room:* A/C, TV, fridge, kitchen.

Le Village St-Jean ★ (Value)   This family-owned cottage colony hideaway, 2km (1¼ miles) from the airport toward St-Jean, offers charm, warmth, and comfort. Lying in the center of St. Barts, a 5-minute drive uphill from St-Jean Beach, it offers one of the best values on this high-priced resort island. A collection of stone-and-redwood buildings scattered about the flower-filled garden and hillside holds five handsomely furnished hotel rooms (fridge only) and 20 cottages and three villas with well-equipped kitchens, tiled bathrooms, sun decks or gardens, tiered living rooms, and balconies with retractable awnings and hammocks strategically placed to enjoy the breeze and spectacular ocean views. A lovely infinity pool comes with killer views of the sea. The **Well-Being Cottage** holds a gym and a relaxation room for massages and other body treatments.

Colline de Saint-Jean (B.P. 623), 97133 St. Barthélemy, F.W.I. ✆ 590/27-61-39. Fax 590/27-77-96. www.villagestjeanhotel.com. 30 units. Winter 220€ double; 260€–650€ 1-bedroom cottage, from 620€ 2-bedroom cottage; off season 135€ double, 170€–350€ 1-bedroom cottage, 400€ 2-bedroom cottage. Extra person 50€–70€. AE, MC, V. Rates include continental breakfast. **Amenities:** Restaurant; bar; babysitting; gym; Jacuzzi; outdoor pool; room service; Wi-Fi (free). *In room:* A/C, ceiling fan, fridge, hair dryer, kitchen (except hotel rooms).

Salines Garden Cottages ★ (Finds)   This is excellent value on pricey St. Barts. Guests stay in stylish gingerbread *cazes* (traditional Creole houses), three with kitchenettes, nestled amid flowering trees and bushes just steps from one of the island's loveliest beaches. Each has a private tiled terrace shaded by bougainvillea. Interiors have brilliant batik fabrics, island crafts in various media, and four-poster or cast-iron beds. Asian and African antiques, collected by the peripatetic owners, enliven public spaces and grounds. Romantics and independent types can cherish utter seclusion while finding sustenance at two fine restaurants within walking distance—and Salines beach is just minutes away.

www.salinesgarden.com. 5 units. Winter 140€–190€ double; off season 90€–120€ double; 30€–50€ additional person. Continental breakfast, airport transfers, taxes, and service charges included. AE, MC, V. **Amenities:** Outdoor pool; babysitting. *In room:* A/C, ceiling fan, hair dryer, kitchen (in some).

Tropical Hôtel The facade of this small, unpretentious hotel looks like a picture-postcard Caribbean colonial inn. Originally built in 1981, it's perched on a hillside about 40m (131 ft.) above St-Jean Beach. Each room contains a private shower-only bathroom, a king-size bed with a good mattress, tile floors, and a fridge. Nine units have sea views and balconies; no. 11 has a porch that opens onto a garden that's so lush it looks like a miniature jungle. The hotel has an antiques-filled hospitality center where guests read, listen to music, or order drinks and snacks at a paneled bar surrounded by antiques. The pool is small, but watersports are available on the beach.

St-Jean (B.P. 147), 97133 St. Barthélemy, F.W.I. ℰ **800/223-9815** in the U.S., or 590/27-64-87. Fax 590/27-81-74. www.tropical-hotel.com. 21 units. Winter 216€–242€ double, 246€–272€ triple; off season 144€–170€ double, 174€–200€ triple. Rates include continental breakfast. AE, MC, V. Closed Sept 1–Oct 15. **Amenities:** Babysitting; outdoor pool; watersports equipment. *In room:* A/C and ceiling fan, TV, fridge, hair dryer.

INEXPENSIVE

La Normandie (Value) This modest, unassuming, family-owned Antillean inn has undergone a transformation: No longer a plain Jane, the Normadie has become a smart boutique inn with completely updated rooms. The owners, however, are committed to keeping the rates down, and lucky for you—this is a very good value. A Brazilian-wood deck connects the two buildings that hold the guest rooms. The Normandie is located near the intersection of two major roads, about 200m (660 ft.) from Lorient Beach.

97133 L'Orient, St. Barthélemy, F.W.I. ℰ **590/27-61-66.** Fax 590/27-58-32. www.normandiehotelstbarts.com. 8 units. Winter 175€ double; off season 125€ double. Rates include continental breakfast and afternoon wine. AE, DC, MC, V. **Amenities:** Outdoor pool. *In room:* A/C, TV (in some), fridge, Wi-Fi.

3 DINING

Fueled by young French chefs and hotel dining rooms that keep ratcheting up the excellence quotient, the St. Barts dining scene is superb. It's also really, really expensive, and prized tables are often booked along with hotel reservations in high season. But the island is not just about five-star hotel dining. You can eat very well at the many casual beachfront, hilltop, and harbor-side restaurants. Many of the island's most popular spots offer an affordable and filling lunchtime *plat du jour* (daily special) for 10€ to 12€. *Note: Entrée* is the French term for appetizer; *plat* means main course. Restaurants offering plats du jour include **La Marine** and the **Wall House** in Gustavia, and **The Hideaway** in St-Jean.

Virtually all the restaurants on St. Barts include a 15% service charge *(service compris).*

IN GUSTAVIA

At press time, the solid Italian food served in the elegant, candlelit **L'Isola** (✆ 590/51-00-05; www.lisolastbarth.com), in the former site of O'Corner, was getting raves.

Note: New ownership has turned the acclaimed restaurant Le Sapotillier into **The B4** (Rue Sadi-Carnot; ✆ 590/52-45-31), and the clapboard-covered Creole cottage set beside a magnificent sapodilla tree had been reconfigured as a small restaurant serving tapas and French classics as well as a late-night bar/VIP lounge.

Bonito Saint Barth ★ FRENCH/ASIAN FUSION Formerly La Mandala, Bonito Saint Barth has been transformed into a striking ceviche bar/fusion restaurant. White is the new black here, with snappy white tablecloths and painted white wicker nicely offset by blue-and-white pillows. A candlelit, white-on-white lounge with nightly DJs has ramped up the hipness quotient. The location alone—a house on Gustavia's steepest street with a dining deck overlooking a swimming pool—guarantees memorable sunset cocktails.

Rue de la Sous-Prefecture. ✆ **590/27-96-96.** Reservations recommended. Main courses 22€–34€. MC, V. Thurs–Tues 7–11pm; sushi and cocktails 5–7pm.

Eddy's ★ ⓥ**alue** CREOLE For some 15 years, charismatic Eddy Stackelborough has satisfied in-the-know locals and regulars with simple but honest island fare (green papaya salad, shrimp curry barbecued ribs, chicken in coconut sauce, passion fruit mousse). The setting resembles a Caribbean translation of *The Secret Garden:* It's a virtual jungle punctuated by ethno-tropic trappings. It's a miracle how Eddy keeps prices affordable by most standards (perhaps the roving location keeps rents down).

Rue du Centenaire (near rue Général du Gaulle), Gustavia. ✆ **590/27-54-17.** No reservations taken. Main courses 15€–22€. No credit cards. Mon–Sat noon–10:30pm.

La Route des Boucaniers ★ FRENCH/CREOLE Having written a five-volume primer, owner/chef Francis Delage is considered an authority on Creole cuisine. The decor evokes a rum shack—there's even a boat wreck—and the fare is simple but hearty. The restaurant has a prime perch overlooking Gustavia harbor. The menu offers such tempting dishes as spiny lobster and pumpkin bisque; coq au vin de Bourgogne; sea scallops and shrimp with crispy risotto and passionfruit sauce; and a traditional West Indian chicken Colombo curry with Creole sauce. The *assiete Creole* (spicy Caribbean platter) is a tasty seafood platter of codfish fritters, conch gratin, marinated Bonito puff pastry of crab, and a *feroce d'avocat* (local avocado recipe and green salad).

Rue de Bord de Mer, Gustavia. ℂ **590/27-73-00.** Reservations required in winter. Main courses 20€–28€. AE, MC, V. Daily 10am–10pm.

Pipiri Palace ★ Ⓥalue FRENCH/CREOLE   The twinkling lights and densely planted gardens fronting a classic Creole cottage make this a romantic spot in the heart of Gustavia. It's a lush, lively spot, with gregarious owner, Pierrot, presiding over the nightly action. The barbecued ribs and grilled rock lobster are specialties, but the local fish, served in a lemony butter sauce or Colombo-style, is equally good. Start with the lobster bisque or homemade foie gras.

Rue General-de-Gaulle, Gustavia. ℂ **590/27-53-20.** Reservations recommended. Main courses 19€–33€. MC, V. Lunch Mon–Sat 6:30–10pm. Closed June–Oct.

Wall House ★★ Ⓥalue FRENCH/CREOLE   New ownership has not diminished the Wall House traditions of warm service, lively ambience, and bistro fare with flair at reasonable prices. The dazzling harbor views certainly don't hurt. In taking over the reins of this local favorite (and retaining most of the old staff), new owners Bernard and Julien Tatin have proven to be warm, gracious hosts. The menu retains a lively mix of ingredients and influences: Look for bacon-wrapped roasted monkfish filet in a black pepper sauce; sautéed foie gras with rhubarb compote in a gingerbread sauce; and the divinely creative lobster and mozzarella on crispy polenta bruschetta with pesto. The three-course prix-fixe menus (29€) and daily *plats du jours* (10€–12€) are remarkable values.

La Pointe. ℂ **590/27-71-83.** www.wallhouserestaurant.com. Reservations recommended. Main courses 18€–28€. AE, MC, V. Lunch Mon–Sat noon–2pm; dinner daily 7–9:30pm. Closed June–Oct.

IN THE GRANDE SALINE BEACH AREA

Le Grain de Sel ★ CREOLE   Set against a rocky backdrop on a wooden deck overlooking the old salt ponds of Salines, Grain de Sel has a sun-dappled, treehouse appeal. It's a casual place that's popular with locals, but the crowd is mixed, with families, hipsters, and beach-goers tucking into delicious, well-priced Creole classics. The seafood is well-prepared, and you can't go wrong with the shrimp, here grilled

> ## *Traiteurs:* **Gourmet Food to Go**
>
> St. Barts can be so expensive that many visitors often go the epicurean takeout route at one of the gourmet *traiteurs* on the island. These *traiteurs* go way beyond the classic French picnic fare of bread, cheese, and a bottle of wine: This is highfalutin' grub, or at the very least an incredibly tasty takeout repast, perfect for a midday beach picnic or a candlelit dinner on your hotel balcony or villa terrace. **La Rôtisserie**—which has two stores: **Gustavia** (rue du Roi Oscar II; ℂ **590/27-63-13**) and **St-Jean** (ℂ **590/29-75-69**)—is a boulangerie, patisserie, bakery, and more, selling wine, mustard, pâté, herbs, caviar, chocolate, and exotic oils and vinegars, as well as takeout *plats du jour* from pâtés to *pissaladière* (onion tart); the Gustavia store is open daily 7am to 7pm; the St-Jean location is open from 6am to 8pm. Also in St-Jean are two more highly recommended *traiteurs*. **Maya's To Go** (ℂ **590/29-83-70**), across from the airport, is operated by the famed island restaurateurs (see below) and offers such takeout specialties as sesame chicken noodles, wahoo ceviche, tuna tataki, meatloaf sandwiches, and more. It's open Tuesday to Sunday 7am to 7pm. American-born I. B. Charneau named **Kiki-é Mo** (ℂ **590/27-90-65;** www.kikiemo.com) after sons Keefer and Marlon. It channels the Italian *salumerias* of her Short Hills, New Jersey, childhood with pizzas, pastas, and panini—and great espresso; it's open 9am to 10pm. **La Route des Boucaniers,** the harborside restaurant in Gustavia, will also do delicious French/Creole takeout meals (ℂ **590/27-73-00**). And if you want to stock up on basic supplies and groceries, St. Barts has a number of grocery stores with excellent selections of imported French delicacies, good wines, and excellent snacks. The **Super-U supermarket** (which recently replaced the old Match) is located directly across from the airport; it's open on Sundays.

on kebabs with a buttery herb sauce or swimming in a heady beer sauce. Local fish is grilled or cooked in a tomatoey Creole sauce. Entrees come with traditional rice and peas.

Plage de Saline. ℂ **590/52-46-05.** Reservations recommended. Main courses 16€–27€. MC, V. Open daily 11:30am–4pm and 7–10:30pm.

Le Tamarin ★ FRENCH/CREOLE   The perfect place for a lazy
afternoon on the beach, this open-air bistro sits amid rocky hills and
forests on the road to Plage de Saline, in a thatched gingerbread cottage with a teak-and-bamboo interior. Lunch is the more animated
meal, with customers dining in T-shirts and bathing suits. If you have
to wait, savor an aperitif in one of the hammocks stretched under a
tamarind tree—or even take a dip in the swimming pool. A new
menu focuses on light, summery fare.

Plage de Saline. ☎ **590/27-72-12.** Reservations required for dinner. Main courses
25€–34€. AE, MC, V. Wed–Mon noon–4pm and 7–10:30pm.

IN THE GRAND CUL-DE-SAC AREA

A casual beachside favorite, **O'Corail Restaurant** ★ (☎ **590/29-
33-27**) opened in April 2008 on the sands between Le Sereno and
the former La Gloriette in front of the Ouanalao Dive shop. It has
terrific views out over the bay at Grand Cul-de-Sac and good, fresh-
tasting food, from burgers to lobster salad to paninis. It's open for
breakfast and lunch Tuesday to Sunday and dinner Friday and Saturday nights.

Bartoloméo ★★ FRENCH/MEDITERRANEAN   It's located
inside one of the island's most exclusive hotels, Guanahani. But Bartoloméo manages to be unthreatening, informally sophisticated, and
gracefully upscale. It's a lovely setting, half inside a Creole cottage
under a lime wainscoted ceiling and half outside on a gaily lighted
wooden deck with tables under big umbrellas beneath the blue-black
sky. Cream-colored walls are romantically lit. The food is impeccable.
If you want *poisson,* try the basted swordfish tataki in lemon and salt,
with baby bok choy. For meat-lovers, there's the 10-hour confit of
suckling lamb knuckle-joint. Starters include black truffle carnaroli
risotto or St. Barts lobster ravioli in a foamy caper juice; the curry
shrimp cannellone wrapped in an outer layer of pasta and an inner
wrapper of braised cabbage is fantastic. Spaghetti with clams comes to
the table tangled in sprigs of dill and sprays of white foam, looking as
if it had washed up right out of the sea.

In the Hôtel Guanahani, Grand Cul-de-Sac. ☎ **590/52-90-14.** Reservations recommended, especially for nonguests. Main courses 32€–44€. AE, DC, MC, V. Daily
7:30–10pm.

Le Restaurant des Pêcheurs ★★ FRENCH/SEAFOOD   The
house restaurant at Le Sereno resort is a lively spot during the day,
but at night it takes on a more somber, less vibrant tenor. Maybe
it's the liberally spaced seating, good for privacy-loving diners but
not so good for optimal feng shui. The food doesn't disappoint,
but it's pricey for what is essentially a fishhouse—alas, this *is* St. Barts.

The menu features a catch of the day, both local (29€) and imported Atlantic/Mediterranean (45€). A deft hand is in the kitchen, that's for sure. The starters include a deeply flavored gazpacho and a lobster trio of carpaccio, mini spring roll, and charlotte with mango dressing. For mains, try the giant prawns in garlic and herb sauce; risotto with grilled scallops, leeks, and green asparagus; lamb shank with Caribbean vegetables; or a perfect pasta with baby clams.

In Le Sereno hotel, Grand Cul-de-Sac. *©* **590/29-83-00.** Reservations recommended, especially for nonguests. Main courses 22€–48€. AE, MC, V. Daily 7am–10:30pm.

IN POINTE MILIOU

The intriguing menus at the two house restaurants in the newly opened **Hotel Christopher** are worth the drive along the daredevil curves in Pointe Miliou. The open-to-the-sea **Taino** ★ offers a French-Caribbean "ingredients cuisine," using sustainably sourced local seafood whenever possible. Lunch is served at **Mango** ★, a 60-seat spot in the sand offering an earthy *"cuisine de bonne femme"*; it's the only official barefoot restaurant on the island.

IN THE PUBLIC BEACH AREA

Maya's ★ INTERNATIONAL   After several seasons, this beach-front *boîte* just northwest of Gustavia remains the island's premier stargazing (in both senses) spot, thanks to its artful simplicity and preferential treatment for regulars. The much-rebuilt Antillean house attracts crowds of luminaries from the worlds of media, fashion, and entertainment. It's the kind of *pieds dans l'eau* (feet in the water), picnic-table-on-the-beach place you might find on Martinique, where its French Creole chef, Maya Beuzelin-Gurley, grew up. Maya stresses "clean, simple" food with few adornments other than island herbs and lime juice. You might follow cold avocado soup with lobster with grilled fish in a Creole sauce or a veal chop with portobello mushrooms. Almost no cream is used in any dish, further endearing the place to its clientele. Views face west and south, ensuring glorious sunset watching.

Public Beach. *©* **590/27-75-73.** Reservations required in winter. Main courses 31€–43€. AE, MC, V. Mon–Sat 7–10pm.

IN THE ST-JEAN BEACH AREA

The Eden Rock Hotel has two excellent dining choices: The chillingly expensive **On the Rocks** ★, serving dinner in a splendid spot high above the Baie St-Jean; and **The Sandbar** ★, open for lunch down on the beach. Call *©* **590/29-79-99** for reservations.

The Hideaway ★ (Value) INTERNATIONAL   How can you not love a place that advertises "corked wine, warm beer, lousy food, view of the car park" with a staff "hand-picked from the sleaziest dives, mental institutions, and top-security prisons?" Savvy locals and celebrity regulars know that the sound system, food, and prices rock at this beloved haunt nicknamed Chez Andy after Brit owner Andrew Hall. Worthy specialties include a duck gizzard salad dressed in a house dressing; shrimp Creole; pastas; and thin-crust pizzas from the wood-burning oven. Andy will finish off your evening (and you) with a bottomless carafe of free vanilla or orange rum.

Vaval Center, St-Jean. ℂ **590/27-63-62.** www.hideaway.tv. Reservations recommended. Main courses 16€–24€. AE, MC, V. Tues–Sat noon–2:30pm and Tues–Sun 7–10:30pm.

La Plage ★ SEAFOOD/FRENCH   This feet-in-the-sand beach bar has been an instant island classic since it opened, with rich tropical colors and comfortable lounges. Tables spill out onto the St-Jean sand under the starry sky. Expect a lively, welcoming scene, with DJ-spun music—but also expect a relaxed vibe and solid food. Dine on grilled fish and lobster and island-inspired flavors.

Tom Beach Hotel, Plage de St-Jean. ℂ **590/27-53-13.** Reservations recommended. Main courses 18€–40€. AE, MC, V. Daily 8–11pm; closed Mon dinner.

AT MORNE LURIN

Santa Fe ★ FRENCH   This informal restaurant is a local favorite and set inland atop one of the highest points on the island overlooking Gouverneur Beach, which makes it a prime spot for watching legendary sunsets from wraparound decks. For decades this place was known as a good burger joint. It still serves a great burger, but the rest of the menu has headed upmarket, specializing in French dishes along with barbecued meats and fresh fish. In addition to the catch of the day, opt for the côte de veau or the flavorful tomato tart.

Morne Lurin. ℂ **590/27-61-04.** Reservations not accepted. Main courses 19€–60€. MC, V. Thurs–Tues noon–2:30pm and 6–11pm.

IN THE TOINY COAST AREA

Le Gaïac ★★★ FRENCH   This swooningly romantic restaurant is for folks who want to dine among the rich and famous at Le Toiny, one of St. Barts' most expensive hotels. Here's the shocker: You don't have to be rich *or* famous to get the restaurant's seamless, pampered service. You dine in an elegant open-air pavilion adjacent to the resort's infinity pool, with a view that sweeps out over the blue-black sea. Lunchtime menu items—black truffle and Parmesan spaghetti, perhaps, or a yellowtail snapper in a lemongrass emulsion—are simple yet exquisitely prepared, and the sumptuous all-you-can-eat "Brunch du Toiny" (43€) is a must. Dinner courses might include a lighter-than-air tuna and salmon tartar with wheatberries. For the main course, try the fricassee of Maine lobster and cepe mushroom or lamb served in three different Creole styles. A new Tuesday-night Fishmarket Menu lets you pick out your fresh filet—which is then lightly grilled—and your choice of sauce, whether a creamy tomato or an old-fashioned *moutarde*. It's all first-rate, from the food to the setting to the impeccable service.

In Hôtel Le Toiny, Anse de Toiny. ℂ **590/27-88-88.** Reservations recommended in winter. Main courses lunch 20€–29€, dinner 30€–40€. AE, DC, MC, V. Mon–Sat 7:30–10:30am, noon–2:30pm, and 7–10pm; Sun 11am–2:30pm. Closed Sept 1–Oct 23.

---

4 BEACHES

St. Barts has some 21 white-sand beaches. Few are crowded, even in winter; all are public and free. Topless sunbathing is common (nudity is officially permitted on two). The best known is **St-Jean Beach ★★**, which is actually two beaches divided by the Eden Rock promontory. It offers watersports, restaurants, and a few hotels, as well as some shaded areas: There's fine snorkeling west of the rock. Just to the east is **Lorient Beach ★**, on the north shore, quiet and calm, with shaded areas. An offshore reef tames breakers save on the wilder western end, where locals and French surfer dudes hang out.

The largest beach on the island is lovely **Flamands Beach ★**, to the west, dotted with a few small hotels and in some areas shaded by lantana palms.

For a beach with hotels, restaurants, and watersports, **Grand Cul-de-Sac Beach ★**, on the northeast shore, fits the bill. It's narrow and protected by a reef. The shallow lagoon waters aren't great for swimming, but the breezy conditions make it ideal for wind- and kite-surfing.

North of Gustavia, the rather unromantic-sounding **Public Beach** is a combination of sand and pebbles more popular with boaters than swimmers. There is no more beautiful place on the island, however, to watch the boats at sunset. Also in Gustavia, **Shell Beach** is awash with lovely little seashells—or it is when the conditions are right. Rocky outcroppings protect the beach from strong waves. It's also the site of popular **Do Brazil,** a favored lunch spot as well (see "Nightlife," below).

In the picturesque fishing village of Corossol, **Corossol Beach** offers a typical glimpse of French life, St. Barts style, facing a bay dotted with bobbing boats. This is a calm, protected beach, with brown sand and a charming little **seashell museum.**

Southeast of Gustavia, **Gouverneur Beach ★★**, on the southern coast, can be reached by driving south from Gustavia to Lurin. Turn at the popular **Santa Fe** restaurant (*©* **590/27-61-04;** stop for drinks on the way back to savor sensational sunset views) and head down a narrow road. The uncrowded strand is gorgeous, ringed by steep cliffs overlooking St. Kitts, Saba, and Statia (St. Eustacius), but there's no shade. You'll find excellent snorkeling off the point. **Grande Saline Beach ★★**, to the east of Gouverneur Beach, is reached by driving up the road from the commercial center in St-Jean; a 10-minute walk from the parking lot over a rocky pathway and you're here. Lack of shade doesn't deter the nude sunbathers (the late JFK, Jr., was famously photographed here).

Colombier Beach ★★ is difficult to get to but well worth the effort. It can only be reached by boat or by taking a rugged goat path from Petite Anse past Flamands Beach, a 30-minute walk. The lookouts here are breathtaking; several adjacent coves are usually patrolled only by peacocks and mules. Shade, seclusion, and snorkeling are found here, and you can pack a lunch and spend the day. Locals call it Rockefeller's Beach because for many years David Rockefeller owned the surrounding property (Harrison Ford allegedly bought his blue pyramidical house).

More than one local has taken me to the fiercely beautiful **Grand Fond,** on the Toiny Coast, overlooking a rock-strewn beach and rough seas. Facing the beach (and on the other side of the two-lane road) is a mossy green hill that rises sharply; here, goats serenely graze the pastoral and undeveloped cliffsides.

5 SPORTS & OTHER OUTDOOR PURSUITS

FISHING Anglers are fond of the waters around St. Barts. From March to July, they catch mahimahi; in September, wahoo. Atlantic bonito, barracuda, and marlin also turn up. **Yannis Marine,** Gustavia (*©* **590/29-89-12;** www.yannismarine.com), charters a 50-foot Sunseeker Carmarque outfitted for deep-sea sport fishing. A half-day trip for nine guests costs 1,300€, which includes a captain, fuel, snacks, open bar, and fishing equipment. Yannis also offers boat rentals, snorkeling trips, and island excursions; sunset cruises (7–11 guests) cost 850€ to 900€.

KITESURFING   Kitesurfing is fast becoming one of the most popular sports here. Former champion Enguerrand Espinassou gives expert lessons at **7e Ciel of St. Barth Kiteschool,** at the Ouanalao Dive center (see below) on Grand Cul-de-Sac (© **690/69-26-90**), open daily from 8am to 5pm. Kitesurfing costs 300€ for a 3-hour lesson, 450€ for a 5-hour lesson, and 800€ for 10 hours. Reservations are recommended, especially in high season.

SAILING   Charter the beautiful *Lone Fox,* a wooden sailing yacht built in 1957, for a day of sailing, swimming, snorkeling, and exploring the St. Barts coastline. You'll have a captain and crew on board to do all the heavy lifting. The maximum number of guests is eight; a full-day charter is $2,000 (© **690/33-27-91;** www.lonefoxcharters. com).

SCUBA DIVING   **Marine Service,** quai du Yacht-Club, in Gustavia (© **590/27-70-34;** www.marine-service.fr), is the island's most complete watersports facility. It operates from a one-story building at the edge of a marina on the opposite, quieter side of Gustavia's harbor. Catering to both beginners and advanced divers, the outfit is familiar with at least 20 unusual sites scattered throughout the protected offshore Réserve Marine de St-Barth. The most interesting include Pain de Sucre off Gustavia harbor and the remote **Grouper,** west of St. Barts, close to the uninhabited cay known as Île Forchue. The only relatively safe wreck dive, the rusting hulk of *Kayali,* a trawler that sank in deep waters in 1994, is recommended for experienced divers. A resort course, including five open-water dives, costs 280€. A "scuba review," for certified divers who are out of practice, also goes for 75€, while a one-tank dive for certified divers begins at 60€. Multidive packages are available.

SNORKELING   Hundreds of shallow areas right off beaches such as Anse des Cayes teem with colorful aquatic life. You can also test your luck at hundreds of points offshore. **Marine Service,** quai du Yacht-Club, Gustavia (see above), runs daily snorkeling expeditions. Half- and full-day group excursions aboard a 13 or 14m (42- or 46-ft.) catamaran, including snacks, open bar, all equipment, and exploration of two separate snorkeling sites, costs from 72€ per person. They also rent snorkeling gear and can direct you to good snorkeling sites.

SURFING   Beach clubs rent out equipment for surfing St. Barts' main surfing beaches, including Anse des Cayes, Toiny, Miliou, and Lorient. Contact the **Reefer Surf Club** (© **590/27-67-63**).

6 SHOPPING

Duty-free St. Barts offers liquor and French perfumes at some of the lowest prices in the Caribbean—often cheaper than in France itself. You'll find good buys, albeit a limited selection, in haute couture, crystal, porcelain, watches, and other luxuries. Gustavia's **rue de la République** is lined with designer boutiques, including Bulgari, Cartier, Giorgio Armani, Louis Vuitton, and Hermès.

Aside from Gustavia, St-Jean is the island's center of shopping action, with several small shopping plazas along the main road leading toward Lorient: **Les Galeries du Commerce, La Villa Creole, La Sodexa,** and **L'Espace Neptune,** each filled with small boutiques. We actually find St-Jean a more satisfying shopping experience than Gustavia—less of the chillingly pricey luxury brands and more of the real-life St. Barts clothing we covet: flirty bohemian-style kurtas and gypsy dresses; sexy, slouchy jersey separates in dusky tones; gold and silver sandals or bejeweled flip-flops. **La Savane Commercial Center,** across from the airport, has grocery stores, an electronics store, and a handful of boutiques.

As for island crafts, the little old ladies from the fishing village of Corossol have traditionally made intricately braided **straw goods ★** (baskets, bags, bonnets) from the dried fronds of the latanier palm. These delicately woven crafts are for sale along the harborside Quai in Gustavia.

Keep in mind that most shopkeepers open around 9am or 10am but close midday for an extended *dejeuner* (lunch) that may last until 2pm or 3pm. Closing times are generally 7pm.

There are **officially designated sales seasons** twice a year, generally the month of May and from mid-October to mid-November. Much of everything is deeply discounted, including couture—so expect to find some great deals during these times.

Diamond Genesis   This well-respected jeweler maintains an inventory of designs strongly influenced by European tastes. Although the prices can go as high as 10,000€, an appealing and more affordable 18-karat-gold depiction of St. Barts sells for around 200€. The selection of fine watches is superb. 12 rue du Général-de-Gaulle/Les Suites du Roi Oscar II, Gustavia. ℂ 590/27-66-94. www.diamondgenesis.com.

Goldfinger   This is the largest purveyor of luxury goods on St. Barts. The entire second floor is devoted to perfumes and crystal, the street level to jewelry and watches. Prices are usually 15% to 20% less than equivalent retail goods sold stateside. Ask about sales when you visit. Rue de la France. ℂ 590/27-64-66.

La Ligne St. Barth ★ The laboratory/shop sells the famed scents and skincare products still produced on-site by the Brins family, island residents since the 17th century. Brewed from the extracts of native Caribbean fruits and flowers, Ligne St Barth products include sun creams and sunscreens (Solaire) made with oils produced from the tropical roucou tree (a natural insect repellent). *Tip:* The shop offers deep discounts on slightly damaged lotions, creams, and more during the sales seasons. Route de Saline, Lorient. 𝄏 590/27-82-63. www. lignestbarth.com.

Le Comptoir du Cigare This place caters to the December-to-April crowd of villa and yacht owners. It's sheathed in exotic hardwood, and enhanced with a glass-sided, walk-in humidor storing thousands of cigars from Cuba and the Dominican Republic. Note to Americans: Smoke the Cubans on the island—it's illegal to bring them back to the United States. There's also a collection of silver ornaments, lighters, pens suitable for adorning the desk of a CEO, artisan-quality Panama hats from Ecuador, and cigar boxes and humidors. 6 rue du Général-de-Gaulle. 𝄏 590/27-50-62. www.comptoirducigare.com.

Les Artisans This top gallery specializes in fanciful crafts and custom jewelry. They can also arrange visits to ateliers of leading local artists in various media (names to watch include Robert Danet, Jackson Questel, and Hannah Moser). Rue du Roi Oscar II. 𝄏 590/27-50-40.

Lili Belle ★ This little shop in St-Jean sells stylish prêt-à-porter clothing from such beloved Parisian designers as Isabel Marant and Claudi Pierlot. Look for big discounts during the sales seasons. Le Pélican Plage, St-Jean. 𝄏 590/87-46-14.

Linde Gallery ★★ The fabulous collection of must-haves includes vintage Pucci and Alaïa, elegantly stylish prêt-a-porter (modern Pucci, Rick Owens, Linde collection), vintage Courrèges and Yves St. Laurent sunglasses from the 1970s and '80s, Melissa shoes, Steidl artbooks, objets d'art, and more. The rigorously curated clothes, including silk tunics and printed caftans, are beautifully wearable. A smaller second shop is located in the **Hotel Christopher,** in Point Milou. Les Hauts du Carré d'Or, Gustavia. 𝄏 590/29-73-86; www.lindegallery.com.

Lolita Jaca ★ Flirty and ethereal, with more than a nod to "hippie chic" styling and East Indian patterning, Lolita Jaca outfits the quintessentially sexy St. Barts femme in soft, candy-hued satins and silks. Les Hauts du Carré d'Or, Gustavia. 𝄏 590/27-59-98. www.lolitajaca.com.

Made in St-Barth The MADE IN ST-BARTH logo is everywhere here: on T-shirts, pants, dresses, baby clothes, bags, purses, you name it. Villa Créole, St-Jean. 𝄏 590/27-56-57.

Mademoiselle Hortense After expressing our admiration for the effortlessly chic ensembles worn by a stylish St. Barts restaurant hostess, she had two words to say: "Mademoiselle Hortense." Rue del République, Gustavia. (C) 590/27-56-57.

Pain de Sucre Inside this Creole house across from St-Jean Beach is a collection of beautifully styled bikinis and beachwear in gorgeous prints and florals. It also has a small collection of darling matching swimsuits for little girls. Pélican Plage, St-Jean. (C) 590/29-30-79. www. paindesucre.com.

Poupette St Barth ★ This frothy little pastel-hued boutique offers gorgeous hippie-goddess dresses, minis, and kurtas in meltingly soft fabrics and embroidered or floral designs. Little-girl dresses are charming mini versions of the grownups' frocks. Rue del République, Gustavia. (C) 590/27-94-49. www.poupette-st-barth.com.

Stéphane & Bernard ★★ For nearly 30 years, this has been the couture playground of Stéphane Lanson and Bernard Blancaneau, who have stocked their salon to the rafters with the latest handpicked Lacroix, Leger, Galliano, Versace, and Missoni creations. Rue de la République, Gustavia. (C) 590/27-65-69. www.stephaneandbernard.com.

---

7 ST. BARTS AFTER DARK

Most visitors consider a sunset aperitif followed by a French Creole dinner under the stars enough of a nocturnal adventure. Beyond that, the lounge and live music scenes have exploded, enlivening the once quiet evenings.

In Gustavia, one of the most popular gathering places is **Le Select,** rue de la France ((C) 590/27-86-87), a 50-year-old institution named after its more famous granddaddy in the Montparnasse section of Paris. Locals love this classic dive with the friendly vibe. It's a glorified shanty, though most patrons congregate at tables in the open-air garden (called "Cheeseburgers in Paradise" in homage to honorary St. Barthian Jimmy Buffett), where a game of dominoes might be under way as you walk in. You never know who might show up here—Mick Jagger perhaps? It's closed Sunday.

Former French tennis star and singer/performer Yannick Noah is one of the owners of **Do Brazil** ★ ((C) 590/29-06-66; http://do brazil.com), right on the Plage de Shell Beach. This bar and café is a great place to hang out after a swim on Shell Beach. It serves a French-Thai cuisine and a sampling of French-Brazilian dishes.

Le Bête à Z'Ailes ★ (also known as the Baz Bar) on the harbor in Gustavia (© **590/92-74-09**) is a sushi bar and live music club, where an eclectic assortment of bands play soul, jazz, blues, urban folk, and indie tunes, accompanied by excellent fusion food.

Draped in red, **Le Ti St. Barth** (Pointe Milou; © **590/27-97-71**; www.ksplaces.com) calls itself a Caribbean tavern, and the setting, in a pitched-roof Creole-style cottage, manages to be both charming and sexy at once. The club has a fashion show nightly at 11pm in high season.

Le Ti St. Barth's Carole Gruson transformed the **Le Yacht Club,** 6 Rue Jeanne d'Arc (© **590/27-68-91**; www.ksplaces.com), into a favored haunt of the dawn patrol, with breathtaking harbor views through billowing white drapes.

Fast Facts

1 FAST FACTS: ST. MAARTEN/ ST. MARTIN

AMERICAN EXPRESS   None of the three islands covered in this book has an official AmEx representative.

AREA CODES   The country and area code for St. Martin is 590/590; the country and area code for St. Maarten is 599/599.

BANKS   Banks affiliated with the **Cirrus** (© **800/424-7787**; www.mastercard.com) and **PLUS** (© **800/843-7587**; www.visa.com) ATM networks are located on St. Maarten/St. Martin. On the Dutch side, several banks are clustered along Front Street in Philipsburg. On the French side, most banks are along rue de la République in Marigot. Check the following banks' websites for exact locations of ATMs (also called ABMs for "automated banking machines"): **Windward Island Bank** (http://wib-bank.net), **Scotiabank** (www.scotiabank.com), **FirstCaribbean Bank** (www.firstcaribbeanbank.com), and **RBTT N.V.** (www.rbtt.com). **Princess Juliana International Airport** in St. Maarten has two ATMs (WIB and RBTT) on the Arrivals floor. A Scotiabank branch is located at the **cruise terminal building** at Pointe Blanche, Philipsburg, St. Maarten. *Note:* Keep in mind that ATMs in St. Maarten give you a choice of dollars or euros, while ATMs on St. Martin dispense only euros.

BUSINESS HOURS   **Banks:** On the Dutch side, most banks are open Monday to Friday from 8:30am to 3:30pm, Saturday from 9am to noon. On the French side, they are usually open Monday to Friday 8:30am to 1:30pm. **Stores/shops:** Although French St. Martin stores open around 9am and close around 7pm, most shopkeepers close to take an extended lunch break from around 12:30 to 2pm, or even later. Dutch side shops stay open continuously from 9am to 6pm (and later).

CURRENCY   U.S. dollars are widely accepted, and prices in hotels and most restaurants and shops are most often designated in dollars as well. On the French side, the official monetary unit is the **euro** (€), with most establishments widely quoting and accepting either dollars or Netherlands Antilles florin (NAf) guilders as well. At press time, the U.S. dollar was trading at $1.20 to 1€. *Prices throughout this book are given in U.S. dollars for establishments on the Dutch side, and in euros or dollars for establishments on the French side.*

DRIVING RULES   See "Getting Around St. Maarten/St. Martin," on p. 26.

DRINKING LAWS   Eighteen is the legal drinking age on St. Maarten/St. Martin. Alcohol is sold in grocery stores and restaurants.

DRUGSTORES   Both sides have several pharmacies, though none are open 24 hours. On the **French** side, try **Pharmacie du Port** (rue de la Liberté, Marigot; ✆ **590/87-50-79;** Mon–Sat 8am–7:30pm, Sun hours vary). On the **Dutch** side, try **Philipsburg Pharmacy** (4 E. Voges St., Philipsburg; ✆ **599/542-3001;** Mon–Fri 7:30am–7pm, Sat 9am–1pm, Sun 10am–noon), **Simpson Bay Pharmacy** (Simpson Bay Yacht Club, 163 Welfare Rd.; ✆ **599/544-3653;** Mon–Fri 8:15am–7pm, Sat 9am–1pm, Sun 5–7pm), and **the Druggist** (Airport Rd., Simpson Bay; ✆ **599/545-2777;** Mon–Fri 8:30am–7:30pm, Sat noon–7pm, Sun 1–3pm).

ELECTRICITY   Dutch St. Maarten and Anguilla use the same voltage (110-volt AC, 60 cycles) with the same electrical configurations as North America, so adapters and transformers are not necessary for Americans or Canadians. However, on French St. Martin and St. Barts, 220-volt AC prevails; North Americans will usually need transformers and adapters. To simplify things, many hotels on both sides of the island have installed sockets suitable for both European and North American appliances.

EMBASSIES & CONSULATES   On St. Maarten/St. Martin, **citizens of the U.S.** are represented by its consulate at St. Anna Boulevard, Willemstad, Curaçao (✆ **599/961-3066**). There is a Canadian consulate at 16A Topaz Dr., St. Maarten (✆ **599/544-5023**). **Citizens of the U.K.** can register with the consulate at 38 Jan Sofat in Willemstad, Curaçao (✆ **599/747-3322**).

EMERGENCIES   For emergencies, call ✆ **911.** On the **Dutch** side, call the **police** at ✆ **542-2222** or an **ambulance** at ✆ **542-2111;** to report a **fire,** call ✆ **911** or 120. On the **French** side, you can reach the **police** by dialing ✆ **17** or 87-50-10. In case of fire, dial ✆ **18.** For an **ambulance,** dial ✆ **15** or 29-04-04.

HOLIDAYS   National holidays are New Year's Day (Jan 1); Epiphany (Jan 6, French side); Carnival (early Feb); Good Friday and Easter

Monday (usually Apr); Labor Day (May 1); Ascension Day (early May); Bastille Day (July 14, French side); Schoelcher Day (July 21, French side); Assumption Day (Aug 15); All Saints' Day (Nov 1); Concordia Day and St. Martin Day (Nov 11); Christmas Day (Dec 25); and Boxing Day (Dec 26). For more information, see "St. Maarten/St. Martin Calendar of Events," on p. 20.

HOSPITALS   On the Dutch side, go to the **St. Maarten Medical Center,** Welegen Road, Cay Hill (© **599/543-1111;** www.sint maartenmedicalcenter.com). On the French side, the local hospital is **Hospital Louis-Constant Fleming,** near Marigot in Concordia (© **590/52-25-25**).

INTERNET ACCESS   Cybercafes can be found in both Marigot and Philipsburg, and most hotels have high-speed Internet access and/or a computer center.

MAIL   On St. Maarten, the **main post office** (© **599/542-2298**) is located on Walter Nisbeth Road. The **main post office** (Bureau Principal; © **590/51-07-64**) on the French side is in Marigot, on Rue de la Liberté.

NEWSPAPERS & MAGAZINES   In addition to several local newspapers (*The Daily Herald* is the leading English-language publication), visitors can pick up one of several useful tourist magazines including *St. Maarten Nature, St. Maarten Events, Discover St. Martin/St. Maarten, St. Maarten Nights, Ti Gourmet,* and *Vacation St. Maarten.*

PASSPORTS   See "Embassies & Consulates," above, for whom to contact if you lose your passport while traveling. For other information, contact the following agencies:

For Residents of Australia   Contact the **Australian Passport Information Service** at © **131-232,** or visit www.passports.gov.au.

For Residents of Canada   Contact the central **Passport Office,** Department of Foreign Affairs and International Trade, Ottawa, ON K1A 0G3 (© **800/567-6868;** www.ppt.gc.ca).

For Residents of Ireland   Contact the **Passport Office,** Setanta Centre, Molesworth Street, Dublin 2 (© **01/671-1633;** www.foreign affairs.gov.ie).

For Residents of New Zealand   Contact the **Passports Office,** Department of Internal Affairs, 47 Boulcott St., Wellington, 6011 (© **0800/225-050** in New Zealand or 04/474-8100; www.passports. govt.nz).

For Residents of the United Kingdom   Visit your nearest passport office, major post office, or travel agency or contact the **Identity and Passport Service (IPS),** 89 Eccleston Square, London, SW1V 1PN (© **0300/222-0000;** www.ips.gov.uk).

For Residents of the United States   To find your regional passport office, check the U.S. State Department website (http://travel.state. gov/passport) or call the **National Passport Information Center** (© **877/487-2778**) for automated information.

POLICE   See "Emergencies," above.

SAFETY   See "Crime & Safety," on p. 35.

SMOKING   While many larger properties offer nonsmoking rooms, there are no regulations against smoking—for now. Legislation has recently been proposed to ban smoking in all St. Maarten restaurants, bars, and casinos—check to see if the law has been passed.

TAXES   For departures to international destinations from Princess Juliana Airport on the Dutch side, there's a departure tax of $30 ($10 if you're leaving the island for St. Eustatius or Saba; if you're leaving by ferry from Marigot Pier to Anguilla, the departure tax is $4). There is a 3€ ($4.50) departure tax for departures from L'Espérance Airport on the French side. *Note:* The departure tax is often included in the airfare. On St. Maarten, a government tax of 5% is added to your hotel bill. On top of that, many hotels tack on a service charge of 10% to 15%. Hotels on French St. Martin add a 10% service charge and a *taxe de séjour,* a local room tax of 4% to 5%.

TELEPHONES   See "Staying Connected," p. 39.

TIME   St. Maarten/St. Martin operate on Atlantic Standard Time year-round. Thus in winter, if it's 6pm in Philipsburg, it's 5pm in New York. During daylight saving time in the United States, the island and the U.S. East Coast are on the same time.

TIPPING   See "Tips on Dining," on p. 29, for restaurant guidelines. Otherwise, porters and bellmen expect $1 per bag. Taxi drivers should receive 10% of the fare, more if they offer touring or other suggestions.

TOILETS   Public facilities are few and far between other than a couple of options in Marigot, Philipsburg, and Orient Beach. Hotel lobbies and restaurants are the best options, though technically you should be a guest or customer.

WATER   The water on St. Maarten/St. Martin is safe to drink. In fact, most hotels serve desalinated water.

2 FAST FACTS: ANGUILLA

AREA CODES   The country and area code for Anguilla is 264.

BANKS   Banks with ATMs are open Monday to Thursday 8am to 3pm, Friday 8am to 5pm. Several banks, including **Scotiabank,** the Valley, Fairplay Commercial Complex (© **264/497-3333**), and **First Caribbean,** the Valley (© **264/497-2301**), have ATMs that are usually accessible after hours.

BUSINESS HOURS   Banks are open from 8am until 2pm Monday through Thursday and Friday until 4pm. Businesses keep widely varying schedules (some boutiques and art galleries close for lunch), although grocery stores are generally open Monday to Saturday from 8am to 9pm and Sunday to noon.

DRINKING LAWS   The legal drinking age is 18. Wine, beer, and liquor are sold in grocery stores and restaurants 7 days a week during regular hours.

DRIVING RULES   See "Getting Around," on p. 127.

ELECTRICITY   See "Fast Facts: St. Maarten/St. Martin," above.

EMBASSIES & CONSULATES   There is no U.S. diplomatic representation on Anguilla. **U.S. citizens** are advised to register with the consulates at Bluff House, English Harbour on Antigua (© **268/463-6531;** ryderj@candw.ag), or Georgetown, Barbados (visit http://bridgetown.usembassy.gov or https://travelregistration.state.gov/ibrs/home.asp). Likewise **Canadian citizens** should register with the Canadian High Commission on Barbados. **Australian citizens** can register with the Australian High Commission in Port-of-Spain, Trinidad and Tobago (© **868/628-4732**).

EMERGENCIES   You can reach the police at their headquarters in the Valley (© **264/497-2333**) or the substation at Sandy Ground (© **264/497-2354**). In an emergency, dial © **911.**

HOLIDAYS   New Year's Day (Jan 1), Good Friday, Easter Monday, Monday after Pentecost (Whit Monday), May 30–31 (Anguilla Day), June 18 (Queen's Birthday), first Monday in August (August Monday), first Thursday in August (August Thursday), August 6 (Constitution Day), December 17 (Separation Day), Christmas Day (Dec 25), December 28 (Boxing Day).

HOSPITALS   For medical services, consult the **Princess Alexandra Hospital,** Stoney Ground, the Valley (© **264/497-2551**). Many of the larger hotels have a physician on call.

INTERNET ACCESS   Most hotels, large and small, offer free Wi-Fi.

LANGUAGE   English is the main language on Anguilla.

MAIL   The main post office is on Wallblake Road, The Valley (*C* **264/497-2528;** www.aps.ai). Collectors consider Anguilla's stamps valuable, and the post office also operates a philatelic bureau, open Monday to Friday 8am to 4:45pm. Airmail postcards and letters cost EC$1.50 (55¢) to the U.S., Canada, and the United Kingdom. *Note:* In January 2009, Anguilla got its first postal code: **AI-2640.** So if you're *sending* a letter to Anguilla from another country, you'll place the new postal code after "Anguilla" and before "British West Indies" (or "BWI").

PASSPORTS   All visitors must have an onward or return ticket. U.S., British, and Canadian citizens must have a valid passport. See p. 22 for information on how to obtain a passport.

PHARMACIES   The **Princess Alexandra Hospital Pharmacy,** Stoney Ground (*C* **264/497-2551**) is open weekdays 8am to 5pm and Saturday 10am to noon. The **Paramount Pharmacy** has branches at Water Swamp (*C* **264/497-2366**) and South Hill (*C* **264/498-2366**).

POLICE   See "Emergencies," above.

SMOKING   There are no regulations against smoking in Anguilla.

TAXES   The government collects a 10% tax on rooms, and hotels tack on a 10% service charge. Effective January 2008, all visitors traveling through the seaports are required to pay an embarkation tax of $20 per adult, and $10 for children 12 to 18 (children under 12 free).

TELEPHONES   See "Staying Connected," p. 39.

TIME   Anguilla is on Atlantic Standard Time year-round, which means it's usually 1 hour ahead of the U.S. East Coast—except when the U.S. is on daylight saving time, when clocks are the same.

TIPPING   Many restaurants include some sort of service charge in the menu pricing. The menu should state whether service is included, but always confirm whether gratuities are added. In many instances, tips are pooled among the staff (including the back of the house), so it's always a good idea to leave something extra if you feel your server warrants it. Give a 10% to 20% tip to boat captains. Bellhops should get $1 to $2 per bag. Be sure to tip beach attendants and leave something for housekeeping (approximately $1 for every night you spend). Tip taxi drivers an extra 10%.

TOILETS   As on St. Martin/St. Maarten, there are few public facilities, although the ferry terminal at Blowing Point has bathrooms. Hotel lobbies and restaurants are your best options.

WATER Water is a precious commodity on Anguilla, and even though the water is potable, it is in short supply. Bottled water is easily available.

WEATHER The hottest months in Anguilla are July to October; the coolest, December to February. The mean monthly temperature is about 80°F (27°C). Rain is most heavy in the winter, but few days are without sunshine.

---

3 FAST FACTS: ST. BARTHÉLEMY

AREA CODES The country and area code for St. Barts is 590/590.

BANKS The two main banks, both of which have **ATMs,** are: **Banque Française Commerciale,** rue du Général-de-Gaulle, Gustavia (📞 **590/27-62-62,** or 📞 **590/27-65-88** in St-Jean); and the **Banque Nationale de Paris,** rue du Bord de Mer (📞 **590/27-63-70**).

BUSINESS HOURS Keep in mind that most shopkeepers open around 9am or 10am but close midday for an extended *dejeuner* (lunch) that may last until 2pm or 3pm. Generally, the closing time is 7pm. Banks are open Monday to Friday 8am to noon and 2 to 3:30pm.

DRINKING LAWS The legal drinking age is 18. Wine, beer, and liquor are sold in grocery stores and restaurants 7 days a week during regular hours.

DRIVING RULES See "Getting Around," on p. 164.

ELECTRICITY See "Fast Facts: St. Maarten/St. Martin," above.

EMBASSIES & CONSULATES U.S. citizens can visit the Consulate General of France in New York, 934 Fifth Ave., New York, NY (📞 **212/606-3600**). Canadian citizens can contact Canada's Embassy of France, 42 Promenade St., Sussex, Ottawa, ON (📞 **613/789-1795**).

EMERGENCIES Dial 📞 **17** for **police** or **medical** emergencies, 📞 **18** for **fire** emergencies.

HOLIDAYS Banks, government offices, post offices, and many stores close for national holidays. *Note:* If a holiday happens on a Thursday, don't expect a business to open until the following Monday. National holidays are as follows: January 1 (New Year's Day), January 3 (All Kings Day), Easter weekend, May 1 (Labor Day), May 8 (Armistice Day), July 14 (Bastille Day) August 24 (St. Barthélemy Saint's Day), November 1 (All Saints Day), November 11 (Armistice Day), and December 25 (Christmas).

HOSPITALS   St. Barts is not the greatest place to find yourself in a medical emergency. Except for vacationing doctors escaping their own practices in other parts of the world, it has only seven resident doctors and about a dozen on-call specialists. The island's only hospital, with the only emergency facilities, is the **Hôpital de Bruyn,** rue Jean-Bart (⟨℅⟩ **590/27-60-35**), about .4km (¼ mile) north of Gustavia. Serious medical cases are often flown to St. Maarten, Martinique, Miami, or wherever the person or his/her family specifies.

INTERNET ACCESS   Most hotels and resorts offer Wi-Fi. **Centre@lizés,** rue de la République, Gustavia (⟨℅⟩ **590/298-989**) is a full-service Internet cafe that also offers cellphone and laptop rentals.

LANGUAGE   French is the official language, but English is widely spoken.

MAIL   The main post office is in Gustavia (rue du Centenaire; ⟨℅⟩ **590/27-62-00;** closed Sun).

PASSPORTS   U.S. and Canadian citizens need a passport to enter St. Barts. If you're flying in, you'll need to present your return or ongoing ticket. Citizens of the European Union need only an official photo ID, but passports are always recommended. See p. 22 for information on how to obtain a passport.

PHARMACIES   The **Pharmacie de Saint-Barth** is on quai de la République, Gustavia (⟨℅⟩ **590/27-61-82**). Its only competitor is the **Pharmacie de l'Aéroport,** adjacent to the airport (⟨℅⟩ **590/27-66-61**). Both are open Monday through Saturday from 8am to 7:30pm; on Sunday, one or the other remains open for at least part of the day.

POLICE   See "Emergencies," above.

SMOKING   While a number of properties offer nonsmoking rooms, there are currently no regulations against smoking

TAXES   You're assessed a 4€ departure tax if you're heading for another French island. Otherwise, you'll pay 8€. (These taxes are included in your airline ticket.) There is no sales tax and no tax on restaurant meals. Hotels now tack on a 5% tourist tax.

TELEPHONES   See "Staying Connected," p. 39.

TIME   When standard time is in effect in the United States and Canada (in winter), St. Barts is 1 hour ahead of the U.S. East Coast and 4 hours behind Greenwich Mean Time. When daylight saving time is in effect in the United States, clocks in New York and St. Barts show the same time—5 hours behind Greenwich Mean Time.

TIPPING Hotels usually add a service charge of 10% to 15%; always ask if this is included in the price you're quoted. Restaurants add a 15% service charge. Taxi drivers expect a tip of 10% of the fare.

TOILETS There are public bathrooms on the Quay in Gustavia (next to the Comité du Tourisme de Saint-Barthélemy tourist office). Hotel lobbies and restaurants are your best options, though technically you should be a guest or customer to use one.

WATER The water on St. Barts is generally safe to drink.

WEATHER The climate of St. Barts is ideal: dry with an average temperature of 72°F to 86°F (22°C–30°C).

FAST FACTS

10

ST. BARTHÉLEMY

INDEX

See also Accommodations and Restaurant indexes, below.

Restaurants